*The story of God's faithfulness
in one missionary's journey
to Africa and back*

Great is Thy Faithfulness

©2006 by Bernice Foss

The right of Bernice Foss to be identified as the Author of this Work has been asserted in accordance with all relevant copyright laws. All rights reserved. No part of this publication may be reproduced, stored in a retrieval system, or transmitted, in any form or by any means, electronic, mechanical, photocopying, recording or otherwise except as permitted by US or UK copyright laws, without the prior permission of the publisher.

First published 2006 by the author.
Reprinted 2007 by Doorlight Publications
PO Box 718, South Hadley, MA 01075

ISBN 0-9778372-4-6

Printed and bound in the United States by Lightning Source Inc. (US)
1246 Heil Quaker Blvd. La Vergne, TN USA 37086

Great is Thy Faithfulness

*The story of God's faithfulness
in one missionary's journey
to Africa and back*

Bernice Foss

To all of my students, African and American,

Without you there would be no story.

You have more insight than your teacher.

(Psalm 119:99)

TABLE of CONTENTS

Foreword	ix
Acknowledgements	xiii
Maps	xvi-xvii
Preface	xix
1. My Childhood Years	1
2. The High School Years	15
3. College Years	27
4. Further Preparation and Call to Missions	43
5. First Term in the Belgian Congo	59
6. The Independence Years	85
7. My Third Term at Singa	119
8. Pioneering at Kasheke Mission Station	149
9. Country Girl Moves to the City	179
10. My Final Term with its Medical Challenges	219
11. The Bonus Years at New England Bible College	273
12. God's Faithfulness Continues	339
Epilogue	373

FOREWORD

When *The Greatest Story Ever Told* was chosen as the title for Fulton Oursler's 1949 narration of the life of Jesus Christ, its appropriateness was never in doubt, at least not in the minds and hearts of individuals who have experienced a life-changing encounter with the central Figure of that story. This classic publication has been read by millions and is, without question, one of the most successful best-sellers of all times. Jesus Christ's story - His birth, His life, His public ministry, His death and resurrection - is indisputably the greatest story that has ever been told. To comprehend the full impact of *The Greatest Story Ever Told*, however, we also need to be alert to the myriads of *mini-stories* that have found their motivation and empowerment in the life of Jesus Christ and that have flowed forth in an exciting rippling effect into all corners of the world.

In the summer of 1977, I was approached by the leaders of the mission with which Bunny served asking me to fill an administrative role to its ministry on the African continent. Accepting this assignment would involve a major change for my family and me - one that would mean being uprooted from the ministry among the Tagbana people in Cote d'Ivoire, West Africa, that had started 18 years previously and leaving the people whom we had grown to love very much. With considerable heart-searching, we accepted this new responsibility but, in so doing, came in contact also with hundreds of gifted missionaries and non-western church leaders who, through the years, have made an indelible mark upon our lives and ministry. It was as a result of this transition that I, and eventually my family, came in contact with Bunny, the author of the story that you are about to read.

It is to our benefit that Bunny has chosen to record her story. Psalm 78 reminds us that our lives and experiences are like a parable that offers enlightenment for the journey of those who follow and provides affirmation of the truths of God's Word so that they "…will know of the glorious deeds of the Lord…will set their hope anew on God…and will obey His commandments…" I believe this is how Bunny viewed her life and ministry. Because of that, it doesn't surprise me at all that she would choose to share her story in written form - not because she was in any way "me-focused" - but rather because she saw her life and lived it as a work that God was doing - bringing to completion that which He had begun earlier.

People-focused ministries tend to become exceedingly demanding on one's emotional and physical resources. In my extended journeys from country to country and from home to home throughout Africa, I found myself being drawn often toward individuals like those Gordon MacDonald described in his book entitled *Renewing Your Spiritual Passion* - Very Resourceful People - people who challenged us to greater faith and Christlikeness. I look back upon visits with Bunny as making this kind of impact upon my life. Her quiet demeanor…her gracious hospitality…the natural way in which she would reach for her Bible at the conclusion of a meal and lead in worship...the single-minded way in which she carried out her assignments...the gentle way that she shared what God was doing in her own life and in the lives of others. Visits with Bunny served as "fuel-stops" for me on my journey throughout Africa. I have a feeling that you will be ministered to in this same way as you read through these pages.

It doesn't surprise me either that when Bunny decided to share her story in writing, she would entitle it Great is Thy Faithfulness. I believe that decision was almost a "given" from the very beginning because as she refers back to her early life in Maine...her 36 plus years of fruitful ministry in the country now called Congo...her recuperation from cancer in our home in Wheaton, Illinois...and the challenging years of teaching at the New England Bible College, she was keenly aware that it was through God's grace and faithfulness that she lived and served and that God, as He had promised, had never left nor forsaken her. It is my hope and prayer that some of the benefit that I have received in my relationship with Bunny down through the years will become yours as you enjoy this mini-story of God's faithfulness to one of His own.

Dick Jacobs
Director of African Ministries, 1977-1995
July 2006

ACKNOWLEDGEMENTS

A number of years ago I was fascinated by Allan C. Emery's book, *A Turtle on a Fencepost*. Mr. Emery pointed out that just as the turtle needed help to reach the top of the fencepost, most people need help to accomplish their goals. For several years family and friends have encouraged me to write my story. I made a slow start in February, 2004, thinking to write that story just for family. The project began to grow and I knew I needed help - lots of help. The following winter, while leading a Bible study for ten ladies in Dexter, Maine, cancer struck. Teaching and writing came to a sudden halt. I began to recover slowly and took up my pen again. One by one, ladies from the Bible study came forward to help me. Rosemary Waller became my editor. Thank-you, Rosemary, for all your time and effort to turn my jumble of words and memories into a readable script. You helped me far beyond the boundaries of duty. When we needed another set of eyes to check the work one more time, Shirley Grant graciously agreed to use her skill and read through the twelve chapters. Thank-you, Shirley, for adding your unique touch to my story. Then Pamela Nadeau, who works full-time for a local newspaper, offered to design the cover and to format the manuscript and make it ready for the printer, complete with pictures. Pamela, I acknowledge your gifted skills which have added such professionalism to my life story. You have worked many long hours to make the story look just right. When I thought the checking was all done, Pamela informed me that the galley copies needed to be checked. Carol Sherburne came forward with her keen eye for checking many classroom papers and helped with the galley checking. I thank you, Carol, for your encouragement throughout the final stage of the process. God is so good to have given me a team of capable helpers from the Bible study group. All live within a few miles of my home - another tangible evidence of His faithfulness.

When I needed a map of the Congo to enhance my story, I called on Harold Salseth, a retired missionary colleague who is also an artist living in Spring Valley, California. Thank-you, Harold, for the excellent map which will keep readers on track as they journey with me in the Congo. Sharon Foster, a friend and neighbor, came to my rescue so many times when I became frustrated and needed help with my computer. My family and friends have encouraged me all along the journey with great suggestions and faithful prayer. My medical team have done all in their power to keep me healthy so that I could complete the project.

Dick Jacobs, who served as director of African Ministries from 1977 to 1995 with World Venture (formerly Conservative Baptist Foreign Mission Society and CBInternational) and my boss for eleven of those years, graciously agreed to do the Foreword without having read the manuscript. Thank-you, Dick. I hope you won't be disappointed when you read the story.

The African Continent

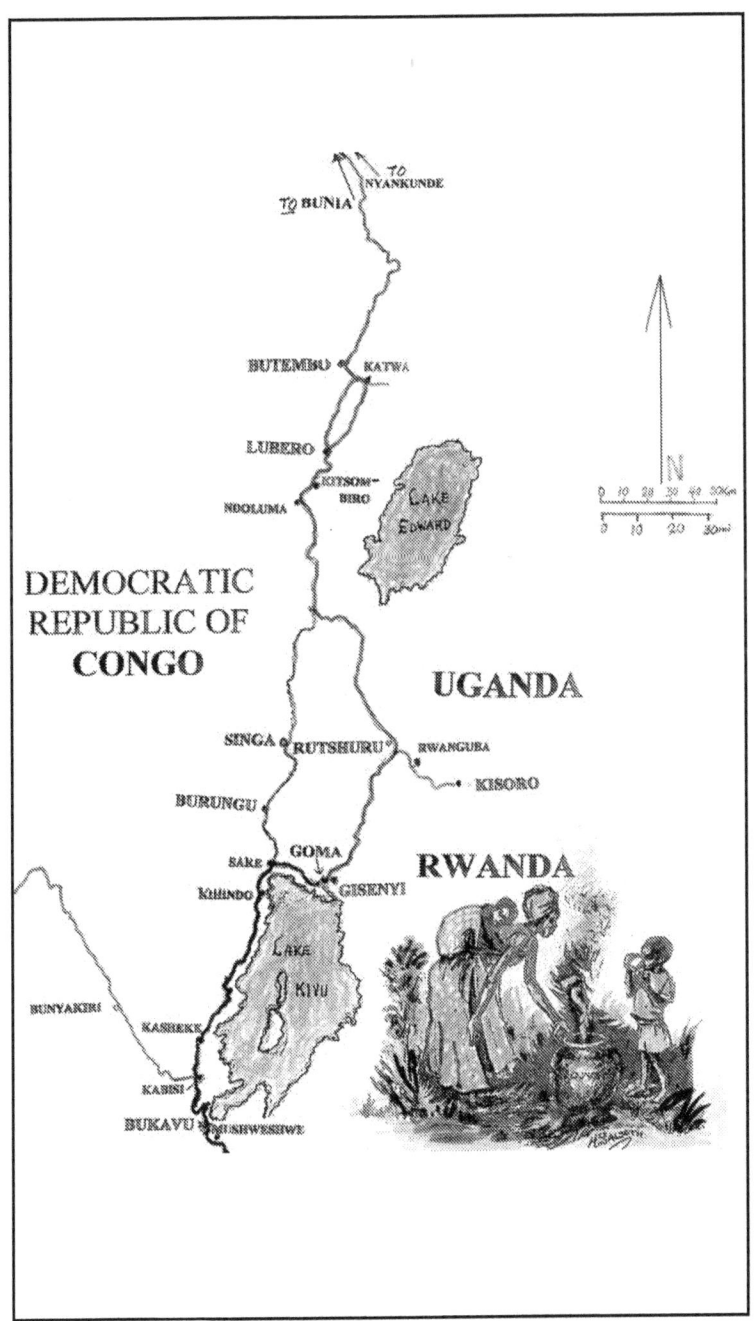

PREFACE

I can still hear the strains of Thomas O. Chisholm's magnificent hymn "Great is Thy Faithfulness" as I walked into Mrs. McDonough's Bible study class in Boston back in 1944. I heard that great old hymn for the first time and soon claimed it as my favorite. The wonderful truths in that hymn - the Lord does not change; He pardons sin; He gives strength for each day; He provides for all my needs - these, and many more, encouraged me and kept me going through life's challenges throughout my nearly eighty years. The hymn went with me all the way to Africa and back again. I knew right from the start of writing my story that the theme would be "Great is Thy Faithfulness." In a sense it is not my story, but the story of God's faithfulness in a life committed to His service.

As you read the story, keep in mind that it was only by God's grace that I had the courage to go to Africa. I could never have gone without His going before me. I never thought of being a missionary as a sacrifice. Rather, it was a privilege to serve the Lord in the Congo. There were trials, sufferings and challenges, but these were only opportunities to see the Lord's great faithfulness again and again.

The prayer of an old saint expresses what is in my heart:

"O Lord, never allow us to think that we can stand by ourselves, and not need you." John Donne (1572-1631)

As you read of the Lord's faithfulness in my life, all the way, may you, dear reader, be encouraged to commit your own life and all its details to His wise, loving and faithful direction. The Scriptures remind us of the hope we have in our God because of His great faithfulness.

> *"This I recall to my mind, therefore, I have hope.*
> *Through the Lord's mercies we are not consumed.*
> *Because His compassions fail not.*
> *They are new every morning; Great is Your faithfulness.*
> *'The Lord is my portion,' says my soul,*
> *Therefore I hope in Him."*
> *- Lamentations 3:21-24 (NKJV)*

Bernice Foss
Dexter, Maine
August, 2006

All Scripture quotations are from the New King James Version unless otherwise indicated.

CHAPTER ONE

**MY CHILDHOOD YEARS
(1926-1940)**

"As for God, His way is perfect" - 2 Samuel 22:31

It was a delightful early spring evening in Boston. I had hopped on the subway from Gordon College, where I was a student, to go to Tremont Temple for the six p.m. service. Dr. Clarence Roddy, a professor at Eastern Baptist Theological Seminary in Philadelphia, was the featured speaker for that evening. He had started his ministry in Cambridge, Maine, next to Parkman where I had grown up, and I was eager to meet him. After the service, when I introduced myself as the daughter of Hazel Stuart Foss, he excitedly called to his wife. It was my thrill to meet the lady who had led my mother to Christ! From that time a friendship began, a mentoring process that continued for many years until the Lord took 'Mother Roddy' home, well after she had passed the century mark. But that meeting was in the mid 1940's. I need to take you, the reader, back to the beginning.

BACKGROUND

My father, Ivan Bertelle Foss, born in Abbot, Maine on August 20, 1897, was the son of George and Rose Hilton Foss. Ivan had one brother, Gardner, who married Annie Barnett; he had three sisters: Bertha, married to Wesley Chase; Celia, married to Alton Merrill; and Esther, married to Wesley Harrington. Their mother Rose died of tuberculosis in 1912. George later married Alice Mosier, who, said my Aunt Esther, 'was good to the children.' George and Alice bought a farm in Parkman in 1919. On May 23, 1925 they sold the farm to Ivan for one dollar and George and Alice moved back to Abbot.

My mother, Hazel Audrey Stuart, born on November 24, 1905 to Harry Berton Stuart and Cora Amelia Crockett Stuart, had an older brother, Elwood, who was married to Verna Bean, and an older sister married to Nelson Gilman, all brought up in Cambridge,

Foss farmhouse with Mckusick twins in foreground.

Maine. The name Stuart is Scottish in origin. Our first ancestor who emigrated to this country was Duncan Stuart who came here during the troubled times of King Charles around 1650 or 1660. This would have been the same period when John Bunyan was imprisoned for preaching the Gospel in England. While in prison Bunyan had written the famous classic, *Pilgrim's Progress*. Duncan had a son, Ebenezer, who built the first Baptist Church in New Hampshire, located near the Massachusetts line and a short distance north of Lowell, Massachusetts. The church was built in 1750 of logs. Ebenezer not only built the church but hired the minister; thus it was called the "Stuart's Church"! Ebenezer's son, Robert, was among the first settlers of the town of Newport, Maine.

EARLY CHILDHOOD
1926 -1932

I was born in the hospital in Guilford, Maine on September 8, 1926 and brought up on the Foss farm in Parkman. My parents named me Bernice Cora Foss. The Cora was after my maternal grandmother, Cora Crockett Stuart. I can still recall the child's prayer that my mother had taught me, "Now I lay me down to sleep." It is difficult to know, after all these years, what I really remember and what I've been told. I do recall the horse and buggy rides over to see my Aunt Esther, an all-day adventure in those days, a ten-minute drive today. Pictures and adult recollections of the brief time we had together give me further samplings of those happy early childhood years. Reverend Martin and Grace McKusick Storms were friends with my parents. I remember an outing at Sebec Lake where the Storms had invited Hilda Hersey to come along as my playmate. We also went over to Cambridge from time to time to visit Uncle Elwood and Aunt Verna so I could become acquainted with their only child, my cousin Alden Stuart. Then there was the day Uncle Elwood came to our house with his newly acquired rumble-seat car and gave me a ride in the rumble seat! I remember as clearly as if it were yesterday the day my father came over to Aunt Esther's with the sad news that my mother had died on August 27, 1931. He had taken her to the Dover hospital with a tubal pregnancy and had left me in the care of Aunt Esther. I was almost five and my small world crumbled. The custom of that day was to bring the casket with the body of the deceased into the home. My mother's body was brought to our home and I can vividly recall the day my Dad let me go into the room and see my

Ivan and Hazel Stuart Foss with Bernice.

mother for one last time. I stayed with "Aunt Ethel" McKusick while the adults went to the funeral at the Parkman Baptist Church and then to the burial at Pingree Center. In later years I have often reflected on such an untimely death. My mother had so much left to offer to her family and students. She had grown up in Cambridge, Maine and had received spiritual training at the Cambridge Baptist Church under the Roddys' ministry. "Mother Roddy" had led my mother to receive Christ as her personal Savior. Mother graduated from N.H. Fay High School in Dexter in 1923, had spent some time at Farmington Normal School and taught in Brighton. Browsing the old yearbooks from N.H. Fay I learned that she was a very shy and retiring person, well-liked by family and friends. My mother was a woman who had a heart for God and I believe she wanted to impart that to me. I still have her copy of the *Christian Worker's New Testament* which Dad saved and gave to me when I was older. It was my very first copy of God's Word. Through the years, people who knew my mother always told me what a wonderful person she was and that I reminded them of her. It has always been a challenge to me to meet their high expectations.

    Life went on for Daddy and me. He cared for me at the farm where he tried to eke out a living with his one hundred acre farm, working with cows, sheep, pigs, and horses. He did all his own haying. In later years we children helped with the haying and I loved to ride the horse who pulled the rope guiding the loose hay to the loft. Dad also raised cash crops, corn, beans and apples, for market. He also cut his own wood for our wood stove in the kitchen and the new wood furnace in the cellar. I remember well when the furnace was installed. I collected the shiny round disks that the furnace man threw away. Those disks became an interesting new toy for me. From time to time we went over to see Aunt Esther and Uncle Wesley on the other side of town. I loved being with my favorite aunt and playing with my cousin Clayton. We played soldiers to please him, and while sitting in empty barrels, we braided grass to please me. The cracks in the tops of the barrels served as holders for the grass we braided.

Bernice feeding sheep.

Eventually, on February 1, 1933 my father married Grace Chesley from Cornville, Maine, the daughter of Frank and Susan Chesley. Grace was born on September 13, 1906 in Woodville, Maine. She came into the marriage with her young son, Philip Chesley, born November 5, 1929. Life changed drastically for me from that point onward. I was going on seven, with a very sensitive nature. Daddy's and my quiet, peaceful home was now invaded by a stepmother, whom I did not particularly like, and a boisterous three-year-old who demanded most of Grace's attention. Somehow I knew that she and Daddy loved each other and that I must try to adjust to my new situation. This was a challenge for me during the rest of my childhood years.

Ivan and Grace Chesley Foss.

GRADE SCHOOL YEARS
1933 - 1940

Schooling for me began at the Pond School, a one-room school one and a half miles from our house. The McKusick family who lived across the road had twin boys who were my playmates. Victor and Vincent were four years ahead of me in school but kindly tolerated my walking with them to the schoolhouse. Miss Bertha Stonier was our teacher in the beginning. Then in 1937 Miss Ada Bates came to teach at the Pond School. I loved school and earned fairly good grades in everything except geography and history! A love for these subjects would come later. In fact, I loved school so much that I remember later setting up a little schoolroom in the attic of our house where we children played school. Of course, I was the teacher.

One very vivid childhood memory I have is the day one winter when our mother's dress caught on fire while she was cooking on the old wood stove in the kitchen. I was only eight or nine years old but I tried to help her put out the fire with water and we tried wrapping a blanket around her. In desperation she finally ran outside and jumped into a snow bank. Her hands and legs were severely burned. When Daddy came home from his work in the woods, he was able to get the doctor and Aunt Ruth came to care for the family. Mother showed great courage during the long recovery period from those awful burns. The scars were with her for the rest of her life.

Our family grew rather rapidly: Marion Ruth was born on August 3, 1933; George Franklin on August 9, 1935; Beatrice on July 28, 1936; Gayland Linwood on September 18, 1938; Charles Edgar on June 3, 1940 and Mary Lou on October 13, 1942. We became a family of four girls and four boys; ten of us around the table with lots of dishes to be washed! But I'm getting ahead of my story.

Sometime in late 1935 our father had to go to the hospital to have his appendix removed. Peritonitis set in and he became deathly ill. How very worried I was about him. I stayed with Aunt Annie and Uncle Gardner in Guilford while Daddy was in the hospital. I couldn't imagine what it would be like to lose my Daddy, too. I have a vivid memory of standing on the stairs at my aunt's house and praying a child's prayer that Daddy would recover. He did recover from the surgery but the doctors discovered that he had tuberculosis. He was taken to the T.B. sanatorium in Fairfield, Maine. This was a major upset to our family. All the farm animals had to be sold. My stepmother, only three years into their marriage, really showed her strength all during that uncertain period. She cared for us all and kept our home going during the year that Daddy was in the sanatorium. Mothers' Aid and other assistance helped her to cope. She was pregnant with Beatrice during much of that year. The townspeople were so good to her. I remember the time that Pastor Cassens drove her to Fairfield to see Daddy and Mrs. Cassens stayed with us. Others in town offered the same service as well and she was able to visit Daddy fairly often. We children went to see our Dad at least once that summer. Although we were not allowed to enter the san (as we called it), we could wave to him when he came out on the balcony. We were fascinated by the huge tower on the grounds. That Christmas, without our father, we had our tree and gifts as usual. Somehow Daddy had managed to purchase gifts for each of us. Mine was a small electric iron and I loved ironing my doll clothes with it. We made it through the year. Beatrice was born in July and eventually Daddy came home. He looked so good! He had put on weight and was declared free of tuberculosis. However, we children had to be tested for tuberculosis periodically for many years after that. Ouch! And ouch again!

Daddy started all over with his farm. Gradually he bought a few cows and sheep and he went into the chicken business. He had a market for eggs and dressed chickens. He also raised beans for the Hartland canning factory. All of this involved help from us children. We all learned how to work hard from our parents. Dad also started raising sheep again. He would shear the sheep in the spring, sell the wool and use the money to buy our school clothes.

I always looked forward to the one week in the summer when I had permission to go to Monson to visit my Great Aunt Alice Crockett Bray who lived with her daughter Sarah and son-in-law Lyman Davidson. They doted on me, Hazel's only child, and encouraged me in many ways. Sarah made me a new dress every summer. I so enjoyed their quiet place by the river, the swing on the porch, and playmates I found in the neighborhood. Since my visits often coincided with Vacation Bible School in their church, I attended the school with my friends. I learned the names of the books of the Bible and many Bible stories as well. Later when I was ready for high school, these relatives provided the money for me to get my first permanent, a great improvement over my very straight hair. They also took me to see beautiful Moosehead Lake for the first time.

There were good times together on the farm. We loved to go down to the big rock in the "big field" and on down to the spring in the "lower field". We would take our lunch and go down to the fields and into the woods to pick all kinds of berries. We loved to play hide-and-seek and kick-the-can. There were green apples in the summer that we ate with salt and gooseberries that we enjoyed from the bush by the side of the lane. In winter we took our sleds out on the hills for rides on the crust. It was extra special when we had permission to cross the road and slide on the bigger hills at the McKusick farm! When I was still quite young, I remember George Burns came by and gave me a ride right down the main highway on his kicksled. During the long winter evenings we played table games: dominoes, parcheesi and Uncle Wiggily. We also enjoyed working on puzzles. I could always be content with a book and was always serious about my homework. One of my favorite subjects was math and Daddy often helped me with my lessons. Roy Nutting, from the church in town, used to come by on Sunday mornings to pick children up for Sunday School. This was a highlight of the week for me! I loved being at church where I heard about missionaries for the first time. Our teachers used to read letters from missionaries in the opening exercises.

At school, our new teacher for the Pond School was Miss Ethel Sawyer, who came after Miss Bates. Miss Sawyer probably made the greatest impact on me of any of my early teachers. A strict disciplinarian, she had our best interests at heart. She was my teacher for grades seven, eight and nine. The ninth grade in those days was preparation for going to high school in Guilford.

In April 1940, my ninth school year, when I was thirteen years old, Miss Sawyer invited me to spend the weekend with her in Dover-Foxcroft. There was to be a big Youth Conference in her church and young people from all over the area were invited. Miss Sawyer's parents opened their home to a number of young people. The Rev. Winthrop Robinson was the pastor at the United Baptist Church in Dover. It was a great weekend for me and I made many new friends my own age. Dr. Howard Ferrin, from Providence Bible Institute in Rhode Island, was the speaker. His song leader was Carlton Booth and together they made an excellent team. That Saturday evening, April 6, 1940, the Gospel was clearly given and I accepted Christ as my personal Savior. This was a new beginning for me. Little did I realize then where that decision would take me. Somehow I knew that from then on my life belonged to the Lord and I wanted to be and do only what He wanted. That, too, involved lots of unknowns to me at that time. After that weekend, I returned to my family wanting each one of them to experience the new joy I had found in knowing Christ. At that point however, I was timid about my new-found faith.

In June of that year I graduated from Pond School in Parkman. A big graduation ceremony was held at the Baptist Church in Parkman. Ninth graders from all the schools in Parkman participated in the graduation. In all we were seven boys and seven girls. My first answer to prayer after becoming a Christian had to do with my graduation dress. All the girls were to wear white dresses. I had found one in the

Sears catalogue and placed an order, but it was late in coming. I really prayed that the dress would arrive on time. It did! It came in the afternoon mail on the day of graduation! For the first time in my brief Christian experience I realized that my heavenly Father was keenly interested in the small details of the lives of His children. I proudly marched with the other graduates wearing my new dress. I was baptized at Pingree Center on June 23 of that same year. It was an overcast day but I can still see how the sun came out late that afternoon. It was shining brightly, as a special benediction, when Pastor Kenneth Cassens baptized me.

REFLECTIONS ON MY CHILDHOOD YEARS

"Amazing grace! How sweet the sound
That saved a wretch like me!
I once was lost, but now am found,
Was blind but now I see."
- John Newton (1725-1807)

As I write this account nearly seventy years after the fact, I see God's hand in so many ways. He gave me a Christian mother for a brief period and then He took her away. In return He gave me a new mother whom I learned to love and respect. I was given seven brothers and sisters with whom I grew and learned to work hard. Also I learned to think of others and to live contentedly without all the extra frills that others may have had. I treasure the lifelong impact made when God brought to our little one-room school a Christian teacher who took special interest in me so that I could meet and accept Christ at an early age. Truly —

GREAT IS HIS FAITHFULNESS!

CHAPTER TWO

THE HIGH SCHOOL YEARS
(1940 - 1944)

"Grow in the grace and knowledge of our LORD."
- 2 Peter 3:18a

It was September 1940 when I entered Guilford High School as a green freshman, straight from the country and my one-room schoolhouse. Our Dad's goal was for each of his children to graduate from high school; he had not had that privilege. As the oldest, I was paving the way for the seven who would follow. There had been difficult years for our family, especially the year Dad was in the sanatorium. The depression years of the thirties were over and Franklin D. Roosevelt was still our President. Living on a farm had great advantages. We raised our own vegetables which

Mother canned during the summer. Dad always had meat for us from the farm animals and it was a special treat in the winter when he would prepare home-made smoked bacon. There were apples from our own trees for apple pies, applesauce and jelly. Dad boiled down the sap from our maple trees outdoors and completed the process on the wood stove in the kitchen providing us with that sweet maple syrup for our pancakes. The grain that Dad bought for the animals came in flowered grain bags which Mother creatively transformed into dresses for the younger girls in the family and also into sheets for our beds. We survived the depression quite well. The country was on its way into World War II by the time I entered high school and the war years were to last all through my high school days.

Dad had arranged a ride for me to school each day with a group of young people from Parkman village. The transition from a small one-room country school to a larger town high school could have been a traumatic experience, but even in my timidity, I survived change. I chose the college course, reasoning that the best choice since I didn't really know what I would do after high school. That first year I took English, Latin, algebra, and civics. I loved algebra and Latin but I struggled with English and civics. Mrs. Elsie Emery was our homeroom teacher that year and she stayed with us until we graduated. We were fifty-one eager freshmen from a number of small country schools in the area. Two friends from the Pond School in Parkman were in my class, Donna Welts and Dolores Boutot. We stuck together for the four years. Very early in my time at Guilford High School I made a new friend, Joyce Prescott. She was to be my best friend all through high school. Joyce came from Guilford Center and her older siblings had paved the way for her at GHS. She was chosen our freshman class president. A keen Christian, Joyce was a great encouragement to me in my new walk as a Christian. One day she came to school all excited about Psalm 141:3, "Set a watch, O Lord, before my mouth; keep the door of my lips." She had just discovered the verse in her Bible and suggested that we memorize it together. This I was more than happy to do and it was the beginning of our memorizing a number of Bible verses together. During our junior and senior years we organized a Bible Club and a good number of students joined the club. Other key people in the club included Beverly and Audrey Crafts, also from Guilford Center and they became good friends of mine. Once in a while I spent a weekend with Joyce in Guilford Center and we enjoyed

Joyce Prescott, best friend in high school.

taking walks in the fields, playing table games, just chatting, and reading the Bible together.

It was the summer between my freshman and sophomore years, I think, that I had my first real job. I took care of two small girls for a family, whose names I cannot recall, in Guilford Center while their parents worked. The grand sum of four dollars a week was mine, plus my board and room. As long as gas was available, they promised to take me home for the weekends. This was, of course, during the war when gas as well as other commodities were rationed. I can still feel the awful homesickness of those days. Even though I was only about eight miles from home, the days were long and the no-gas cloud hung over my head all week. After a few weeks of that agony, a job opened up right in Parkman, less than a mile from our home, and I was able to return to Parkman. A neighbor, Phyllis Gilman, asked me to stay with her while her husband was away at his work all week. I did a few household duties but basically my job was to keep Phyllis company. My pay was the same, I was sure of being home for the weekends, and I could go to church in Parkman and put my forty cents tithe in the offering plate.

Our family was doing fairly well. Dad was working hard on the farm and Mom cared for us children. I did plenty of baby-sitting for my younger siblings during those years and there were always dishes, cooking, and cleaning and more dishes. As the younger ones grew older, each learned to help with these tasks; the boys helped on the farm and the girls in the house. Mother spent any free minutes she had knitting mittens and sewing clothes for all of us with her knack of making over old hand-me-downs that had been given to us. For several summers Dad planted beans for a local factory. All of us, boys and girls, had to help pick the beans. When the bean man said they were ready, they had to be picked. How crestfallen I was when he came one Saturday and announced that the beans had to be picked the next day which meant I wouldn't be able to go to church and Sunday School.

By then Pastor Bernard Estes had come to our little church in Parkman. He and his lovely wife, Grace, took a personal interest in me. They had no children of their own and encouraged me in my walk with the Lord. Once in a while they invited me to have Sunday dinner with them. They gave me Bible studies to work on at home. I would study the lessons and write out the answers to the questions at the end of each lesson which they corrected and returned to me. In this way I received my earliest study of God's Word. They were discipling me in their own way. As time went on, Pastor Estes and his wife started talking about college and encouraged me to think about going to college after high school.

As I gained new friends and became more involved in our little church, I sensed a growing tension between my stepmother and me. There were often caustic remarks from her, leaving me confused and bewildered. All I knew was that I was happier with the folks at church than with my own family. This didn't seem right to my young heart but that was what was happening. I tried hard not to neglect my duties around the house. One Thursday night Daddy helped me with the dishes so that I would be on time for prayer meeting. Even though I didn't want to be the cause of friction between my parents I could see that happening. Maybe it would be better if I wasn't around any longer — I stood in front of the medicine cupboard in our old pantry and wondered what I could take to make that happen. In my heart I knew it would be wrong to take anything and did not. Wanting my life to end before God's time never happened again.

Sometime in the spring of 1942 an evangelist, whose name I cannot recall, came to our church for a whole week of meetings. At some point my parents and sister Marion began attending the meetings. I was elated the night that Marion responded to the invitation to accept Christ; she went forward and both Dad and Mother followed her. This was the answer to my prayer of two years for my family. I was excited and began to notice small changes around the house. My Dad made an effort not to take the Lord's name in vain. Later that summer the three of them were baptized. In October of that year, the last of my siblings, Mary Lou, was born. From then on Mother could concentrate on caring for the eight of us without the added burden of another pregnancy. She and Dad gradually became involved in church

My first Sunday School class.

activities and I was allowed more freedom to be involved. I even taught a small class of girls in Sunday School. Although over sixty years have passed, I still keep in touch with some of those girls: Arlene Gilman, Betty Ayer, Marion Foss, Florence Kimball, Bea Foss, Marilyn Gilman and Janet Knowles.

In the fall of 1942 I entered my junior year and took English, French, geometry, and history. Anything to do with math I loved. I guess I inherited this from my Dad. He, too, loved math and I remember how he used to help me with my homework in the evenings. The A's came easily in any math course, but French was a totally different story. I really did not like French and I felt the teacher was overwhelming in her insistence on correct pronunciation. Had I realized at the time that I would be teaching for thirty years in the French language, I'm sure I would have taken the course more seriously.

I don't recall too much else of that junior year. I did begin noticing the boys but did not date any of them. Joyce and I were still the best of friends. We always ate lunch together and often took walks during the noon hour. She was involved in after-school sports activities. I had to choose activities that took place during school hours as I could not miss my ride back to Parkman. I was elected to be the Chief Librarian in school that year. I loved the library, browsing in the books, keeping them in order and trying to make sure all books came back on time. Because there was a war still on, our school was involved in selling Defense Stamps. I was on the Stamp Committee and helped sell the stamps at recess and the noon hour. I really enjoyed doing that for my country. I was also elected as a Student Council representative during my junior and senior years.

Then came another summer of helping out on the farm, picking beans, haying and doing household chores. I made the usual visits to my aunts in Parkman and in Monson. There was even time to pick beans for a neighbor for pocket money. I worked hard and was able to buy new clothes for my senior year. A happy weekend at Sebec Lake with my friend Joyce and the Craft girls provided more memories of that summer. Joyce's older sister, Madolyn, a student at Gordon College, was there, too. I was greatly impacted by this kind lady who knew her Bible so well and took a personal interest in me. She encouraged me in my walk with the Lord.

September of 1943 came and I could hardly believe I was a senior in high school! My first ever birthday party was a special treat for me. Usually we celebrated birthdays in our family with cake and ice cream at home. Mother invited my friends to come to the house for cake and ice cream for my seventeenth birthday. At school I took all the final requirements in the college course: English, history, general science, and Problems of Democracy. I also asked permission to take typing for the first half of the year, a decision that helped me in years to come when I had to type college papers. Mrs. Emery was still our homeroom teacher. That Christmas she gave everyone in the class a Christmas card with a little poem she had written for each one personally. I still have that card:

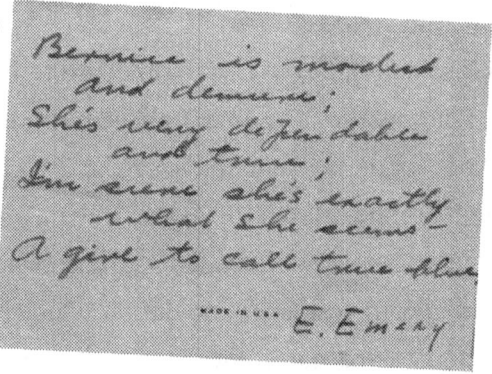

I knew that she could not see inside me the tendency to sin but I was flattered with her evaluation and really tried to be all that she thought I was. Senior year was a flurry of activities: the senior class play, the annual prom, sports of all kinds. Many of these I was unable to participate in because transportation was always a problem. However, I was involved with the Literary Club and our Bible Club which met during school hours.

My sights were set on college, a dream encouraged by

Pastor and Mrs. Estes. My friend Joyce had decided to take nurses' training. She applied to the New England Baptist Hospital in Boston and I applied to Gordon College of Theology and Missions in Boston. Joyce and I talked a lot about our decisions and encouraged each other. We were excited that we both would be in Boston and close enough to see each other from time to time. Because of our decisions to go to college, we both decided we would save our money and not go on the class trip to Quebec. Word got around of our decision and on the very morning of departure, we were called into Principal Clark's office. We entered in fear and trepidation, sure that he was going to scold us for not going on the trip. Instead he told us that money had been provided anonymously for the two of us to go on the trip. We raced home for permission from our parents and to pack suitcases for the evening departure by train. We had a wonderful time in the quaint old city of Quebec, where we stayed in the Hotel St. Roch. It was a new experience for Joyce and me to stay in a hotel. Mrs. Emery, of course, went with us. I still treasure a picture of her and

Mrs. Emery and some of our class in Quebec.

some of the girls in a horse drawn wagon!

Graduation was the next big event in my life. I was chosen to give the address to the undergraduates and prepared my talk around four virtues: cooperation, service, honesty and gratitude. At the graduation ceremony I was given, along with several others, a certificate of membership in the National Honor Society of Secondary Schools. This award is still based on scholarship, leadership, service, and character. Since I had not been particularly popular in high school, this was a great surprise to me and a very great honor indeed. It also helped me realize that one does not have to be popular to make an impact.

The summer of 1948, following graduation, I had an opportunity to live and share a home in Boston with Madolyn Prescott and she invited four other girls to also share the rather large house. Madolyn was taking care of the house for some of her friends who were away for the summer. I had a job in a pill factory which helped with expenses as I anticipated entering Gordon in September. It was a great summer as I became used to the big city, churches in the area and new friends. One special detail I recall was standing in line to buy nylon hosiery. With war still on, some items were being rationed. As I became more at ease and confident in the city, I felt I was ready for my next adventure in the unknown world of college.

REFLECTIONS ON THE HIGH SCHOOL YEARS

> *"May I run the race before me,*
> *Strong and brave to face the foe,*
> *Looking only unto Jesus*
> *As I onward go."*
> — Kate Wilkinson (1859-1928)

While those four years were not my happiest, they were years of growing and maturing. I look back with gratitude that I had parents who made it possible for me to go to high school. I also learned the benefits of hard work as I performed my duties around the house and on the farm. I was very blessed to have my special school friend, Joyce. Pastor and Mrs. Estes were a constant encouragement to me. I read my Bible, did the Bible courses that the Estes provided and grew in my faith and knowledge of God's Word. The wonderful summer in Boston served as a bridge that spanned my adolescent years into the beginning of adulthood and also helped me develop more self-confidence. God graciously used all the details of my high school years to make me a more mature person, stronger and braver, ready to face the next step in my life.

GREAT IS HIS FAITHFULNESS!

CHAPTER THREE

COLLEGE YEARS
(1944-1948)

"The fear of the LORD is the beginning of wisdom, and the knowledge of the Holy One is understanding."
- *Proverbs 9:10*

SEPTEMBER, 1944

An exciting adventure awaited me as I left for my first year in college! I loved the train rides on the Maine Central Railroad from Pittsfield to Boston. The whistles, the jostling along, time to read and think are all pieces of my memories of those train rides, as well as pulling into North Station and learning to find my way by subway out to Gordon College on the Fenway. Truly an adventure for this timid girl from the country, learning to travel by myself to the big city.

The girls' dormitory at Gordon College was called

Wood Hall. Evelyn Lothian from Limerick was my roommate for that first year. A Sears and Roebuck store was within walking distance of the college; my second day at the dorm I hiked to the store and bought some curtains and throw rugs to brighten up our room.

Gordon College on the Fenway.

Dr. T. Leonard Lewis was the newly chosen president at Gordon College. He was a stately, godly man with a great vision for the future of the college. I loved the setting of Gordon from the first day. While Gordon didn't have a campus as such, right across the street was the Fenway. It was a large area with trees and lovely green grass and students could use the area freely. It was wonderful being in a school with Christian professors and Christian students. That first year I took both Old Testament and New Testament survey courses, Greek I, and other required courses. We had daily chapel services with assigned seating and were expected to be present. Singing hymns together with messages from the Word by professors and missionaries were some of the special things I loved as I started my college years at Gordon.

When I began my college years, I already knew I

would have to earn my own way through college, including tuition, board, room and spending money. My plan was that summer jobs would take care of tuition and I would earn my board and room as I went along. One was able to do this back in the forties! I continued working on a part-time basis at the pill factory where I had worked all summer. Eventually I found a job at the college in the kitchen and dining room where I worked for the rest of my college days. This was a much nicer situation. I didn't have to take a trolley to work and the kitchen and dining room were all in Wood Hall where I lived. Gradually I became involved in various college activities. One of these was Hospital and City Missions, an outreach ministry from the college. Usually on Sunday afternoons a group of us would go to the hospitals in the area to sing, give testimony and to visit with patients. That first year I also helped at Friendship House, a ministry to children in a slum area of Boston. Foreign Missions Fellowship was a student-led group that brought missionary speakers to the college on Wednesday evenings. I tried to support those mid-week meetings. My favorite missionary speaker that first year was Mrs. Ruth Stull from Peru. She was an outstanding speaker and I was enthralled by some of her amazing stories of life in the Peruvian jungle. We divided into prayer groups on those Wednesday evenings and I chose to pray in the China group. We were all proud to have a celebrity, Gil Dodds, on campus that year. A noted runner who had set the world's record for the indoor mile, he received his degree from the Divinity School in the spring of 1945. It was during my first year at college that I received my first ever telegram. My Dad sent the sad message: "Aunt Ethel died." She had been our neighbor who lived across the road from us in Parkman. Aunt Ethel always had time for us children. We really loved her and her loss was keenly felt.

Many new friendships were formed that first year in college: Violette Gerrish, Arlene Bartlett, Lois Farr, Ruth Crocker, Bob Ginn, Pauline Kolodinski and many others. I roomed with Violette, Vi as we called her, one year and with Arlene another year and Polly was my college "little sister." I still keep in touch with many of those early college friends. Some of us worked together in the kitchen and dining hall, and some of us did our Christian service together in the same church in Watertown. It was second semester when I began teaching a Sunday School class of young women at the Armenian Church in Watertown. That class became my special ministry for the remainder of my years at Gordon. In May we saw the war in Europe grind to a close. I recall the joy on campus when we received word that the war was over.

SUMMER 1945

The summer following my freshman year I found a job in Falmouth, Massachusetts working at the Tanglewood

Hotel as a waitress. It remains the most wonderful summer so far in my seventy-plus years. The setting was gorgeous, the lovely buildings were on beautifully kept grounds, and all this within walking distance of the Falmouth beach. There were adequate living quarters for the workers, all of whom were Christian, from the lady manager down to the grounds' workers. There was a fascinating old tower on the grounds that I used to climb all the way to the top for my early morning Bible reading and quiet time with the Lord. I made many new friends that summer and kept in contact with a number of them for several years. That summer was a time of further spiritual growth for me, as well as learning how to minister to others in the Body of Christ. I still have an old autograph book from that period, filled with my friends' words of appreciation and confirmation.

SEPTEMBER 1945

Memories of my sophomore year at Gordon are not as clear as those of my freshman year. Violette Gerrish from Rockland was my roommate this time, the beginning of a life-long friendship. I took my first missions course with Miss Carrie Tarbell who had been a missionary in India. This was the beginning of another long friendship. We kept in touch until the time of her death many years later. I learned so much from Miss Tarbell. She was a simple but godly lady, who believed that a missionary should go out to the mission field not expecting an easy life but to represent the Lord Jesus in word and behavior. She encouraged the class to work toward strong self-discipline as a prerequisite for persevering in a foreign country. Miss Tarbell was very happy and proud when she learned that I was on my way to serve in Africa.

Ruth Beaumont from York, Maine entered Gordon that year as a freshman. Ruth had a beautiful singing voice and we called her the "song bird." Her commitment to the Lord was outstanding and she truly wanted to do only what would please her Lord. Ruth and I soon became the best of friends. At Thanksgiving Ruth invited me to go home with her over the break. It was a wonderful Thanksgiving Day at their church with all the church families sharing the meal and fellowship. I loved Ruth's parents and spent many special times over the years at their home in York.

Ruth Beaumont my best friend.

I continued to be very busy with my work in the dining hall three times a day and my studies. I took six courses that year and continued to teach my Sunday School class in Watertown. I didn't have much time for activities outside the college. I was elected class treasurer, but I don't remember that I was responsible for all that much money!

It was a year of growth and change for Gordon College under the able leadership of Dr. T. Leonard Lewis. The college grew by leaps and bounds. Growth for Gordon was reflected in class size. For example, there were only thirty-seven in my class and the next incoming class was twice that number. The apartment buildings adjacent to the school became part of the college property. A beautiful mansion in Brookline became the new home for Gordon Divinity School.

At home in Parkman in April of 1946, my nine-year-old sister, Beatrice, developed osteomyelitis, an infectious, inflammatory disease of the bone in her leg. She had surgery at the Children's Hospital in Portland and there she spent the next nine months. Every time I went through Portland on the train to or from college, I would stop and hike up to the hospital to see her. She was a brave little girl and recovered from the ordeal. However, that right leg has always been weak.

My sophomore year at Gordon College was a year of being stretched spiritually for me and I began to think of what I would do with my life after college. There were desires and concerns that I constantly had to turn over to the Lord. My friend, Ruth, was my faithful confidante. It was about this time that I met the Roddys at Tremont Temple. The encounter with that godly couple helped to bring perspective to my life. Their interest in me because of my mother, as well as their personal concern for me, made a great impact on me at that time.

Early in June I was chosen to be a bridesmaid in Lois Farr's wedding when she married Harley Rowe who was from Skowhegan, Maine. My dress was already purchased and I was really looking forward to this experience, a first for me, when just a few days before the wedding I came down with the old-fashioned measles and was put in the hospital in Boston, under quarantine. It was at the close of the school year and everyone had gone home. It was a lonely time for me in the hospital and a huge disappointment not to be in the wedding. I recovered and was able to go home to Maine before starting back to my summer job at Tanglewood.

SUMMER 1946

There are few recollections of my second summer working at Tanglewood. The hotel had changed hands and many of my old friends had not returned. I was placed in charge of the dining hall and had more responsibility than the previous summer. One memory I do have is missionaries who were coming home from China. The Communists had taken over the country and missionaries were no longer welcome or safe in the land. The Gripsholm, a Swedish ship known as "the mercy ship," chartered by the U. S. and protected by the Red Cross, brought missionaries home from China. A young couple, whose names I cannot recall, had come to the states on the Gripsholm and worked at Tanglewood. We enjoyed hearing their tales of China and their adventurous escape to safety.

SEPTEMBER 1946

Back at Gordon for my third year, I settled into my dorm room, this time with Arlene Bartlett from Rockland as my roommate and formed another lifelong friendship. I still worked in the dining hall and in our newly renovated cafeteria. I was so grateful for the financial security that job gave to me. My junior year I took six courses. The one I remember particularly well was Philosophy I with Dr. Edward J. Carnell. His book, *Introduction to Christian Apologetics*, had just come off the press and we all had autographed copies. His class was my first exposure to philosophy and I felt I was being forced to really think for the first time. However, I'm quite sure that Professor Carnell was not impressed with my early attempts, for he marked my first paper with, "Nice try!"

A number of extra activities that year included being the secretary of our junior class, member of the Student Council, president of Beta Gamma Theta, on the board of the Foreign Missions Fellowship, and a member of the China Prayer Band. The paramount interest of the Student Council was to promote the spiritual welfare of the college. It also attempted to cooperate with the Administration of the college in solving student problems. There were times when this meant frequent and long meetings. Beta Gamma Theta was an organization of the girls of the college to build a high standard of Christian womanhood and to create social ease and grace. The big event for Beta Gamma Theta that year was a ladies' spring banquet. As president of the group, I was responsible for that function. It was a lot of hard work but went off well. The faculty women joined the female students for a delightful evening.

It was a very busy year with these extra responsibilities. I didn't lack for dates to all the important college functions, but "Mr. Right" never seemed to be on the horizon. The young Armenians in my Sunday School class in Watertown were becoming closer to me. I learned so much as I taught them from week to week, including some of the cultural differences of the Armenian people and how much they had suffered before taking refuge in our country. I also learned to enjoy their foods, especially their delicious dessert called baklava.

SUMMER 1947

The summer of 1947 was my first exposure to Rumney Bible Conference, a ministry of the New England Fellowship of Evangelicals, located among the stately pine trees in Rumney, New Hampshire. My job was working in the kitchen and dining hall and being in charge of the working girls' dormitory. At that time the dormitory, now used as a snack center and called the Snack Shack, was the square building in the center of the conference grounds. I was neither much older nor more mature than most of the girls, so it was a summer filled with new learning experiences for me. I learned some valuable lessons about leading people. There are some rare and amusing memories as well. One day the girls and I were outside the kitchen peeling carrots. "Daddy Hall", an eccentric man from New York City, came by, horrified to see all those carrot peelings going to waste. He asked permission to take them back to his cottage where I suppose he cooked them and who knows what he did with them after that! "Daddy Hall" gave us other good chuckles. When he would meet three girls together, he would call out, "Faith, Hope and Charity!"

 The highlight of that summer was when Dad, Mother, and Aunt Esther stopped by to visit me on their way to see the White Mountains. I was so pleased to show them the place where I was happily employed and to introduce them to some of my friends. At the end of the summer I returned to Maine to see my family. My brothers and sisters were all growing rapidly. Each return home included attending church where Claire Harrington always slipped a fifty-cent piece into my hand. It was his way of saying he was happy that I was in college and he wanted to help. A lot could be done with fifty cents in those days.

SEPTEMBER, 1947

Now I was a senior in college. Never had I thought in my wildest dreams it would be possible for me to reach that point. It was all because of the faithfulness of our Heavenly Father. As a senior I was allowed to have a single room. What a special joy it was to have a room all to myself for the first time in my life! My friend Ruth also had a single room right across the hall from me. In many ways my senior year was the most stressful one. I entered the year without the faintest idea of what I would do after graduation. Many of my friends had plans for marriage but, while I had dates, there was no steady "beau." A number of activities occupied my time that year. I was senior advisor to the Beta Gamma Theta, feature editor of our school paper, the "Gordon Herald," president of the girls' dormitory and a member of the House Council. All these took more time than I really had to give and as a result my grades were not the best for my final year. The ten courses on my schedule gave me the thirty-two credits necessary for graduation. One of my favorite courses that year was music appreciation, with instructor Robert E. Dan. A whole new world opened to me as I began to appreciate Bach, Beethoven and Brahms. Though not truly musical, I have been ever grateful for that course and I learned to enjoy and appreciate the great masters.

One of the big events for seniors is what was known as

the "Senior Sneak." The idea was to sneak away from campus without the juniors knowing. Above all, we seniors did not want the juniors to know where we had gone. Our plan was to spend a weekend in Farrington, New Hampshire in mid-winter. We engineered a very successful sneak. Somehow we were able to sneak our suitcases out of the dorms a few days ahead of our actual departure. I was scheduled to meet Esther Wilbur, DeForrest Cole and John Burgess at a certain point in Boston where one of the men would drive us in his car to New Hampshire. Each group sneaked away without a hitch. Most of our sixty-two classmates were able to be there and enjoy the weekend together for fun in the snow. Our meals were catered and our evenings were spent with games, singing and great fellowship. Sunday was a very special day when Professor Edwin K. Gedney, our class advisor, opened God's Word to us in the morning worship time. In the evening George Sweeting, our class president, did a chalk drawing with a missions theme, followed by a challenging message on missions from God's Word. Before the weekend was over, the juniors did find us and a number of them came to Farrington to prove their discovery! When we returned to campus we found our rooms in terrible disarray. All part of the price of being a senior and all in fun.

In the early spring, Mrs. Helen Baugh from Youth Home Missions, a home mission based in Fort Wayne, Indiana, spoke in chapel. Mrs. Baugh and Mary Clark, another representative of YHM, remained on campus for several days. A dynamic speaker, Mrs. Baugh presented a ministry that very much interested me. I learned that YHM was sponsored by Christian Business and Professional Women of America and Christian Women's Clubs. Since I had been earnestly praying about my future, I felt led to talk with her about her ministry. After a delightful personal encounter with both Mrs. Baugh and Mary Clark, I was led to apply to become a home missionary with their group. To my joy, I was accepted to work with them beginning in the summer of 1948. One of my classmates, June Browning, was also accepted by them. I had a certain sense of relief knowing that I had some specific ministry to do right after graduation.

Gradually plans were made for all the graduation activities. I looked forward to Dad, Aunt Esther and Miss Sawyer coming to Boston for all of the graduation events. They came on the train, a new experience for each of them. They were present for our senior banquet and for the graduation ceremony itself which was held at Park Street Church in Boston. At that time I was honored to have been chosen as a member of "Who's Who in American Colleges and Universities," a very great honor, comparable to the "National Honor Society" in high school. Seven seniors had been chosen by the faculty that year: George Sweeting, Linwood Bishop, Jack Lord, Harold Burchett, Robert Draper, Goldie Stocker, and myself. All seven of us were on our way to serve the Lord in some capacity. Graduation is always a bittersweet time. One is elated to have completed the four years successfully, but sad to part with the many friends made during those four years. After taking part in Ethel Mann's wedding right after graduation, I returned to Maine for a little rest and to prepare for heading to the midwest, where I was to begin to serve with Youth Home Missions.

Proud Daddy.

✌

REFLECTIONS ON THE GORDON COLLEGE YEARS

"O Jesus, I have promised To serve Thee to the end;
Be Thou forever near me, My Master and my Friend:
I shall not fear the battle If Thou art by my side
Nor wander from the pathway If Thou wilt be my guide".
- John E. Bode (1816-1874)

College had opened up a whole new world to me. I

made new friends from all over New England as well as from other states. Living and learning in a Christian setting was also a new and delightful experience. Studying under Christian professors was both a blessing and a challenge. The friends, the courses and the instructors all helped to stretch me spiritually. My faith grew by leaps and bounds. Constant exposure to missionaries opened my eyes to the needs of the world, although I was not seriously thinking of foreign missionary work during those years. My involvement in various college activities helped to develop my leadership skills. For me, college was a growing time as well as a scary time because I knew I had to face life out in the world once my college years were completed. There were struggles, I must admit, as I really expected God to give me a life mate while at college. When the expected did not happen, I learned to trust Him all the more as I stepped out into the world, alone. I learned that real wisdom is knowing and fearing the Lord. When He is the foundation of our lives, we can trust Him for all that is to come. I was so grateful to be able to graduate debt free, all my college bills paid. Truly the whole experience was another indication of God's leading in my life.

GREAT IS HIS FAITHFULNESS!

CHAPTER FOUR

FURTHER PREPARATION AND
CALL TO MISSIONS
(1948-1952)

"You did not choose Me, but I chose you and appointed you that you should go and bear fruit, and that your fruit should remain..." - John 15:16

SUMMER 1948 - SPRING 1949

Before my next adventure in life there were some good times in Maine with family. We enjoyed family picnics and hikes in the fields and woods on our farm. In mid-summer I made my way to Massachusetts to connect with June Browning. Her brother and family were to drive the two of us to Ogden, Michigan, for Orientation to the ministry of Youth Home Missions. The trip itself was uneventful, but our arrival in Ogden in the middle of the night was not the best way for new missionary candidates to make their first appearance. June and I expressed deep regrets to our hosts the next day and we were forgiven for having awakened them from their sleep. The week of orientation, led by the leaders of Youth Home Missions, was very practical. A guest pastor gave daily Bible studies and we were instructed in how to conduct ourselves in the homes where we would stay. We were also instructed on home visitation and were given outlines of studies we would be teaching in the schools. During the week each person was paired up with a co-worker; Maxine Parrott from Ohio was my teammate and we became known as Polly and Bunny. I had been given the nickname Bunny back in college and it seemed to stick with me.

Our first assignment was in Buena Vista, a small southern Ohio town along the Ohio River. Polly had a driver's license and was able to drive us to our appointments when a vehicle was available but otherwise we used the bus.

Polly and Bunny.

We loved our ministry of teaching Bible in the schools, visiting homes, and conducting evening evangelistic meetings in the churches. Polly was the musician and we took turns speaking and teaching. Pastors of small churches invited us to come and give them a boost in their church work. Although most of our assignments were in Ohio, we did have a two-week period in rural Michigan. We served together until the spring of 1949. Polly's health was not good and she began to feel the pace was too much to cope with. When she was forced by ill-health to resign, I, too, felt that I needed to move on to the next step in my life. From the beginning of my time with YHM, I had felt I was not in that particular work for a life-time, but that it was a stepping stone for my real-life ministry. I greatly respected the outreach of YHM and was very grateful for all the learning experiences I had with them. Many years later, while I was visiting the Holy Land on my way home for furlough from Africa, I bumped into Mrs. Baugh, the director of YHM, in the Garden Tomb. It was a wonderful encounter and reunion with this godly woman who had impacted my life for a brief period of time. I have followed the work of YHM through the years. Their headquarters were moved from Fort Wayne, Indiana, to Hickman Mills, Missouri, near Kansas City under the name of "Stonecroft." They branched out into "Village Missions" sending pastors into rural areas to open closed churches. Today "Village Missions" has become an independent entity with headquarters in Dallas, Oregon, sponsoring over two hundred missionaries in rural areas of the United States and Canada.

I decided to resign and return to Maine, especially grateful for my friendship with Polly, which continues to this day. While working with Polly, who had studied only two years in a Bible School, I was constantly aware of how well she knew God's Word, so much better than I, who had completed four years of college. For some time while working with YHM, I had been thinking about pursuing further training in the Bible. I chose the Graduate School of Missions at Columbia Bible College in South Carolina. I knew I would receive excellent Bible training at Columbia and also receive credits towards a Master's degree should I ever want to go in that direction. In order to go there I realized I needed to work for a year and save money. I applied for a teaching position in Parkman and learned that I would have to take some summer courses in order to earn a teaching certificate.

SUMMER 1949

At the beginning of the summer, I directed a Vacation Bible School in Dryden, Maine where Walter Wakeman was the pastor. Walter had married my college roommate, Arlene Bartlett. The two-week school was in the morning and children came with the excitement to learn more about Jesus and God's Word. There were some willing helpers from the church who taught classes, organized games, and led the craft program. This was another learning experience for me, leading people and organizing a program. I still have the memory of two marvelous weeks in Dryden.

I then went to Farmington State Teachers College and took three education courses for my accreditation with the State of Maine. This was my first experience living and studying on a secular campus. It didn't take long to find some Christian friends. We were seven who enjoyed doing things together: Bible studies, mountain climbing and weekend trips. I was especially happy to be at the same college that my birth mother had attended years earlier. In her day the school was known as Farmington Normal School.

FALL 1949 - SPRING 1950

In the fall of 1949 I taught at the Pease School in Parkman, my home town. It was a one-room school way up in the woods. The roads were not paved and the spring-time mud became my biggest adventure to that point! I boarded with the Morrison family and walked to school early every morning to start the fire in the old wood stove. I was the only teacher in my little school for twelve children, grades one through six. It was a wonderful year for me. I was happy to be a real teacher and learned as many lessons myself that year as did my students. I had a lot of free time during that year and I took a Bible correspondence course on Scripture Memorization from Moody Bible Institute. I worked on this course each morning sitting by the wood fire waiting for my students to arrive. By this time, my Dad owned a pick-up truck and he and Mother came after me every Friday afternoon. I spent the weekends with my family on the farm and stayed involved in my church.

SUMMER 1950

My year of teaching over, I started the summer of 1950 by being a bridesmaid in my best friend's wedding in York, Maine. Ruth Beaumont married Paul Pretiz, and shortly afterwards they left for Panama where they were to serve as missionaries. Later they transferred to Costa Rica where they served under the Latin American Mission until their retirement. Several years later, I was privileged to visit them in Costa Rica on one of my furloughs. After their wedding I went to Rumney, New Hampshire to serve as senior counselor for Camp Cathedral Pines at the New England Fellowship Conference where I had worked in the summer of 1947. My responsibilities included overseeing six to eight young girls in White Cliff cabin and teaching Bible classes to the older girls. The summer was filled with a variety of activities, some with the campers and others with the counselors. We went on hikes with the campers and climbed mountains with them. On Sunday mornings everyone in the girls' camp walked to the conference center to worship in the tabernacle.

Jane Finch, a friend from Gordon days, worked in the Snack Shack at the conference center. We spent a lot of our time-off together. A special memory for me was when we met on a little island in the pond for prayer together. Later that fall Jane married Harold Burchett. Harold and Jane became close friends and years later they had a profound impact on my discipling ministry in Africa.

One of the highlights of the summer for me was a second encounter with Dr. and Mrs. Clarence Roddy. Dr. Roddy was an invited speaker at the conference for a week. I invited Mrs. Roddy to come to the girls' camp and speak to one of my Bible classes. The girls responded well to the words of an older woman. From that moment on Mrs. Roddy and I always kept in close contact by mail. At the close of that summer all counselors, wearing Camp Cathedral Pines sweatshirts, went on a boat trip on Lake Winnepesaukee. For me, that marvelous summer was a time of maturing my faith, when I cried out to the Lord to help me be a good counselor to my cabin of girls. New friendships served to encourage and strengthen me in my walk with the Lord.

Bernice at "White Cliff" cabin in Rumney, New Hampshire.

FALL 1950 - SPRING 1951

In the fall of 1950 I traveled to South Carolina to

attend Columbia Bible College, now known as Columbia International University, where I enrolled in the Graduate School of Missions. Little did I realize that this next step would change the direction of my life forever. I rode to South Carolina in a car with friends from Guilford, Ernie and Joyce Prescott Ireland. Joyce's sister, Ethel Prescott, was to be my roommate for the year. This was my first experience in the Deep South. I will never forget the day on our trip when we bought a whole big watermelon along the side of the road for a mere twenty-five cents.

The year at CBC was a year of studying the Bible in depth and more exposure to missions. I had some outstanding instructors including Mr. James Hatch, Mr. Frank Sells, and Dr. Robert C. McQuilkin, who was the President of the College at that time. I took every Bible course that was available and how I delighted in each one. Caroline Kreimann, also a graduate student, was my assigned "big sister" and she was the best. Caroline was headed for Japan as a missionary to serve under the Conservative Baptist Foreign Mission Society. She was a great encouragement to me when I began to think and pray about becoming a full-time missionary.

As the year went along, I knew that I had to make more solid decisions about my future. I was given two Christian Service assignments that year: one, teaching Sunday School in a black church and another, teaching Bible in a black public school. These contacts with the black community served to broaden my vision for ministry. I learned to love the black people. We were constantly having missionary challenges placed before us in chapel. Caroline told me about the great mission board with which she was connected. More and more I came to believe that God was leading me in the direction of missions, but I needed to be sure.

Early in the spring semester, I knew I needed some time-out for prayer and fasting to seek God's direction for my life. One Friday noon I went to the little prayer room, where, on my knees, I started reading the book of Acts with concentrated prayer for God's direction in my life. I did this for a number of consecutive Fridays, until I felt certain that God was directing me to go to serve Him on the mission field. As a result of my soul searching and prayer, I sent an application to the Conservative Baptist Foreign Mission Society to serve in Africa.

Sunday School class in Columbia, SC.

SUMMER 1951 - FALL 1952

The summer of 1951, at the age of twenty-five, I

served again as senior counselor and Bible teacher at Camp Cathedral Pines at Rumney, New Hampshire. In the fall I returned a second time to teaching, but this time at the Pond School where I had spent nine years as a

Pond School.

pupil. There were seven of these one-room schools in my small home town. At the Pond School that year there were twenty-one pupils, grades one through six, my youngest brother Charles and my baby sister Mary Lou among them.

Sister Mary Lou on the farm.

I boarded at home and rode the school bus with the students every day. I recall preparing my lessons in the evening using the old hectograph to make copies... a far cry from the delightful printer that makes my copies as I type this manuscript! Near the end of our happy year together we prepared a

Brother Charles, one of my students.

twenty-nine page "Pond School Memoirs" with pictures, poems, stories and history, all prepared by the pupils, with copies made on the trusty hectograph. I still have my copy, old and battered, but still a very special memory of that year.

My application to the Conservative Baptist Foreign Mission Society was being processed during that year. I had had a preliminary interview earlier in New Jersey, so I felt somewhat confident I would eventually be invited to meet the full board of directors in Chicago. The board invited me to go out to Chicago in January for more interviews and a possible final appointment. I requested a substitute teacher and took the long train ride to the "Windy City." On January 24, 1952, I was accepted by the board and appointed for service in the Belgian Congo. They requested that I return to Columbia Bible College for the summer to complete the work for my master's degree.

Back in Maine, I completed the school year and began to make plans for returning to Columbia for the summer of 1952. It had not been in my plans to return to more studies, for I was eager to start my service in Africa. However, thirty-six years later I was thankful for that decision. My endurance was stretched as I took several required courses and began work on my thesis, a requirement for graduation. My thesis subject was "The Personal Nature of the Missionary Call." I really loved working on it! I sent out questionnaires to eighty missionaries, read many biographies of missionaries from all over the world, and conducted interviews where possible. Once the course work and research for my thesis were completed, I returned to Maine and settled in with my Aunt Esther in Hartland to write my thesis.

To my sadness and disappointment, things had taken a bad turn in our little church in Parkman. The American Baptist Convention objected to our church having missionary speakers from the Conservative Baptists. This brought about a split in our church and in my family. Since I had chosen to go out under the CBFMS, it seemed best that I absent myself both from my church and from my family for the time being. That was a very difficult decision and a difficult period in my life. I really wanted to do God's will, but it seemed that Satan was out to stop me in whatever way he could.

FALL 1952 - SUMMER 1953

Aunt Esther was a great encouragement to me. I had a quiet spot, with few distractions, for working on my thesis. She lived closer to public transportation and it was easier from Hartland to visit prospective supporting churches. I began visiting churches and raising my support seriously in the fall of 1952. I completed my thesis! It took a while to be processed, but finally I was granted my degree of Master of Arts in Biblical Education on August 6, 1953. Because of time constraints I was unable to be present for the graduation ceremonies. Eventually I, along with about twenty others from the Parkman church, transferred our memberships to the Cambridge Baptist Church. The Cambridge church became my home church for all the years that I spent as a missionary in Africa. I felt at home in my new church situation and was happy to be out of the previous conflict.

CBFMS had a policy that each missionary had to raise financial support before going to the field. In order to do this missionaries visited churches and shared their testimony and burden for their chosen field. We were not allowed to leave for the field until our full support was designated. My support came in quickly from churches all over New England, from Buffalo, New York and Philadelphia, Pennsylvania. By the summer of 1953 I was making plans for my departure for Belgium, where I was to spend a year studying the French language and other required courses before going to the Belgian Congo. I was commissioned by Cambridge Baptist Church on July 22, 1953 and sailed for Belgium on August 14. Arthur and Althea Folsom, dear friends from my church, drove Aunt Esther and me to New York City to catch my boat for Europe. On the way we stopped at Barrington Bible College in Providence to attend a Bible Conference going on at that time. Dr. Clarence Roddy was the speaker; this was my third encounter with this man of God. Later he and Mrs. Roddy took on some of my annual support. "Mother Roddy", as we lovingly called her, was a faithful prayer warrior all the years I remained in Africa. After Dr.

Roddy died, she lived with her daughter in Montana. We kept in touch until she reached 100 and was unable to correspond, although she lived several years after that. I'll never forget the delightful setting there at Barrington with the lovely trees and flowers. It was a perfect spot to be able to relax for a few days before crossing the Atlantic to begin my life's work of serving my Lord.

The Sibajak.

Maxine Parrot, Aunt Esther and Bernice.

From Providence we drove to New York City where we spent one night. Roy Watson, our mission representative, then drove us to Hoboken, New Jersey, to my boat, the MS Sibajak, a gorgeous ship of the Holland

American Line. The E.J. and Esther Kile family, also missionaries, were sailing on the same boat. Twenty-eight friends had made their way to the big city to see me off. Before saying our good-byes, we sang "Great is Thy Faithfulness" and prayed together and I was off for my next, and very new, adventure!

REFLECTIONS ON THE FINAL YEARS OF PREPARATION

"Am I a soldier of the cross, A follower of the Lamb,
And shall I fear to own His cause,
Or blush to speak His Name?
Must I be carried to the skies, On flowery beds of ease,
While others fought to win the prize,
And sailed thro' bloody seas?
Sure I must fight, if I would reign; Increase my courage, Lord!
I'll bear the toil, endure the pain,
Supported by Thy Word."
- Isaac Watts (1674-1748)

Once I knew that I was destined for Africa to serve as a missionary, I was eager to be on my way. However, there were some important lessons to be learned and remembered. God's timing is perfect and He is never in a hurry, although we often are. I am very grateful for the experiences in Youth

Home Missions, the two years of teaching in rural Maine, the studies at Columbia Bible College and the discipline of having to complete the work for my master's degree which had not originally been in my program. The heartaches connected with the church and family split only served to make me a stronger person. Satan's attacks to try to keep me from going to Africa made me very aware that I would be dealing with his tactics all along the way in my life and in my work. He did not want the Gospel to gain further entrance into darkest Africa. I learned that the Lord is more powerful than Satan. I praise Him for working out so many details that brought me to the point of walking up the gang-plank of the MS Sibajak on that August morning of 1953.

GREAT IS HIS FAITHFULNESS!!

CHAPTER FIVE

FIRST TERM IN THE BELGIAN CONGO
(August 1953 - May 1959)

"And when He putteth forth his own sheep, he goeth before them." - John 10:4a KJV

After saying "Good-bye" to each of my friends, I located my state-room on the Sibajak. There on my bunk was a cablegram from Japan! It read "HE GOETH BEFORE HIS SHEEP." The message had come from Caroline, my graduate school "big sister" who was already in Japan studying the Japanese language in preparation for her ministry there. That little message came as a great encouragement to me. In the days, weeks and months that followed, I was able to prove that He had indeed gone before me.

Ten days on a large ocean liner was, and still is, a marvelous experience. Leisure travel on an Atlantic crossing is most enjoyable for those who want time to be quiet. There were three hundred passengers and one hundred Jamaican workers plus the ship's staff on board. There was time for rest, reading and writing. I spent much of my time either on deck or in the library. Mrs. Roddy had given me a copy of *Hudson Taylor's Spiritual Secret* to read on the Atlantic crossing and I delighted in that spiritual classic. I still have the hard cover and have read it many times with great spiritual benefit. For the most part it was smooth sailing. Ten days later we docked in Rotterdam where missionary friends met and guided us to our final destination, Brussels, Belgium. I'll never forget the sea of bicycles around Rotterdam. It seemed that everyone in the city was on a bicycle.

FRENCH LANGUAGE STUDY IN BELGIUM

Because the Belgian Congo in 1953 was a colony of Belgium, the Belgian government provided special training for their colonists and missionaries going out to the Congo. Since French is the official language of the Belgian Congo, we were immersed in the French language for the next ten months.

Madame Janssen, my Belgian hostess.

There were classes at a government school and we had private tutors as well. During the year I was in Belgium, I boarded in a Belgian home (pension) at 71 rue de la Victoire. There were three ladies from our mission; Ruth Uhlinger, Elfreida Pruitt and myself who lived in this home. We had our meals at the pension and every day we were able to practice speaking French with our Belgian hostess, a great advantage to us. French was not easy for me. With the many exceptions to the rules and the difficult accent, I made many mistakes in the learning process. At the market one had to be careful when asking for "poisson" (fish) not to say "poison," the word for poison!

I loved the city of Brussels with its cobblestone streets, magnificent old buildings, many museums and monuments of all kinds, and the intriguing street markets. The Grand Place, at the center of the city, is famous for the City Hall with its tower that stands above the rest of the buildings. The bakers' shops are encircled by numerous trade buildings that were prominent during the seventeenth century. The well-lighted area is breathtaking at night. The Belgian lace makers,

Elfreida and Ruth, my housemates in Belgium.

known throughout the world, held a special fascination for me. There had been some devastation to the city during the war but they were recovering nicely. We attended a small Baptist church within walking distance of our pension. To worship in French was a big boost to our language learning. Communion from the common cup, practiced every Sunday morning, was a new experience.

Our days were filled with the study of the French language until it seemed as if our heads would burst. A break from the routine was necessary from time to time. Elfreida and I took two interesting trips while we were in Brussels. During our Christmas break we took the train to Paris for a long weekend. Paris is another world in itself, with the Arc de Triomphe, Notre Dame, the Eiffel Tower, the huge Louvre Museum, and crusty French bread in long loaves! We also visited Versailles. Later in the year Elfrieda and I flew to Geneva, Switzerland, my first time to fly. It was another delightful trip seeing the Swiss Alps, riding on dogsleds pulled by huskies. We saw the Monument to the Reformers and the church where Huldrych Zwingli (1484-1531), one of the leaders of the Swiss reformation, had preached.

Arc de Triomph, my favorite monument in Paris.

When our French studies were completed, we had to take the famous "Colonial Course," twelve different courses to help further prepare missionaries for living and serving in Belgium's great colony of Congo. We studied the history of Belgium, the history of Congo, the geography of Congo and hygiene, to name a few of the courses. All were helpful, but it was a grueling time because an oral exam had to be passed on each of the twelve courses, in French, of course!

While in Brussels, I also took advantage of the good prices on Bavarian china and purchased a lovely tea set for twelve in the Winterling pattern. The china set went with me to the Congo, was used on many special occasions and bits and pieces of the set are still with me here in Maine. Finally, studies, exams and retakes were all completed to the satisfaction of the Belgian government and we started making final plans for our journey to the Belgian Congo. We had to apply for visas, make plane reservations and say our good-byes. Elfreida and I would be traveling together; Ruth had gone earlier.

We flew from Brussels on October 1, 1954 on Sobelair, a Belgian airline that offered a special itinerary for those flying to the Congo. We stopped in Rome where we stayed in the Hotel Majestic. The package included a tour of the city and we saw the famous St. Peter's Church with lovely mosaics all around the plaza. We visited the Colosseum, the Pantheon, the Arch to Constantine, and the old Roman Forum. From Rome we flew to Athens, Greece to refuel and have lunch. In Cairo, Egypt we had time to go into the desert to see the great pyramids, the Sphinx, an Egyptian Museum and even camels. That evening I had my first experience with bargaining the African way and purchased a lovely camel skin bag and hassock. An African chief, his son and their little white Lula dog were on the plane with us and that added to our amusement. We finally arrived at Irumu, Congo, just north of the Equator, on October fourth. A note written in my journal before we landed at Irumu says: "Excitement and joy increases as we get nearer to Irumu. What is Congo going to be like? Will I be happy there? Am I going to let the Lord use my life to the fullest? He has been so gracious to lead me up to these moments and I long that my life and service bring glory to Him." Two missionary ladies from Katwa station met us and for six hours we drove over winding, narrow, dirt roads south to Katwa mission station. My feet finally touched Congo soil and it was not a dream! It was real, the culmination of all my hard work.

Pyramid and Sphinx in Cairo, Egypt.

SWAHILI LANGUAGE STUDY AT MUSHWESHWE

Before going into further language study, I was encouraged to try to visit all eight of our Conservative Baptist mission stations located in Kivu Province in eastern Congo. This was a major feat since there were three hundred miles, going north to south, from Katwa to Mushweshwe, with some stations off the major route and all on unpaved roads! I wasn't able to see all of the stations right away but I was impressed with what I saw. Rolling green hills, palm, banana and bamboo trees, friendly Africans and their grass huts everywhere, volcanoes towering around us and some nice, warm, sunny weather — all of these made me love Africa right from the start! Remember, this was the Belgian Congo with Belgian officials in every major location. They ran the government, the schools, the hospitals, took care of roads and gave a sense of security. I felt safe, wanted and happy. Eventually, in November I found a ride to the city of Goma where I took the boat down Lake Kivu, a five-hour ride, to the city of Bukavu. Bob and Marie Bothwell met me and drove me over the hills to Mushweshwe station which would be my home for the next five months while I studied Congo Swahili, the trade language of eastern Belgian Congo. In the Belgian Congo there were over two hundred different tribes, each with its own tribal language. Each area also used a trade language which was understood by all the tribes of that area.

Bob and Marie Bothwell and their four children were the missionaries at Mushweshwe, a rural mission station where life was very relaxed. Marie was to teach us Swahili. There were four newly-arrived missionaries sent to do language study together; Don and Peg Penney, Elfreida Pruitt and myself.

My first Congo house at Mushweshwe.

Elfie and I lived in a mud hut with a thatched roof during that time of study. There was a cement floor in the hut and very simple furnishings, a bed for each of us, a dresser that we shared and one card table. Since there wasn't a lot of lighting in the hut, we often put the card table outside and did our work in the open air. We ate our meals with the Bothwell family. After the year of our grueling studies in French, learning Swahili was a "piece of cake." We had formal classes with Marie in the morning and spent time with an African informant working on conversation in the afternoon. From time to time Bob worked with us on an individual basis along with the African informant, who told a story to us in Swahili. We then told the same story back to Bob in

English as proof that we had understood. Soon we began to see progress in our understanding of Swahili. Learning the grammar with Marie was quite easy, but speaking Swahili took practice and more practice. At least once a week I hiked over the hills with the Bothwell children. I tried speaking with the Africans we met along the way and was always pleased and encouraged when they understood my faltering efforts to speak their language. Not only did I thoroughly enjoy the hikes, I loved visiting in the African homes and talking with them in my limited Swahili. Actually progress in fluency was rather fast. We had our first instruction in Swahili near the end of November, and in early February Marie gave us an assignment to prepare a Bible lesson in Swahili to be given to the African school children the next week! This assignment was a big challenge. I chose the story of Mephibosheth for that first lesson. Every week after that we had to prepare a story in Swahili and each time it became easier.

    Not only did Bob and Marie teach us the language, but day by day they taught us valuable lessons on the culture of the African people. They had lived and worked among the Bashi tribe for over ten years. We learned customs unique to the Bashi people and other customs of the scores of different tribes all over the country. I saw the Bothwells as an ideal missionary family who loved and disciplined their children and had a good working relationship with the Africans. Even though Bob and Marie had the extra burden of teaching and feeding all of us, they carried on their regular missionary duties among the people of the Mushweshwe area.

The Conservative Baptist Mission in the Congo held an annual Field Conference at various stations where all the missionaries gathered for fellowship and to discuss mission business. The Field Conference had given me my assignment which was to start as soon as the study of Swahili was completed. I was to go north to Ndoluma station to work in the home and school for the mulattoes. After we had successfully completed our Swahili exams, Don and Peg Penney offered to drive me to Ndoluma. On April 11, 1955, the Penneys, their two children and I started on the long drive to my new home. We arrived two days later, dusty and weary, and were greeted warmly by the mulatto children out by the road. Ndoluma mission station is located on a side road about a half mile from the main road and the children and missionaries had all come out to the main road to welcome us with a huge welcome sign and great singing. After greeting each one, we went to the mission and had a delicious supper with the missionaries who would be my co-workers at Ndoluma, Ray and Clara Jensen and E.J. and Tudy Kile.

MY FIRST ASSIGNMENT: THE MULATTOES AT NDOLUMA MISSION STATION

Ndoluma was one of our "northern" stations, located at an altitude of about seven thousand feet. When I arrived in April, 1955 the whole mulatto project had only recently been moved to Ndoluma, a new mission station. Early mornings and evenings were very cold and we were grateful for fireplaces and the availability of wood to burn. Two large dormitories had been built, one for boys and one for girls. I was given a small apartment in a corner of the girls' dorm and the Kile family were in the larger apartment just across the hall from me. The Kiles were responsible for the girls' dorm and I was to be one of the teachers. The boys' dorm, where the Jensens lived and were in charge, was on a hill a short distance from the girls' dorm.

Mulatto children with girls' dormitory in background.

When I arrived there were about sixty-five children on the station. The mulattoes were half-caste children, mostly with African mothers and white (Belgian or Greek) fathers. Because of their brown skin, they did not easily fit into either the black or the white society. Our mission saw the need to minister to these unwanted children with a home and a school at Ndoluma. Several years earlier the mission had a small ministry for Mulatto girls at Katwa station and a ministry for the boys at Kitsombiro. The mission made the decision to open up Ndoluma where both boys and girls could live and go to school. In June I was to begin teaching the third and fourth grades — in French. Woe is me! Would I ever be able to separate English, French and Swahili in my head?

I had fun getting my first apartment settled. I collected bits and pieces of furniture from here and there and it really was quite comfortable. There was a small corner fireplace in the living room which also served as a dining area and study area. My Dad had sent me ten dollars for a birthday gift and I had a local carpenter make me a new desk - yes, for only ten dollars and that desk served me all my years in Africa. Ever since I used to play school with my younger siblings, I had dreamed of one day having my very own desk!

My desk and the carpenters.

One of my first big adjustments was having African house-help. It was almost impossible to have much time for teaching and other ministry without hiring some Africans to help with the day-to-day household tasks. For example, our water had to be carried up from the valley about a quarter of a mile away, so I hired Simoni as my "water boy." Every day he would make several trips to the valley to bring back two five-gallon buckets at a time to fill the small reservoir near my apartment. Another "boy," the term we used to refer to our househelp, Philipo, a twenty-five-year-old married man, helped with the inside chores. He kept the wood fires going, did my cooking, washing (by hand), ironing and general house cleaning. These two African Christian men were invaluable to me and gave me the time to teach and to minister to people in the African village. I appreciated their help but I still loved the day of the week when they were off and I had my house to myself.

Before the school term started, I was invited by Glenn and Dorothy Lawrence, missionaries from the neighboring station of Kitsombiro, to go on an evangelistic safari with them. This was a new and wonderful experience for me. We drove about one and half hours and then hiked another hour to the village of Ikabula. There we camped in one of their huts for four days among these bush people. I learned more about African life as we witnessed a baptism, a wedding and took part in a big church conference with over two thousand people in attendance. I learned that a man of the Wanande tribe had to pay ten to twelve goats to the bride's parents before he could marry their daughter. On Saturday morning I gave a little message on Jonah, in Swahili, while an

African male leader translated into Kinande, the tribal language. I began to see the warm, friendly, generous, hospitable spirit of the African people — I liked what I saw.

King Baudoin of Belgium made a visit to the Belgian Congo early in June. A large group of Africans, mulattoes and missionaries gathered out at the main road to wait for the king to pass by. The three-hour wait was a little disappointing when the king passed so quickly that we hardly had a glimpse of him but he did wave to us!

Various missionaries offered much appreciated help in the mulatto work from time to time, especially when we regulars needed a little break from the many responsibilities involved in caring for all of those children. When Deighton and Alice Douglin arrived on the scene to work with the mulattoes, we were greatly encouraged to have some full-time workers who had hearts for these unwanted children. The Douglins settled in at the boys' dorm and began seriously to fit into the routine at Ndoluma. Deighton would teach the upper grades and Alice, a nurse, helped with the medical problems and general work at the boys' dorm. She also had charge of the meal-planning for the children. This was the beginning of a life-long friendship for me. We three were co-workers for most of our thirty plus years in the Congo.

I had not worked and lived with the mulattoes for very long before I began to recognize some of the deep emotional problems they faced. A lot of time after school was spent listening, talking and praying with individual girls who had special problems. I learned that most of them suffered from low self-esteem, most of their pasts were a mystery and they had little hope for the future. Our greatest challenge as missionaries was to introduce them to Jesus Christ, who offered forgiveness for the past, love and security for the present and a blessed hope for the future. This became a greater challenge when our help and encouragement and teachings were so often met with resistance. There were, however, encouraging signs as our team of missionaries worked together to bring spiritual hope to these special young people. Besides the daily sharing of the Word with them in the classroom and our private encounters, there was worship, Sunday School and an evening evangelistic service on the weekends. Gradually, one by one, the children began to accept Christ as their personal Savior.

Our closest neighbor mission station was Kitsombiro, about five miles from Ndoluma. The Lawrences lived there as well as a nurse, Eileen Bader, who was in charge of the local dispensary, and Louise Buness who was in charge of the African elementary school. Louise and I became close friends and I loved taking a little respite from my responsibilities to spend time with her at Kitsombiro and she, in turn, came to visit me. Another special friend was Ruth Uhlinger, a widow lady, who lived at Katwa station, two hours from Ndoluma. When I visited Ruth she took me out to the African villages to visit the women in their huts. Ruth had already been in the Congo for four years and had established a good relationship with the African women. I learned from her example. With our own families so far away, these missionary friends became a family.

Ndoluma was surrounded by Africans, little villages of fifty to one hundred people in every direction. Very close by was one of those villages with a small African church pastored by Mariko Muhindo from the Munande tribe. I loved to go to that village and visit with the women. Gradually I ventured out with some of the African Christian leaders to bring the Gospel to the heathen villages in the area. Then I began to invite some of the key mulattoes to go with me on these weekly treks. I had no vehicle so we walked everywhere. I felt that these Tuesday afternoon trips helped to link our mulattoes closer to the Africans.

One day in April, 1956, I was the only missionary on the station as the others had gone to do various errands in different directions. One of our younger mulatto teen girls, Katy, came to tell me she had been bitten by a snake. There was a truck on the station and one of the older mulatto boys knew how to drive, so we rushed Katy to Kitsombiro for medical help. The medical people at Kitsombiro sent us north to Katwa station where there was a hospital with missionary doctors and nurses. The trip took over two hours. Katy was given a shot of anti-venom serum to fight off the poison and we returned home that night. Five days later Katy came to show me her cold and purple foot. Something had happened to her foot and I knew she needed to get to the doctor right away. Even though it was already evening and darkness comes to the Congo at six, we took off for Katwa. The medical staff at Katwa were warned by radio of our problem and that we were on our way. After another two-hour journey, we arrived at the hospital at eleven p.m. I shall never forget the worried, serious looks on the faces of the doctors and nurses when they saw her foot. They had never seen anything like it, but they knew they had to do something immediately. With their medical books to guide them, they were able to cut some nerves to release the pressure and blood. I stayed in my room and prayed; Psalm 116 was my encouragement. At three-thirty a.m. word came that the surgery had been a success and circulation had returned to her foot. My prayers turned to praise! For the next three days I stayed to care for Katy, a dear, sweet girl. As a result of her experience with the snake bite, she committed her life to the Lord. As the years went by we saw great spiritual growth in her. She led several of the younger children to Christ and was so helpful to us in the work at Ndoluma. Today Katy, married with children of her own, lives in Nairobi, Kenya.

Katy and her little friend.

When the Kile family moved to another station and

assignment, I had the joy of moving into the larger apartment. I had a much larger kitchen, a separate room for my desk and school materials, a larger living room and two bedrooms upstairs. This gave me more room to have the mulatto children in my home and to host missionary guests as well. Although I had not seen other missionaries inviting the Africans into their homes, I felt strongly that I wanted to share my larger home with Africans as well as mulattoes and missionaries. I carefully planned for my first African guests, the African Pastor in the nearby village, his wife Tabita, and their six children. My faithful cook, Simoni, prepared plenty of rice, chicken, corn, bread, jam, tea and peanut cookies. I enjoyed this family so much and their children were especially good all evening. I knew then that this would not be the last time to invite Africans to my home.

Priscilla and Simoni, my cook.

For Easter of 1957 we planned our first mulatto homecoming and spiritual life conference. Those who had graduated came back and enjoyed a special speaker, music, fellowship and food. The Kiles returned to see the children and to lead the singing for the weekend. Paul Okken, the missionary at Kihindo station with his wife, Nellie, came to be our weekend speaker. We were encouraged to see a number of our alumni return for the happy weekend.

Following the conference we had a break from school and I went on a trip south with Ruth Uhlinger. We spent a night at each of our stations along the way and finally came to Mushweshwe, where we spent a long weekend in order for me to see all my friends from Swahili language study days. On the return trip we visited Burungu station and saw Elfreida, her home, and her work in the school. It was a special reunion of we three who had lived together in Belgium. That was my first time to see Burungu, located about thirty miles from the main road, and it completed my initial assignment of visiting all of our Baptist mission stations in eastern Belgian Congo. Truly I was humbled to be a part of such a great missionary endeavor there in central Africa.

The next months at Ndoluma went well and I began to look forward to my first furlough in 1958. Furlough, now called "home assignment," was a time planned by the mission for missionaries to return to the states for a period of rest, medical check-up, debriefing and orientation at mission headquarters and visits to supporting churches. I made my plans to go home via Belgium soon after the mulatto homecoming weekend and spiritual life conference at Easter. The second homecoming was even more popular than the first and many more mulattoes returned for the special weekend. We missionaries planned weeks in advance and worked hard to have everything in readiness for our guests. We invited Mel Lyons, missionary from Raunguba, to be the speaker. He really challenged us with lessons from the life of Joshua. We all enjoyed an early morning Easter sunrise service. Then we went to Kitsombiro for a baptismal service and returned to Ndoluma for a banquet at noon. The tables in the girls' dining room were beautifully decorated and a delicious chicken dinner was served to all the mulatto family and guests. The Kitsombiro missionaries joined us for the evening service and there was a final service on Monday morning before everyone returned to their homes. Truly it was a blessed weekend together and we were encouraged to see spiritual growth in the lives of our former students.

After the conference I took a few days away from Ndoluma to work on my correspondence and to complete the writing of a Swahili tract on prayer that I had started several weeks before. When I returned to Ndoluma I had to pack my personal things and leave my apartment ready for Mary Fletcher who would replace me for the year I would be in the U.S. The mulatto girls prepared a special farewell for me and welcome for Mary when she arrived a few days before my departure in early May. Marj Hudson and Edna Camp, missionaries from Katwa station, drove me south to Bukavu to catch the plane for the first leg of my journey back to the States. It was hard saying "Good-bye" to my missionary friends and the mulatto children who had been such a part of my life during my first term, but I looked forward to seeing my own family again.

HIGHLIGHTS OF MY FIRST FURLOUGH

I flew from Bukavu to Bujumbura and then on to Leopoldville, the capital of the Congo, where I connected with missionary friends Elwin and Lois Pelletier who were also going home on furlough. We had a day or two to see the sights of the lovely capital city on the Congo River before flying on to Brussels. It was 1958, the year of the World's Fair in Belgium, so I remained in Brussels a few more days and enjoyed the fair with my friend, Louise Buness. She was brushing up on French in Belgium before returning to the Congo. From Brussels the Pelletiers and I flew to New York City. All these cities were quite an attraction to those of us who had been in rural Congo for four years. I called my parents from New York before flying on to Chicago where I could take care of the required medical check-up before returning home to Maine for my furlough year. When I reached Maine I was surprised to see how much my younger brothers and sisters had grown and I had to become reacquainted with them all over again. We had some good family times together. My parents helped me make the rounds to see aunts, uncles and cousins. One morning after breakfast Dad and Mother took me to the cemetery to see where brother Philip was buried. He had been in the navy and, while home on leave, was killed in an automobile accident in California. I chose to settle with Aunt Esther in Hartland again since she was located closer to all the public transportation I needed. I still did not have a car and did not know how to drive. In fact, I was the last one in the family to get my driver's license. One of the first things Aunt Esther and I did together was to go shopping for a hat, gloves and heels for me, since we just did not wear these in the Congo. Anyway, styles had changed in the five years I had been away.

The purpose of furlough was to reconnect with family and to report to supporting churches. That first furlough year seemed like one big rush from one meeting to another. Not only was I visiting my own supporting churches, I was also trying to meet other demands of those who wanted to see "a real live missionary." In order to get around I took trains, buses and even the mail coach. I was still able to spend time with my family and we enjoyed Thanksgiving and Christmas together.

The Beaumonts were dear friends in York, Maine, the parents of my best college friend, Ruth. Since they were conveniently located near the New Hampshire and Maine border, their home was a refuge when I had meetings in the Massachusetts and New Hampshire area. I recall I hadn't seen much television and I was especially fascinated to see the Reverend Billy Graham preaching on television.

Near the close of my furlough I became aware of cycles I had gone through since my return. At first I'd felt like a fish out of water and longed for the quiet security of the African way of life. This was followed by not being sure I wanted to return to Africa when I began to really like the American way. Finally, the longing to see Africa again came and I knew I was ready to return! By April, 1959, I was making plans for return to the Congo. On the thirteenth my home church had a farewell service for me with the Reverend Roy Bohanan from Rockland bringing a challenging message from God's Word. I asked for a favorite quote to be on the program, "No reserve, no retreat, no regrets," taken from *Borden of Yale* by Mrs. Howard Taylor. The Lord Jesus said it even more poignantly in Luke 9:62: *"No one, having put his hand to the plow, and looking back, is fit for the kingdom of God."* These words expressed how I felt as I faced my second term in the Belgian Congo. I knew I was going in obedience to God's call on my life and there would be no turning back. I was to go by boat again and this time my parents and Aunt Esther drove me to New York to catch my boat. Again many friends came to see me off. This time was a little different for I knew what I was going back to...or did I?

REFLECTIONS ON MY FIRST TERM AND FURLOUGH

"Lead on, O King Eternal, we follow, not with fears;
Strong in the strength which God supplies through
His eternal Son;
Strong in the Lord of hosts, and in His mighty power,
Who in the Strength of Jesus trusts is more
than conqueror."
- Charles Wesley (1707-1788)

I knew from the moment I set foot on African soil that I loved the country and the people. That fact never changed as the years went by. I am still grateful for all the people involved in helping me to learn two new languages, a painful process, but so worth it. Without learning the language of the people, a missionary is seriously handicapped. Africans are a very hospitable people and they are so grateful when we, in turn, show these qualities to them. I was glad for the courage to begin to reciprocate their hospitality. I also learned some important lessons as Africans worked with me in my home. I learned to be very careful not to accuse of a wrong-doing without definite proof and to keep all monies locked up in a safe place at all times. I learned that mulattoes can be transformed by the grace of God and that they can become useful tools in God's hands to bring blessing to their own people. The experience with Katy and the snake taught me more about trusting the Lord and how gracious He is in our time of great need. I am grateful for all the new people and places I was able to experience during my first term. Truly it was a great privilege and honor to serve the Lord in the Belgian Congo and to have so many faithful supporters standing with me in prayer and financial support. While on furlough I loved visiting these supporters and trying to help them see the Congolese as I saw them. I was encouraged to see our own family relationships begin to heal during my first furlough.

GREAT IS HIS FAITHFULNESS !!!

CHAPTER SIX

THE INDEPENDENCE YEARS
(April 1959 - June 1965)

"The LORD on high is mightier than the noise of many waters, than the mighty waves of the sea."
- Psalm 93:4
"...neither know we what to do; but our eyes are upon thee." - 2 Chron. 20:12

Little did I realize all that was to be involved in the "noise of many waters" as the years of my second term unfolded. I am glad that my feet were secure in the Lord, the Almighty. The verses above were a constant reminder to me of who really is in control of our lives and our destinies.

The second trip across the Atlantic was on the SS Nieu Amsterdam, another lovely Dutch passenger ship. I loved the ten days free of all responsibilities, a great way to prepare for another term in Africa. I regret that it was my last time to go by ship. Two other missionary women, Maryen Baisley and Jane Winterling, were on board and we ate our meals together in the gorgeous dining hall and enjoyed being on the deck where we could exercise and breathe fresh air.

Mom and Dad seeing me off on the ship.

Elisabeth Elliot's *Shadow of the Almighty* had just come off the press and before sailing I purchased a copy with the idea of reading it during the crossing. Since then I have read everything Elisabeth has written and consider *Shadow of the Almighty* her masterpiece. I was so blessed reading the book and have reread it several times since. The ten days on board ship came to a close all too quickly and we disembarked at Rotterdam, where Phil Claar met us and helped us with taxis to Brussels. My new friends, Jane and Maryen, were also going to Belgium, so we all traveled together.

THREE MONTHS OF FRENCH REVIEW IN BELGIUM

My plans were to spend three months in Brussels for French review, a very necessary and profitable time before returning to the work in the Congo. I had made arrangements to board at the same place where I had stayed in 1953, grateful to have the upstairs bedroom overlooking the lovely gardens. I quickly settled in and registered at the "Alliance Française" for French study and found a private tutor for the three months. Besides my formal French lessons, I did a lot of reading in French to help my progress and fluency. I read a number of biographies of the early Protestant Reformers, including Martin Luther, John Calvin, Ulrich Zwingli and John Knox.

I enjoyed being back in Brussels, that old and fascinating city where I had a few friends, especially at the little Baptist church which I had attended in 1953. It was so good to be able to understand and speak French this time; it made life in a foreign land much more enjoyable. One never ceases to be fascinated by the "Grand-Place," the oldest section of the city, dating back to the seventeenth century. There is the shining "Atomium" of the great Exposition (World's Fair) of 1958, which stands as a twentieth century testimony to the progress in Belgium. The famous "Congress Column" is a constant reminder of Belgium's independence gained from The Netherlands in 1830. Although wars have interrupted Belgium's progress from time to time, the bravery, courage and perseverance of the Belgian people through the years have been remarkable. I was seeing all of this for the second time but with a new and deeper appreciation and understanding. A special gratitude goes to Belgium for allowing missionaries the liberty to take the Gospel to its colony, the Belgian Congo.

King Baudouin, King of the Belgians, had been visiting the United States for three weeks and returned to Belgium while I was there studying. My Belgian hostess, Madame Simone Janssen, and I went in to the city to join the crowds gathered to welcome him home. Madame Janssen's friend invited us to watch the royal parade from her third-story balcony, providing us with a close look at the King. While in Belgium, I had one other touch with royalty when the King's brother, Prince Albert, married Princess Paola of Italy. All of Brussels came out to see them drive to the Brussels Palace for the civil ceremony and then on to St. Gudulle church for the religious ceremony. It was all so impressive with black limousines, the police force on horseback, and then the open car with the lovely couple. My Belgian hostess and I had balcony seats with an excellent view!

All too soon it was time to leave Brussels and return to the Belgian Congo. My plans were to fly out on August 4, 1959. News coming from the Congo was unsettling and we sensed that the Congo was changing very rapidly. They were demanding independence from Belgium at any cost. The Belgians had a four-year plan to train key leaders to run their own country. This did not satisfy the Congolese; they wanted their freedom NOW! Thus there was strong conflict between the Belgian government leaders in the Congo and the up and coming political leaders among the Congolese.

This uncertainty and unrest left a heaviness over all of us who were serving in that great land, a country eighty times the size of Belgium.

Fifty years earlier King Leopold, the second King of the Belgians, had purchased the Congo with his own money and had given it to his country, Belgium. At that time the Congo was in a more primitive state. The naked Congolese respected the white man and began to appreciate his influence in their country. The Belgians built roads, schools and hospitals to the delight of the Africans. Missionaries entered the land with the Gospel which the Congolese heard and received. Many turned from their fetishes and evil spirits to receive Jesus Christ. Actually, in those early days they came by the hundreds, and indigenous Congolese churches were established throughout the Congo. We missionaries saw our big task to be that of training African pastors to take over these churches. A Bible Institute was established at Ruanguba, one of our central stations. Now with the spirit of independence in the air and facing my second term, I wondered what the future held for the work that we had labored so hard to establish.

BACK HOME AT NDOLUMA

On August 7, 1959 I arrived back at Ndoluma. The Madsens were filling in while the Douglins were on furlough. I became better acquainted with Dick and Marilyn and enjoyed working with them. My first task was to organize the school program in order to start classes on time in September. Dimitri, one of our older mulattoes, would be teaching grades one and two; Katy, grades three and four; and I would have the fifth and sixth grades. Before the opening day on September first, the three of us sat down with each of the children individually to talk about their school work and to pray with each one. I felt that our new school year was off to a good start. I was especially happy to see a partial outworking of one of my goals for the mulatto work, that of involving mulattoes ministering to mulattoes. Truly, Katy and Dimitri were pioneers with us.

At the same time, the small African church at Ndoluma had a fall Bible Conference over one weekend. I attended as many of the meetings as was possible with my work schedule. On Sunday we all hiked down to the valley where there was water for baptism and we witnessed ten Africans and Stephen, one of our mulatto young men, being baptized. I recall how very happy I was and remarked that this was how I wanted to spend the rest of my life. I loved the rural setting, the ministry I had with the mulattoes, and the contacts with the African church. However, for those missionaries working in the African churches and schools, the "clouds" of nationalism in the Congo were mounting. Earlier in the century, when the first missionaries came to the area, they had established Christian schools which were independent of government subsidies. Without dependency on the subsidies, there was the freedom to hire African Christian teachers and to include Bible and chapel in our curriculum. Students had to pay a small fee to attend the Mission Christian school. With independence very much on their minds, the Africans pressured the mission leaders to turn all the mission schools over to the government. An emergency conference was called by the mission leaders for all missionaries in late September. There were long sessions with lots of discussion and prayer. We all knew this was a very serious situation, and to hold out any longer for mission control over the schools could mean the end of our ministry in the Congo. Finally we made the very difficult group decision that we must accept the government subsidies. This meant that now the teachers' salaries would be paid by the government. A Belgian education inspector came into our area to help us with the transition. Actually, the Belgian authorities were very happy for the missionaries to continue running the schools as we had been doing. The Congolese were happy to have the recognition gained by attending a subsidized school. Along with the transition, it was decided that Ndoluma's fifth and sixth grades should begin attending the Kitsombiro subsidized school. I would go with them and help teach in the African school. So much for my nicely organized school year for Ndoluma! However, I soon saw God's hand in this new assignment. He makes no mistakes as He works out the details of our lives.

My friend Louise was in charge of the African school

at Kitsombiro, our neighbor mission station. I commuted every morning to Kitsombiro with the fourteen mulattoes. My assignment was to teach the sixth grade, a class of about thirty Africans and seven mulattoes. I felt blessed to see how well our mulattoes adjusted to their new school system. They were only fourteen in a black school of four hundred, but they entered into the school life very readily and made some real friends among their African classmates. The classroom competition in the sixth grade was keen as one of our mulatto girls and an African fellow vied for first place in the class of thirty-seven students. Our classes were all taught in French, of course. The mulattoes were fluent in French since that was the language used in their classes at Ndoluma. I was grateful for my months of refresher time in Brussels as I entered this new and challenging adventure in the African school system. Elwin and Mildred Peters, missionaries at Burungu station, were asked to move to Ndoluma and give a hand in the emergency situation. They moved in with me and I turned the kitchen over to Mildred, an excellent cook. Every night when I came from Kitsombiro I looked forward to her delicious meals of meat and potatoes, fried bananas, hot biscuits and some kind of pie. The Peters also took care of all the responsibilities of the girls' dormitory.

MOVE TO KITSOMBIRO

Meantime, political unrest was mounting all over the

country. News of riots in Leopoldville, the capital city, reached us in Kivu Province. In light of the unrest and tension, our mission leaders made a very difficult decision in December of 1959. They decided we should close down our ministry to the mulattoes and begin returning the children to their white fathers or black mothers as soon as possible. It was also decided that I would move to Kitsombiro in order to teach full-time in the newly subsidized African school. The move came right after Christmas of that year. These decisions were not made lightly or in haste and it was a sad time for those of us who had come to love the mulattoes and to have a vital ministry among them. The Peters stayed at Ndoluma and headed up the very difficult task of returning the younger mulatto children to their parents.

Since I had also developed an interest in the Africans I was not at all averse to making the move and working full time in the African school. For a time, at least, our fourteen mulattoes would continue to attend school at Kitsombiro and I would see them every day. With the Christmas move, I settled into a missionary house and became better acquainted with Louise Buness, my teacher friend, and Eileen Bader who was the nurse there. Eileen was preparing to go on furlough and insisted on teaching me to drive. She succeeded and I was able to get my license after taking my test with a very serious Belgian police officer in the neighboring town of Lubero. I've been ever grateful to Eileen for her insistence that I learn to drive. I enjoyed going out to the little African villages in the area for weekly evangelistic meetings where both African and mulatto students joined in these ventures. On Sundays Louise, who had a car, and I often went on longer safaris to more distant villages. I also enjoyed entertaining African families in my home with meals and fellowship. Gradually I became accustomed to my new situation at Kitsombiro and really enjoyed my new assignment. I was slowly beginning to understand a very important spiritual principle which Isaiah 55:8-9 clearly states: "For My thoughts are not your thoughts, nor are your ways My ways, says the Lord. For as the heavens are higher than the earth, So are My ways higher than your ways, and My thoughts than your thoughts." I wanted to follow in God's way and did not want to miss out on anything He had in mind for my life. Shortly after I moved to Kitsombiro, Dick and Marilyn Madsen were also assigned to the work in Kitsombiro. Dick helped at the school along with his evangelistic work in the villages while Marilyn cared for their growing family.

"Independence" was the by-word in those days. We approached the big day with some trepidation, although day-to-day life for us went on quite normally. We were busy preparing for our first sixth grade graduation. Since I lived in the largest house, we turned my living-dining room into a big banquet hall. I had fun preparing an evening banquet for our thirty-three graduates and four missionaries. The evening was a joyous occasion. We enjoyed rabbit, rice, carrot sticks, bread, tea, cake and bananas. There was singing, stories and mime which the Africans do so well. On a more serious note, students shared testimonies and Dick brought a brief devotional. The next morning at nine-thirty we all gathered for the graduation ceremonies at the church which had been colorfully decorated by students. Trumpet and accordion music guided the graduates as they marched into the church and down the aisle. Our special speaker was a godly man, Paulo Buha, the father of one of our graduates. "Great is Thy Faithfulness" was beautifully sung by all the graduates. Zakayo, an African boy, was awarded first place and our mulatto girl, Jano, came in second. We were all very proud of both of them.

After the graduation activities, we missionaries tried to keep busy as June thirtieth approached. There would be no more formal school classes until September. One of the African church leaders had asked me to help with Children's Church for the summer. I also had a Scripture memorization program going with individual students. I was happy to have something specific to occupy my time during those uncertain days.

JUNE 30, 1960 - INDEPENDENCE DAY AND EVACUATION

At the stroke of midnight on the thirtieth of June the celebration and excitement began with drums, horns, and voices — no more sleep for the weary! We gathered for early morning prayers at the African church when they raised the new Congo flag. On the surface things seemed to be quiet and peaceful and I kept busy with my little extra projects. Our peaceful lives were disrupted when one week later we heard that serious trouble had broken out in Leopoldville and white people were fleeing the Congo. On July ninth missionaries from another station came to encourage those of us at Kitsombiro to leave the country as soon as possible. We said quick good-byes to some of our African leaders and started on our way, the Madsens in their truck, Louise and I in her car. We drove north and crossed over into Uganda with no trouble. We had the experience of being cared for in refugee camps for the next two nights as we made our way over to Kampala, the capital. All the whites in the country were attempting to leave the Congo. Because we had the advantage of working in eastern Congo we could more easily cross to safety. In all, there were about seventy missionaries plus children with our mission at that time who fled from the Congo. We all reached places of safety either in Uganda, Rwanda or Burundi. There was much rejoicing when we all were finally together in Kampala, Uganda! We knew that God had been with us in a special way and there was no doubt in our hearts that He still had a work for us to do in the Congo.

For the next six weeks we stayed in Kampala, making frequent contact with our African Christians back on the Congo-Uganda border. By late August the unrest and uncertainty seemed to have settled down enough for us to return to the Congo. Dr. Milton Baker, the foreign secretary of our mission, came out from the States to meet with us at Ruanguba Station. To keep in touch with the new spirit of independence in the land we invited some key African leaders to meet with us to discuss the future of missionary work in their country. There was no doubt in the minds of the Africans that missionaries were still very much needed to help train Africans for leadership roles in their churches. After a couple of days of healthy exchange of ideas, we dispersed to our various stations. I was back home at Kitsombiro on September eighth — a great birthday gift!

The next four months were probably the most difficult of all my years in the Congo. Political tensions were mounting and an anti-white, anti-missionary spirit pervaded the country. The indifference among even our own Christians hurt us the most. The people we had come to love and trust were now acting like our enemies. As a result, our spiritual ministry among them was cut nearly to zero. There was an underlying spirit of rebellion among some of the church leaders and they made demands on the missionaries that we were unable to meet. This spirit of rebellion caused division in the association of African churches. There were a very few faithful, thinking people who wanted to stand with us and see God's work go forward and those few would suffer much in the days to come. The faithful few were cut off from the rest of the African community and we whites were given the same treatment. It was almost impossible for us to serve in that forced ostracism. We prayed and waited, hoping for better days to come.

An unexpected sadness and loss occurred during those unsettled times. Mary Fletcher, a missionary nurse serving in the Katwa hospital to the north of us, came to Kitsombiro to check on the African-run medical dispensary at Kitsombiro. She borrowed Louise's car to return to Katwa and on the way she collided with a big truck. Mary and one of her African passengers were killed instantly. Mary was an unusual lady and we felt her loss keenly. However, life had to go on. I continued to work in the school and had the opportunity to have a ministry with a few individuals. For the most part contacts were limited because of the spirit of fear among the Congolese, who had been told by politicians to have nothing to do with the missionaries. Nationalism, political instability and spiritual apathy combined to completely blind the eyes and hearts of our key Christian leaders. As time went by, we sensed that another evacuation was imminent and we kept our bags ready to leave on a minute's notice.

JANUARY, 1961 - SECOND EVACUATION AND SIX MONTHS IN UGANDA

Word came on Sunday, January fifteenth, that we should leave the country immediately. By now our missionary group was composed of Dick and Marilyn Madsen and their three children, Jack and Jean Swinborne and their four children, and Louise and I. Since I had no car and Louise's had been demolished in the accident, we each went with a family, with limited baggage, of course. Hoping to avoid Congolese officials we left in the night and took a route around the town of Butembo, expecting to go east and cross over into Uganda without a problem as we had done on the previous evacuation. To our surprise and consternation we came upon a road block guarded by the most evil-looking African men I had ever seen. They forced us to go into Butembo to obtain a travel permit. We knew then that we were caught in a trap and that it had been sprung. One soldier ordered me to get out so he could ride up front. I found a spot in the back of the truck and Louise had to do the same in the Swinborne vehicle. On arrival at Butembo, the "soldiers" ordered all of us out of the vehicles. They took the two men off to prison and we women and children were put under house-arrest at a small hotel. We were allowed to keep our bags but the soldiers then drove off with our vehicles.

By now it was Monday morning. We women and children were settled into our cabins which were part of the hotel and actually were quite comfortable. Our big concern was for the men in prison and we women feared the soldiers who made the hotel their headquarters. We learned later that some faithful African men were also in prison. The wives of the African prisoners brought food to the prison daily and then they came by to encourage us, read the Word and prayed with us. Our main prayer was that all the men, African and missionary alike, would be released unharmed from prison.

In the meantime, other missionaries had reached safety earlier. Unbeknown to us, they were in Uganda asking the United Nations to come to our rescue. Late Tuesday afternoon the missionary men were released on the condition that we all return to Kitsombiro. We could not obtain the required travel permit and anyway, they still had our vehicles. We couldn't figure out their riddle. Louise and I continued to be very uneasy in the presence of so many evil-looking soldiers. The Lord gave us a very precious promise in Jeremiah 39:17-18 that "…thou shall not be given into the hand of the men of whom thou art afraid." We were so grateful that they did not harm us during that awful week. The days wore on and we kept praying that we would be released from our "prison." On Thursday the African men were released, a happy day for all of us.

On Saturday morning I recall waking early for time in the Word and prayer. Then I washed my hair and clothes and began to help Marilyn with her washing – all of this done by hand out in the sunshine, using soap and buckets that we had brought with us …lessons learned from the first evacuation! About nine-thirty I heard someone call "Bunny, Bunny, the blue hats are here!" and sure enough, a United Nations lieutenant with about thirty Nigerian soldiers had come to escort us out of the country. They gave us ten minutes to throw our stuff, wet clothes and all, into their jeeps and we were off. On our way out we stopped at Katwa station to rescue Dwight Slater and John Slater, the two missionary doctors who had been forced to remain behind when their families had escaped earlier. Since we had left in such haste, we had no food but the soldiers shared their rations with us. My portion was a can of beans, a special Saturday evening treat for this Maine girl! The UN contingent had orders to take us south to the city of Goma instead of traveling east for the shorter two-hour journey into Uganda. This extended journey only added to our adventure. We arrived in Goma in the wee hours of Sunday morning and were given lodging at the UN temporary headquarters in Goma. My journal records my thoughts on January 25, 1961:

Louise and I will never forget that first night when the two of us had to share a single camp cot in the section of the building that was designated to be the girls' dormitory. We settled in there for several days until we had permission to cross over into Rwanda. Eventually permission was granted by the Congolese authorities and we were escorted to safety by UN Indonesian troops.

As we made our way over to Kampala, Uganda we connected with other missionaries who had reached safety earlier. Louise and I traveled with Dr. Dwight Slater who was driving a car with no brakes, and springs that were tied up with a rope, thanks to the Congolese soldiers who had helped themselves to our cars in Butembo. Upon our arrival in Kampala, two days later, Louise and I were taken to a gorgeous home on Acacia Road where Eleanor and Geneva were already settled. The four of us enjoyed the luxury of a bed for each of us for about a week before the owners returned from their vacation and we had to find other lodging. While we were together we shared table devotions using *Streams in the Desert*. We pondered long over a statement from that popular devotional classic "How much is lost for lack of losing all." Each of us had left our possessions in the Congo and never expected to see them again. Our daily prayer was that we would be willing to lose all for the Lord so that we would not lose out on the good things He had in store for us.

Most everyone sensed that this journey away from the Congo was final and that there would be no return for a long time. Gradually, most of our seventy missionaries were sent in different directions. Some of the medical personnel went directly to Senegal, where there was an immediate need for more doctors and nurses. On February fourteenth a chartered plane brought our Conservative Baptist missionaries and those from other missions back to the States. Sensing that it was God's will for me to remain in Uganda I asked for permission to stay. I had so recently returned to Africa and there were still some things I could accomplish in Kampala. In all there were six of us who remained in Kampala.

Anna Best, one of our missionary nurses, an Asian girl named Joy, and I located an apartment on Prince Charles Drive. The apartment, which we rented for two hundred U.S. dollars a month, contained hard furnishings, a table, chairs, and beds. We settled in well with our limited equipment, each in her own room. I was able to purchase my first car from one of the missionaries returning to the States. It was a green 1960 caravan-type Opel. I had to do some serious practice driving in a country where they drive on the left and city driving was also new to me. One of the couples who remained, Dr. and Mrs. Paul Hurlburt, started a small worship group in their

My first car.

home. I had the joy of teaching the young children every Sunday morning. I had been translating some Sunday School lessons, helping translate *Halley's Handbook* into Swahili and developing a ministry with college students in the area. I kept busy and the six months went by very quickly. Within a few weeks of our living together, Anna flew to a new assignment in Morocco where there was a need that she could meet. Joy eventually moved to another location and I used the apartment for ministry with the college young people. Gradually I became acquainted with Christian students at Makerere College and invited them to my home for home-cooked food and fellowship. They in turn took me to their homes. My life was enriched by the contacts with these keen young Ugandans.

In June the request came for me to return to the Congo. A teacher was needed at Ruanguba station for a group of Congolese students trying to complete their school work so they could enter teacher training in the fall. I prayed long and hard over this. I had found a routine in Kampala and was reluctant to step into the unknown again. However, I sensed this was

Volcanoes seen from Ruanguba.

God's call and the real reason He had me remain in Uganda.

Trusting the Lord, I made plans to return to the Congo.

BACK IN THE CONGO - JULY 5, 1961
RUANGUBA STATION

I spent the next three years at Ruanguba station about four hours south of Kitsombiro, a gorgeous location with eight volcanoes in the distance. On a rare, cold morning we could see snow on some of them. Ruanguba means "hill of lightning" and we did have some terrifying electrical storms there. Earlier missionaries had built a hospital, a Bible school where pastors were trained, a school for missionary children, and the elementary school for African children. There was plenty of missionary housing at Ruanguba and I was given a small house very close to where I would be teaching. Joann Kile had lived there and the house was just as she had left it six months earlier. I settled in using her household equipment. My first task upon arrival was to help a group of twenty young African students complete the work to qualify them for entrance to the Teacher Training School that our mission offered. The students and I worked very hard and early in September I arranged an official graduation for them. Gradually other missionaries began returning not only to Ruanguba but to other stations as well. We were beginning to sense that the Congo was finally recovering from those awful independence traumas.

I always tried to supplement my teaching with intentional ministry to individuals. It was during this period while

I was at Ruanguba that I started seriously discipling African women on an individual basis. Ancilla, a lovely Mututsi young lady, asked if I would help her with God's Word. We met weekly as I took her through the truths of the Gospel of John with great spiritual blessing for both of us. Later I was to learn how better to do this. However, I did see some real growth in Ancilla's life during this time and, even before we finished the study, she had received Christ as her personal Savior. She was baptized by the African pastor.

Toma, Ancilla and baby Caroline.

Later in the year a fine Christian Mututsi nurse who worked at the hospital asked Ancilla to marry him. Ancilla asked me to be her maid-of-honor. I tried to protest but she would not take "no" for an answer. This was indeed a rare privilege for me. In due time she gave birth to a baby girl and she asked me to name her. I called her Caroline after my graduate school big sister who was now serving in Japan.

During those years at Ruanguba I learned some very special lessons from the Africans. I recalled that in graduate school when I read the book of Acts in the little prayer room and prayed about my future ministry, I sensed then that I would have a simple low-key ministry but one that would still impact individual lives. At that time I wasn't sure how it would all unfold but to me it made sense that getting close to the people and getting to know them and understand their culture was at least a beginning. I had learned in Swahili language school when I walked over the hills with the Bothwell children that the Congolese loved having us come into their huts. I thoroughly enjoyed seeing their delight when I sat around the fire with them and made those early efforts to share God's Word. Right from the beginning, I wanted to identify with the Africans. As time went by, I began to see that each missionary had differing ideas of how to do this. I observed that when an African would come to see a missionary, the missionary would stand outside and talk with the African. This was the old colonial way but it didn't seem right to me. When we would go to their homes, the Africans always welcomed us into their huts and offered us a place to sit. Gradually I came to understand that all they really wanted was to be treated as they treated us…with selfless friendliness.

After completing the special assignment with the group of twenty, I was asked to teach a class at the teacher training school and to help in the elementary school. Eventually I was given the responsibility of teaching a "sixième sélectionnée," a class that prepared the young Africans for entrance to high school. I thoroughly enjoyed teaching those young people, the cream of the crop, who had been hand-picked for the special training. They were sharp, keen Congolese who were serious about their education. Mine was the privilege of teaching them and guiding their thinking, not only in secular subjects, but especially in God's Word.

1964 Graduates with "Miss Foss" and Principal Ryabahika.

Student house that my class built.

We suffered significant losses in our mission family while I was at Ruanguba. Earl Camp lost his wife Ida to cancer and Dick Madsen lost his wife Marilyn to cancer when their fourth child was born. Earl was an unusual missionary, born and raised in the Congo by missionary parents. He easily identified with the Africans as few others did. He and his first wife, Ida, served in evangelism in the Kihindo area just south of the city of Goma. After Ida died, Earl married Edna Doughten. Earl continued with his evangelism out in the villages and Edna served as our mission treasurer for many years. Dick had been left with four small children to raise. In due time Dick married Louise Buness. They had a lovely wedding at Singa where Louise was stationed and I was privileged to be her maid-of-honor. As the saying goes "always the bridesmaid but never the bride" seemed to be my lot but not really my choice.

Even though we missionaries were beginning to feel quite secure in the Congo, there was still a lot of persecution going on for the faithful Christian African. One day one of our missionaries, traveling with three Congolese, was stopped by "policemen" and had to watch while his three faithful Congolese were beaten unmercifully and then tossed into prison, not even sure of their crime. These kinds of senseless beatings happened frequently during the period of transition from colonial authority to an independent nation. In such cases the white person had to stand by, helpless. About this same time one of my students had a difficult experience. We had had a two-week break at Easter and on the opening day of classes this particular student was not present. We prayed for him daily. Four days later he appeared and shared his story with us. He had left his village early on the Friday morning of the previous week accompanied by his aging father. At the little government post, a few miles down the hills from their home, they were stopped by "policemen" who demanded to see their identification.

Because they were not of the "right tribe," they were badly beaten and thrown into prison. When they were released four days later, father and son said, "Good-bye." The father climbed the lonely hills and returned to his anxious wife and children. The son continued his way back to school. Through tears he shared his story with us and then said, "I thank the Lord for taking care of me during this time, but we must pray for my tribe and please pray for my father who was beaten so badly." Following his testimony we talked about righteousness and justice and how we, as children of the King, must stand as shining lights of righteousness in a land where each man was doing "what is right in his own eyes." We talked about the oneness that we as Christians have in the Lord Jesus. I remember glancing around my class and noting the various tribes represented. I wanted so much for my students to live above the deep tribal feelings of those days.

One other day stands out vividly in my memory — the day we received word that President Kennedy had been assassinated. It is in times of such national crisis that one longs to be home with his own American family but our missionary family stuck together. We had times of special prayer together for the Kennedy family and for our beloved country. Thanks to Voice of America radio we were able to keep abreast of what was happening and we sorrowed with all Americans at that time.

The three happy years at Ruanguba went by all too

quickly and as July 1964 approached I began making plans for my second furlough. There was the usual end-of-the-school year activities. I always tried to celebrate with those who were completing the year and going on to higher studies. We had a proper graduation for them and I made lots of doughnuts and tea which we enjoyed together before the students returned to their home villages. The next day Harold and Joan Salseth drove me to Kampala where I caught my plane for the Holy Land!

SECOND FURLOUGII
JULY 1964 - AUGUST 1965

For some time I had had the desire to visit the Holy Land and, although I had to travel alone, I felt the time had come for me to take the adventure. Dr. and Mrs. Thomas A. Lambie served the Lord together for many years in Ethiopia. Following the Italian invasion of Ethiopia they served for a while in other North African countries and eventually were assigned to Jordan. After Dr. Lambie's death, his widow remained in Bethlehem and was delighted to have a special ministry to missionaries who wanted to visit the Holy Land. She ran a small guest house and made all the arrangements for missionary tourists. I had contacted Mrs. Lambie earlier and she reserved a room for me and arranged for me to take day-trips with a young English couple who were to be in her guest house at the same time as I. When my plane landed in

Jerusaelm, I was amazed to see Mrs. Lambie there at the airport to meet me. Nearing her seventies, she was a stately woman full of energy and enthusiasm for the land of Christ's birth. With well-prepared lunches, she sent the English couple, their four-year-old son and me off on a new adventure every day. She had a private chauffeur who drove us to the interesting places that Mrs. Lambie had chosen for us to see. We saw the shepherds' fields and the place of Christ's birth in Bethlehem. We visited the River Jordan and the Dead Sea. We went into Samaria and saw Jacob's Well where we had a refreshing drink of water. We had a full day in the old city of Jerusalem, walked the Via Dolorosa, saw Golgotha, and Gethsemane with its ancient olive trees. We visited old churches and had time to browse in many gift shops. Our chauffeur-guide was a faithful Muslim and we were impressed to see him stop for prayer every time the summons to prayer was cried by the muezzin from the minarets. There was a visit to the Garden Tomb where I bumped into another tour group and saw my old friend Mrs. Baugh from Youth Home Missions days. Another day we went to Petra and on the way visited Abraham and Sarah's burial place. Each evening we would return to the guest house to enjoy a delicious evening meal with Mrs. Lambie and her younger co-worker. We shared our experiences of the day and our many questions were answered. There was always an abundance of fresh fruit to enjoy, a special treat for me, having just come from central Africa where fresh fruit had not always been that available. I was so grateful for the five-day visit which gave me new insight into the land where our LORD had walked. From Jerusalem I flew on to Chicago and our mission headquarters for the required de-briefing and medical examinations before returning to Maine to be with family.

My second furlough brought me some special family times as I contacted all of my relatives and became acquainted with new nieces and nephews. There were the usual meetings in churches to keep my faithful supporters abreast of all the changes in the Congo. As the year went on, the crisis in the Congo seemed to get worse and word came that the missionary women and children were again staying over in Rwanda. This was a constant prayer concern as I visited my churches. Another note from my journal dated January 1, 1965:

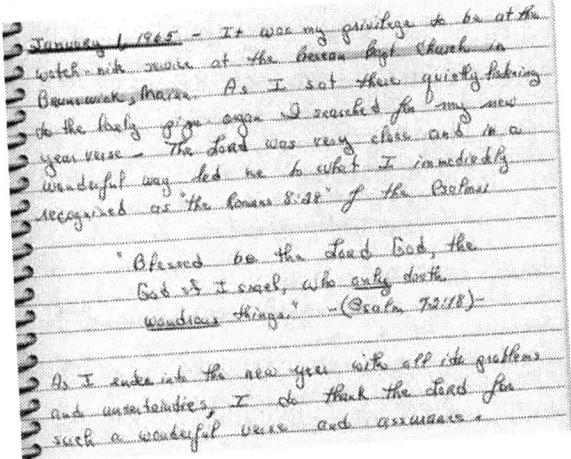

That special evening was followed by a number of

speaking assignments in the Brunswick area. Later in January, we witnessed via television the inauguration of President Lyndon Johnson. In the midst of our American joy and gaiety, all England was sorrowing as Sir Winston Churchill hovered between life and death.

There were many memorable encounters as I went from church to church. Church people were especially kind and thoughtful of missionaries in those days. I never lacked for a place to stay or a meal as I made the rounds of my supporting churches. I spent many profitable hours with the Harold Burchett family in Dover, New Hampshire as Harold and Jane shared with me the system of discipling they had worked out following the Gospel of John. This was to be a great guide for me as I worked with many individual women in the days to come. I had their permission to translate their work which they called *Spiritual Life Studies* into Swahili. I followed their guide as I later discipled many African women. We did a study of the truths found in the Gospel of John and made practical application of the truths in the individual's life. I found that this was a great tool to help individuals grow in their spiritual lives.

Furlough time came to a close and my home church planned another farewell for me. They invited Harold and Jane Burchett from Dover, New Hampshire to be the special speakers. Three of their four children were also present. Their oldest son Jon played the violin, Harold and Jane sang a duet, and Harold brought a powerful message on "Looking unto Jesus" from Hebrews 12:1-4. My dear friends, Ed and Lois Beaumont from York, Maine were also with us for the evening. It was an evening long to be remembered and cherished as I made my way back to Africa.

For the first time I was able to fly out of Bangor airport which made it possible for family and Maine friends to see me off. I left on July 5, 1965. Our Dad always had a goal to eat fresh peas from his garden on the Fourth of July. He wasn't always successful but that year he and Mom picked fresh peas and cooked them for me the evening before I had to leave. We had a family picnic just outside of Bangor before I had to be at the airport at three p.m. I flew to Boston and there were friends there to see me off. From Boston I flew to New York and to my amazement found two more friends there to greet me, Lois Farr Rowe, a college friend, and Erasmia, one of our mulatto girls. These special encounters in airports add so much to the trip and help with the painful "good-byes."

REFLECTIONS ON MY SECOND TERM AND FURLOUGH

"Jesus call us; o'er the tumult
of our life's wild, restless sea,
Day by day His sweet voice soundeth,
Saying, "Christian, follow Me."

> *Jesus calls us: by Thy mercies,*
> *Saviour, may we hear Thy call,*
> *Give our hearts to Thine obedience,*
> *Serve and love Thee best of all."*
> — *Cecil F. Alexander (1823-1895)*

Little did I realize all that would take place when I returned to the Congo for my second term of service. Giving up the ministry to the mulattoes whom I had come to love so much was heart-rending but God was good to quickly give me a love for the work in the African school. I was just beginning to feel at home in that ministry when we experienced our first evacuation from the Congo. After six weeks, to be able to return to the Congo on my birthday was a special blessing for me. The next five months were an extremely difficult period. The anti-white, anti-missionary atmosphere hung over us like a very heavy cloud. The second evacuation seemed so final. There were new lessons to be learned in all that confusion — lessons in trust and confidence in our sovereign Lord. Amy Carmichael, missionary to India, often encouraged me with this statement from her *Edges of His Ways,* the July 11 reading:

> *"Settle this in your minds so that you will not have to settle it again; there is no promise of ease for any soldier on any field. Search the New Testament; you will not find one such promise. It is made quite*

clear that things are not going to be made easy. Why...we are not told; but we are told that there will be this sort of thing, and that it is 'not worthy to be compared with the glory.'"

By then Africa was "in my blood" and I had no thought of turning back. I wanted to serve the Congolese people and help to build them up in their Christian faith. God was very gracious to allow me to be among the first to return to the Congo when the door began to open once again. He gave me those three happy years at Raunguba, a wonderful trip to the Holy Land, and a great furlough with my family and supporting churches. The Lord brought me to the end of those trying years still singing

"GREAT IS THY FAITHFULNESS!"

CHAPTER SEVEN

MY THIRD TERM AT SINGA
(1965 - 1970)

"Blessed be the LORD God, the God of Israel, who only does wondrous things." - Psalm 72: 18

Flying across the Atlantic on a Sabena jetliner was quite different from a relaxing ten-day ocean voyage, but I was happy to be back in Brussels. I had only six weeks for French review this time. Again I was able to board with Madame Janssen. While in Belgium I reconnected with many of our mulattoes who had been evacuated from the Congo in 1961 and settled in the Brussels area. I always found that Belgium was an excellent "stepping stone" back into the Congo. My progress in the French language made this time in Belgium so much more interesting but I still had a lot to learn. I quickly enrolled in classes at the Alliance Française for advanced lessons in French. The best times to use my French were a number of opportunities I had in the homes of Belgian believers.

My sister, Marion, was married to Russ, an Air Force service man, stationed in Ramstein, Germany. They invited me to visit them while I was in Belgium and before returning to Africa. I had so much fun picking out just the right Belgian stuffed dog to take to my nephew David. The train ride from Brussels to Cologne, Germany and on down the Rhine to Ramstein was delightful and I saw some of the beauty of Germany for the first time. I spent a lovely weekend with my sister, brother-in-law and little nephew, my first experience on a military base. Years later I learned what a hit the toy dog had made on David and how he carried it with him everywhere he went.

Back in Brussels final preparations were made for my departure to the Congo. On Saturday, before I was to leave, I enjoyed an evening with Pastor and Mrs. Berge. The Rev. B.J. Berge was the pastor of the little Baptist church which I attended every time I returned to Belgium. They took me to a delightful Chinese restaurant near the Grand-Place. On the eve of my departure I had some rare moments with Madame Janssen, my Belgian hostess. We read Psalm 121 and had prayer together, not realizing that this would be our last time together on earth. Madame Janssen died before I returned to Brussels again. On August 17, 1965 I left Brussels for the long flight to Africa and sixteen hours later I was back in the Congo, having stopped in Athens and

Cairo for refueling. Missionaries Marjorie Hudson and Nellie Okken met me at the Goma airport. The first Sunday that I was back I worshiped in Goma. Only a year earlier a handful of people had met in Ruth Uhlinger's living room to worship the Lord. Now the number of worshipers had grown greatly and they were ready to build their own place of worship. I was greatly encouraged to see what had taken place in such a brief period of time and in the midst of so much unrest in the country.

By the fall of 1965 the political situation in the Congo had settled down considerably and missionaries were returning to their stations of ministry. Our educational ministry had grown and high school training was offered to qualified Congolese. One of these schools was opened at Singa Station, where another teacher was needed. I returned to the Congo just in time to meet that need and our mission leaders asked me to serve at Singa. I moved to Singa Station, in a rather remote area where I would spend the next four years. My ministry would be varied and included school, women, discipling, Sunday School, hospitality, visitation and evangelism in the surrounding area. The adjustment to the bush area and the smaller mission station was not easy, but gradually I began to feel at home, and by the end of the four years, I considered the Singa experience my happiest up to that point!

A little blue Volkswagen Bug was my means of transportation. The trip from Ruanguba, my former location, to

Singa took from four to five hours depending on the condition of the roads and how many "waits" in the park for elephants to decide to get out of the road. In order to go to Singa from Raunguba, we missionaries had to drive through a section of a National Reserve Park area where the wild animals were protected from us. However, our protection from them was not guaranteed. During that four year period I had various co-workers, including Bill and Florence Hunter, Marj Hudson, Dick and Louise Madsen, Paula Warner and Earl and Edna Camp. Fellow missionaries became family as we shared so much together: joys, when we saw spiritual growth in the lives of the Congolese, burdens, when there was resistance to leadership, and frustrations, especially when it came to doing things on time. Then there were the meals we shared together and the prayer times as well as trips to nearby African countries. Our hearts became bonded together as we served the Lord together in the Congo.

Singa was a typical bush mission station with a local church pastored by a trained African, a primary school run by Africans and a medical dispensary staffed by a trained African nurse. At Singa there was the addition of a secondary school and it was to this school that missionary teachers were asked to serve. At that point in time, 1965, we offered grades seven and eight to a limited number of qualified students from all over the area. The school building was on top of a windy hill while down in the valley was the student village supervised by an African. There was a dormitory and several student houses. The students came prepared to do their own cooking in small groups over an open fire in outside kitchens. This "boarding themselves" also involved carrying water from a not-too-far-distant spring, cutting wood for their cooking fires, as well as going out to buy their own food from the local market. All of this was done on a very limited budget. Then they did their own laundry at the town "laundromat," the small stream that ran through the valley. It was always refreshing to see their courage and joy as they lived and worked together. We seldom heard them complain about their work.

Students preparing supper.

Our teaching was all done in French. My first year I taught French grammar, history of the Congo, Bible, geography, English conversation and art. We had to put in a certain number of hours per week, as the salaries of the schools were paid by the Congolese government. One African university graduate taught with us. Several tribes were represented in the school, each with its own tribal language, but since French was the official language of the country all schools were taught in French.

There were several missionary houses on the station, three single residences and two family dwellings. I enjoyed "fixing up" my house which was located closest to the school. I painted the rooms, made curtains and planted flowers. Each house had a fireplace which was used most evenings. My house became a cozy haven which I enjoyed sharing with missionary and African guests. We missionaries often ate with each other on Sunday noon and I took my turn inviting them to my home for a meal and fellowship. Weeks, and even a month, would go by without seeing other white people, so we made every effort to entertain amongst ourselves.

The school program was very demanding but there were timely breaks and holidays. I insisted on having a ministry both in our local church and out among the village people. Very early on I started to disciple individual girls and women — this became a part of my regular ministry all the rest of my years in the Congo. I gradually got into other ministries as well. I felt God had blessed me with the gift of hospitality and I sought to use this in very practical ways. When a

Bernice and Verena with her children.

woman came by just to chat, I would invite her into my home and serve a cup of tea. At other times, such as Sunday afternoons, I would invite one of our leader's families for tea and fellowship. These times gave me an opportunity to get to know the local people better and to share something from the Word with them. When I would do visitation in their villages, I was likewise welcomed into their homes. The Africans never failed to offer me tea or a soft drink. I always felt badly to be offered a soft drink for I knew they paid a price for it that they could not afford on their meager salaries.

During my first year at Singa I made a great eighty-dollar investment — a small, portable, hand-run Singer sewing machine. I made my own clothes, wedding dresses for African girls, curtains and other items for my house. How I enjoyed using that machine and I regret that I didn't bring it back to the States with me! The machine stayed with me to the end of my years in Africa when I donated it to the girls' school to be used in the sewing classes. When I came back to the States a friend updated her electric machine and gave me her old one which is still serving me well.

I developed life-long friendships with some very special African people during my years at Singa. One of these was Esteri who had known the Lord for many years before I arrived at Singa. She was beloved by her own people and missionaries alike, a maiden lady "who'd rather be single than wish she were." She had had only one year of formal schooling but her life was rich with experience. She worked for a number of years as the "baby-sitter" for several of our missionary families. Before coming to Singa, she was employed at one of our mission hospitals where she learned nursing and even delivered babies. Esteri, working under the supervision of a trained African nurse, served as a mid-wife in the dispensary at Singa. Christ was the center of her life and she made a point not to miss an opportunity to tell others about her Savior. Esteri was a jovial person and I enjoyed having her come by my house for popcorn and fresh orange juice as we sat on the lawn on a quiet Sunday afternoon.

Esteri nursing my tropical ulcer.

My first year at Singa went by all too quickly. When school was out I took some time away and vacationed in Kampala, Uganda. We missionaries always loved going to the big city where we could shop, eat at a Chinese restaurant, drive on the left side of the road, and enjoy fellowship with other missionaries serving in Uganda. We did our regular grocery shopping in Kisoro, Uganda, just across the border from the Congo, a four-hour trip from Singa. However, on our annual trip to the city of Kampala we bought goodies not available in the smaller stores, including nuts, chocolate, cocoa, molasses. We ladies always had fun picking out material for a new outfit.

1966 - 1967

After the wonderful vacation in Kampala it was back to Singa to prepare for the new scholastic year. There were some staff changes. Bill and Florence Hunter left for Madagascar where they were assigned to open up a new work for the Mission; Marj Hudson had returned to the States for her furlough; the Camps and the Madsens, just back from furlough, joined our staff at Singa. There was to be a new program at Singa, an internship or practice teaching program, for those young Africans who were taking teacher training at the mission school in Goma. The students would do practice teaching in the Primary School at Singa. Paula Warner was in charge of this program.

Paula and I had a wonderful year together. Her house was next to mine and we spent many happy evenings together, sometimes in front of her fireplace and other evenings by mine. We enjoyed sharing books we were reading and also what we were reading in God's Word. We also shared special meals with each other. My life was enriched with Paula's friendship and the hours we spent together. We also did some evangelistic safaris together in near and far away villages. One of the trips stands out in my memory. Yorime, Paula's house-girl, who lived quite a distance from Singa invited Paula and me to go to her village and meet her family. One Sunday morning we filled Paula's and my car with students, drove for about an hour and then hiked for two hours with Yorime guiding us to her village. Yorime's extended family was waiting for us. The family gathered in their living room and we presented the Gospel to them. Paula shared her testimony, our students sang a hymn and I taught a Bible lesson to the children using flannelgraph figures. The family, in turn, served us a delicious African meal of chicken and hominy. We took pictures of this special day in the bush and then started on the long hike back up over the hills to our cars.

During that eventful year the volcano, Nyiragongo, erupted with a vengeance. The lava flow and the gorgeous glow at night were awesome but the devastation that comes with eruptions is heartbreaking. Houses were burned and crops were destroyed. Famine eventually came to the whole area. For several months we could see the glow of the volcano every time we drove south to take care of business in town.

The vast majority of our students were young men, but that second year we did have three courageous girls among the seventy-two young men. Those three girls were a special challenge for me. Girls did not have much opportunity for advancement in those days. They married very young, were expected to bear many children and care for the gardens, besides all of the other daily duties that fell to them. They carried water, cut wood and cooked the food over an open fire. The three girls lived together in a small hut in the regular African village. Every Wednesday evening I met with them for prayer and we read our way through Proverbs and *The Pilgrim's Progress* together. The status of girls changed dramatically through the years that I was in the Congo and many more girls were able to take advantage of the opportunity to receive a secondary education. Now, fifty years later, even though Africa is still very much a man's world, women are allowed places of leadership in schools, hospitals and even in politics.

As my second year at Singa drew to a close, we again sensed political uneasiness in the land. Both Paula and I had applied for government tickets to return to the States, and there were times when it seemed that we would not be able to leave because of lack of efficiency in offices and delays that were not explained to us. However, after a month of waiting, we finally were on our way. I had a good two months back in the States with family and visited some of my supporting churches. While I was gone, missionaries had to evacuate once again from the Congo. This time they took refuge just across the border in Gisenyi, Rwanda.

1967 - 1968

I returned to Africa in mid-October of 1967 and spent the next five or six weeks in exile in Rwanda with the rest of our mission family. The three of us involved in educational work were able to start classes in Goma, Congo, which meant we worked in Goma during the day but spent the nights in Rwanda. We could walk the distance although most of the time we went together in one vehicle. There was always danger, but for the most part we were safe in the daytime and felt as though we were making small contributions during the time away from our regular ministries. By November the unrest began to settle down and survey trips to check on general conditions in the areas where the mission had ministry were made to the north and to the south. I was sent with two other missionaries to do the survey in the Singa area. We were delighted to find our houses intact and the local people waiting for our return. Some of our students had already arrived and were eager for classes to begin. After my departure to the States, word had reached Singa that all US citizens were to leave the country. The Singa missionaries hid my car in the forest so that it would not be confiscated by rebel soldiers. While on the survey trip, I rescued my VW from the forest where it had been hiding and we drove back to Gisenyi with our report. Very shortly thereafter our Singa team returned from exile in Rwanda and settled into our ministries. Our team then was composed of the Camps, Madsens, Paula Warner and myself. We were so grateful to be back home again. I knew this was one of the "good things" the Lord had promised to give me at beginning in 1967. My verse that year had been "But those who seek the Lord shall not lack any good thing" (Psalm 34:10b). My mind often went back to the lines of Madame Guyon, a French lady of the seventeenth century:

> "While place we seek or place we shun,
> My soul finds happiness in none;
> But with my God to guide my way,
> "Tis equal joy to go or stay."

In November, with our very late start in the school year, we made every effort to try and catch up. By Christmas we had made good progress and the students went home to be with their families over the Christmas break. Marj, Michelle, Helen, Pat and Elfie, single lady missionaries from Rauangua and Goma, came to Singa to spend Christmas weekend together with me. That was fun for me because I loved having guests. Paula and I shared caring for our guests. We all attended the special Christmas services at the African church, a big conference on Sunday and a baptism where eighty-nine

In one of my classes.

Africans were baptized. Hundreds of Christians from all over the area came to Singa to celebrate the birth of our Lord. Christmas Day was on Monday and there was another service at the African church with Communion. The Africans did not have evening services because of a lighting problem, so we ladies kept some of our own traditions in the evening. Paula prepared a tuna roll for our Christmas Eve supper and we sat around her fireplace and a small decorated tree to exchange gifts of lace from Belgium, copper from Katanga, beaded spears from the local area, calendars from Uganda. My special gift from Paula was "Sunburnt Africa" by Kent Cottrell, a gorgeous book done in 'pencil, paint and prose.' On Christmas Day I served a canned ham dinner with mashed potatoes, peas, lime-pear jello salad, homemade bread and rhubarb pie for dessert. The Camps invited all the ladies to their house in the evening to play games. It was a delightful weekend and a wonderful break in our demanding schedules. After our company left and we were facing a new year, I spent some time choosing a verse for the new year of 1968. Reading in the Living Psalms, I found *"Oh God my Strength! I will sing Your praises, for You are my place of safety."* (Living Psalms 59:9). This verse was so appropriate for me, living in the uncertain and sometimes dangerous times in the Congo. I took great comfort knowing the Lord was my "place of safety."

As we entered into 1968 and a new semester, we teachers at Singa were able, for the first time, to arrange our schedules so that each one of us had one day off in the week. This was especially welcome since we were required to teach classes Monday through Saturday noon. I chose Friday as my day off because this was the day the Singa women met for their weekly meetings. The women met once a week for teaching in the Word of God. They took turns leading their own meetings and I was constrained to spend more time with them and to try to help with the teaching as well. That was the beginning of my many years of ministry to women in the Congo. The Singa women often asked me to speak to them from God's Word and I was able to encourage and assist some of their leaders to prepare brief devotionals. We planned evangelistic safaris together when we went out to near-by villages to preach the Gospel. These extra times with the women helped me to really bond with them.

At the same time the Singa church leaders asked me to help organize a Sunday School. They gave me names of people of whom they approved to work in a Sunday School. One young man, Deo, was chosen to be our leader. I met with Deo and the group of volunteers on several occasions to discuss how we would run the Sunday School. The group was concerned that the children would not come to Sunday School and I reminded them that if we teachers would seriously commit ourselves to the task, we would have the children. The first Sunday we had one hundred fourteen children! I taught the sixth graders with great joy and blessing.

My ministry was widening and I loved every part of it. I was so thankful to the Lord for having led me to the Congo and especially to Singa where I had the opportunity to use my gifts of teaching, organization and hospitality to the fullest. Truly, the Lord knows what is best for each one of us in every situation.

One Tuesday in January 1968, Dick Madsen became the proud possessor of two baby lion cubs! An African had brought them to Dick, wanting him to purchase the cubs. Dick bought the cubs and they became real pets and a great attraction in our whole area. I even took my turn petting the cute things! The time came, as they grew larger, that Dick realized he could no longer keep them and he arranged for them to be taken to Kinshasa, the capital, where they were received by the National Zoo. Who says life in Africa is boring?

We were well into the second semester of the school year when an invitation came from the Hunters to spend my vacation with them in Madagascar.

Bernice and Victor Madsen with the lion cubs.

Bill and Florence Hunter and I had worked together my first

year at Singa. I was excited to think about going to a new place and it didn't take me long to make up my mind to accept their invitation. I began making plans to go to the large island off the east coast of Africa. Madagascar, formerly a French territory, became a republic of the French Community as the Malagasy Republic in 1958 and in 1975 became the Democratic Republic of Madagascar. The Hunters had been sent by our mission to open up a new ministry on the island. They lived in the capital city, Antananarivo, and from there carried on their ministry to outlying areas. I really looked forward to going to Madagascar for the first time to see missionary work there and, of course, to visit with my friends. Paula was due for furlough that year and the two of us went to Kampala together, she to catch her flight to the States and I to catch mine to Antananarivo.

I enjoyed two delightful weeks on the island with Bill, Florence and their youngest daughter, Audrey, in their cozy apartment in the city. It surely was a welcome change from the rural living I had experienced in recent years. It was a rich experience for me to meet the warm, friendly, brown-skinned Malagasy people who are of Indonesian and African origin. One of my first days there, Florence took me to the large open market where you could buy everything from delicious fruit to well-crafted furniture. We walked to the market and returned by a taxi driven fast and recklessly by local drivers. My first Sunday there was another rich and memorable experience. We went to the 8:15 service where there was a baptism. The little church filled up quite rapidly with children in the front rows of seats, men on the left and women on the right. The youth choir, sitting in front of the congregation, was directed by the pastor's son. At eleven o'clock we went to the Cultural Center for a service in English where Bill preached an excellent message and I met several of their American friends. We went home for a quick lunch and then back to the church for a three o'clock service. Just before the service began the local pastor asked me if I would give a little report of my work in the Congo. He told me he would translate my report into Malagasy. On such short notice I wasn't exactly at ease but the Lord helped me to share with them my ministry at Singa. Later I learned that I was the first woman to stand in that pulpit "in many a moon." Back at the Hunter's apartment we were enjoying some popcorn when the door bell rang. Bill opened the door and there stood about twenty Malagasy women who had come with gifts for me! They brought a woven purse, two small drums, another woven doily, and a gorgeous tablecloth and napkin set that was embroidered with poinsettias, the national flower of Madagascar. I was overwhelmed with this gesture of their love. I cherished their gifts and still have the tablecloth with me today. We were never at a loss for interesting things to do during my two-week stay. One day the Hunters drove us out into the country to a village called Mormanga where we visited a small church pastored by the son of the pastor in Antananarivo. We were received so graciously by these simple country people. I still remember the sugar-coated peanuts that they served and the time of fellowship in the church before we had to leave.

The two weeks went by all too quickly but I was so grateful for the experience of seeing missionary work in Madagascar and for the time to renew my friendship with the Hunters. I saw their burden not only to evangelize the island of Madagascar but to reach out to other smaller islands in the area. Bill and Florence had hoped I might want to come and join them in the ministry in Madagascar and work with the women especially but I knew, as I had always known, that my call was to the Congo. Refreshed in body and spirit, I was ready to return to my own ministry at Singa.

The long journey home to Singa meant a three-hour flight to Nairobi and another forty-five minute flight on to Kampala. Mt. Kilimanjaro from the air was an awesome, unforgettable sight. I took care of a dental appointment and shopped while in Kampala. The long eight-hour drive back to the Congo, overnight at Ruanguba, and the five-hour trip up to Singa, and I was back home exactly one month after I had left for a vacation. We missionaries were allowed a month of vacation each year and we were encouraged to get away from our stations during that time. I rarely took the whole month but that time I fully enjoyed the whole month.

My first project back at Singa was to help two of our

mulattoes, Emmanuel and Françoise, get ready for their wedding. My kerosene refrigerator needed to be lit and running properly, drinking water needed to be boiled, beds needed to be made ready for guests and the church was waiting to be decorated. The Singa missionaries had done a lot of the preparations before my arrival and I tried to help with some of the many last minute details. Food and the wedding cake had been prepared. The next day the wedding went very well and we missionaries were delighted to see these two young mulattoes united in a proper marriage, special fruit from our years of ministry among them.

Before the end of the month there were rumors that another wedding would take place at Singa. Daniel Mayeur, a mulatto professor in the mission secondary school at Goma, made frequent visits to Singa and one day he approached me to ask if I would help make a wedding dress. He had asked Dina, one of my former students and the daughter of our Singa Pastor, to marry him. He made the request for the dress on Sunday and the wedding was to be the next Saturday. All of our Singa missionaries loved Pastor Lazaro, his wife Marata and their lovely daughter Dina. I wanted to do anything I could to help make a special wedding for them. Out came my trusty Singer portable, the bride produced the material and we went to work on the dress. With Dina's help we completed it on time, as well as a simple dress for her mother. Dick and Louise Madsen stood up with the couple. Early on the wedding day, using flowers from missionaries' flower gardens, I prepared bouquets for Dina and Louise. Dina came to my house to bathe and dress. Then I drove Dina and Louise to the church which had been decorated by village girls. Dina's baby sister, Judy, was the flower girl. After proudly marching his daughter into the church, Pastor Lazaro proceeded with the ceremony. He began by asking a very pointed question to Daniel, "Who are you going to serve?," to which Daniel replied very positively, "God." The invited guests were pleased with the unusual procedure which showed concern and conviction on the part of Pastor Lazaro and father of the bride. The wedding was followed by a big reception at the school. Edna Camp made a lovely cake for the occasion. The newlyweds left for a brief honeymoon in Bukavu at the southern end of Lake Kivu in the Congo. Once again we missionaries were delighted to have had a part in uniting another young Christian couple whom we hoped would serve the Lord. They did serve for a time in the Congo and later moved to Belgium where they now live and serve.

1968 - 1969

This was an unusually good school year. Thankfully, the political situation had calmed considerably. President Mobutu came to power in 1965 and brought a measure of stability to the country after the turbulent years of Lumumba and Kasavubu. Trying to hold together over two hundred disparate tribes from the capital of Leopoldville (Kinshasa) located on the far western border of the Congo was a feat indeed. We who lived in Kivu Province, a thousand miles away, were very aware of the frustrations faced by the political leaders.

Our students who had completed the second year (eighth grade) had moved down to Goma to enter high school. We at Singa continued to teach a new group of students in our seventh and eighth grades. I continued my ministry to the Singa women and the Sunday School. The women and I went on a number of evangelistic safaris to villages in the Singa area. As a result of our trips I saw spiritual growth in the lives of our women and new joy among them as together they reached out to other villagers. I also continued to disciple individual women, taking them through the truths of the Gospel of John. I served as mentor to the head of the Sunday School, as well as teaching my own class of sixth graders. There were the usual monthly trips to Goma, five to six hours away, to do our shopping and pick up our mail that was flown in from Nairobi once a week. We always enjoyed the occasional visit from a pastor or mission executive from the States when we could catch up on specific news from the States and share the blessings and burdens of our work. During my last semester before furlough we were all called to Ruanguba for a special missionary conference. Another time we had a joint staff meeting in Goma of the educational missionaries from Singa and

Goma. This was a helpful time of discussion and sharing ideas. We all welcomed the times away from our regular routine.

I noted in my journal for this period that malaria was hitting me rather frequently and sapping my energies. I tried faithfully to take a prophylaxis, but when one is especially tired malaria hits more often. By taking the prophylaxis, and the cure when a malaria attack hit, I managed to keep going. My furlough was due as soon as the school year was completed and I wanted to be able to finish the year without a major upset. As the year came to a close, there was the usual preparation and giving of final exams, student evaluations, graduation ceremonies and parties that I delighted to prepare for students. In the midst of all the activity I was planning my furlough itinerary. My household and personal things had to be packed away in case someone needed my house during the year I would be absent. There were the special "farewells" both from missionaries and Africans. Those times were very meaningful as I saw the love and appreciation that had developed over four years of working together. It is never easy to say "good-bye," especially when we had no way of knowing when we would see one another again. Dick and Louise offered to drive me to Kampala where I would catch a PAN AM 707 Boeing Jet that would take me on the first lap of my journey home. We spent one night at Ruanguba before crossing the border into Uganda. At Ruanguba there were more "good-byes" and farewells. The next morning we crossed the border into Uganda very early and I declared the ivory carvings that I had purchased to take home. That evening we were in Kampala, weary from the long dusty ride, but so grateful to have arrived safely.

FURLOUGH - JULY 1969 - JULY 1970

My furlough plans included a visit to Paul and Ruth Pretiz, dear friends from Gordon College days, who were serving as missionaries in Costa Rica with the Latin American Mission. In order to reach Costa Rica from the Congo, I flew northwest from Kampala, Uganda to Dakar, Senegal, with fueling stops at the gorgeous big airport in Accra, Ghana and again in Monrovia, Liberia. Anna Best, another missionary serving in Thies, Senegal, met me in Dakar. I was pleased to spend a long weekend in Senegal seeing first hand the work of our Conservative Baptist missionaries in that land before going on to Costa Rica. I spent the weekend with Anna, who had evacuated from the Congo in 1961, had served for a while in Morocco and was later sent to serve in Senegal. Don and Peg Penney, also evacuees from the Congo, also had been assigned to Senegal. It was a special joy for me to spend some time with these former co-workers. I worshiped with them on Sunday morning with two Africans in attendance. My heart ached for our missionaries who were giving of themselves to bring the Gospel to the Senegalese, without seeing the response we saw in the

Congo where hundreds attended church on a Sunday morning. I left Senegal with a real burden on my heart and prayed more fervently for those working among the Muslim people. Our Conservative Baptist missionaries had been working in Senegal since 1962. I understand that today, nearly forty years later, finally, in God's timing, they are beginning to see real fruit from their years of ministry there.

From Dakar I flew Lufthansa, a German plane, to Rio de Janerio, Brazil where I had less than two hours before my onward flight. I asked a taxi man to drive me to see the famous Copacabana Beach. He drove in and out of all the little tunnels until he finally came out of the last tunnel and there was the most beautiful white sand beach. Along the way he pointed out "Christ of the Andes," the famous large white statue of Christ high up on one of the mountains. The taxi man took me back to the airport in time to catch my flight to Panama City, where I had to spend the night in a hotel. I'll never forget the luscious grapefruit that I ate the next morning for breakfast, a treat I had not enjoyed in over five years. I caught my flight for San Jose at seven a.m. and we landed one hour later at seven a.m. having crossed into a new time zone. What a reunion at the airport, with my friend Ruth, her husband Paul, Grammy Pretiz, and David and Millie, two of Paul and Ruth's four children! How we enjoyed catching up on the nineteen years since we had seen one another. They showed me around San Jose including an inactive volcano, hot springs and waterfalls, all of which reminded me very much of the Congo. The climate and temperature were much the same as I experienced in the Congo. I visited their churches and schools and saw their nationals serving alongside the missionaries. I felt lost most of the time because I did not speak Spanish. I met many of their co-workers and shared meals with some of them. I did some sewing for Ruth and played Scrabble with the children — who always won! While there I read two books; *No Graven Image* by Elisabeth Elliot and *Christ the Tiger* by Tom Howard. My wonderful visit came to a close all too quickly and I had to fly off to Chicago. From San Jose I flew to Mexico City, stopping at all of the Latin American capitals to pick up passengers. From Mexico City, I flew on to Chicago where I was met at the airport by Kirkie Hunter, the daughter of my friends in Madagascar. After the required round of medical tests and debriefing with mission executives, I flew on to Boston where Ed and Lois Beaumont, Ruth Pretiz's parents, met me and took me to their home in York, Maine. I spent a few days with the Beaumonts sharing with them my time with Ruth and Paul and the grandchildren, before taking the bus to central Maine to be with my family.

Mom and Dad on our trip to Niagra Falls.

Since I had used a month of my two months allowed for visiting family and friends, I had only one month to spend with my family. I had decided to spend my third furlough with my parents on the farm in Parkman. I purchased a second hand Volkswagen Bug to get me around for my meetings in churches. I enjoyed the year so much, being with my family and seeing friends in my supporting churches. Reporting to my churches involved telling them about my specific ministry during the past term in Africa. I did this by showing slides of my work and explaining to them the burden on my heart for the Congolese people. Of course they wanted to hear all the details of the evacuations I had experienced. Each time I reported to a church I tried to give time for their questions as well, and I gave them specific things they could pray about.

There were several homes especially open to me during this furlough. I often stayed with Ted and Annetta Harmon when I had meetings in the Portland area. I enjoyed a visit with the Beaumonts in York when I was scheduled to speak in their area. I spent time with Harold and Jane Burchett in North Kingston, Rhode Island when I was in their area. Homes away from home mean so very much to weary, travel-worn missionaries on furlough. Near the end of this furlough I relaxed for two quiet weeks in Parkman when I stayed with Franky, our special needs brother, while Dad and Mom flew to Louisiana to visit our sister Marion and her family.

My third furlough was a wonderful year for me. The climax was a family reunion on July fifth at Harlow Pond where twenty-five of us spent the day together. There was a fellowship time at the Cambridge church that evening. On July sixth over fifty family and friends gathered at the Bangor airport to see me off for another term of service in the Congo. At Logan Airport in Boston a group of eighteen friends gathered for another farewell service for me. Truly

Family gathering at Harlow Pond.

farewelled and blessed I made my way back to Africa for my fourth term with a fresh sense of commitment and dedication to my Lord and to the task that lay before me.

REFLECTIONS ON MY THIRD TERM AND FURLOUGH

> *"What He takes or what He gives us,*
> *Shows the Father's love so precious.*
> *We may trust His purpose wholly,*
> *'Tis His children's welfare solely.'"*
> — *Lina Sandell (1832-1903)*

Going through my diaries of this period, I note that it was an especially happy term. I loved every phase of my ministry, the school, the women, visitation and trips to the villages to bring the Gospel. I especially enjoyed getting the Singa Sunday School up and running. From time to time I did struggle with loneliness but I knew that the best therapy for that was to go out among the people and I tried to do this regularly. The Africans continued to teach me so much. They were constant models to me of warm friendliness, generosity and sincere hospitality. The Bible talks of these qualities in the Epistles especially, and it helps to have live examples. I developed life-long friendships among the Africans, including Esteri, Pastor Lazaro and Marata, Pastor Barnabas and Rhoda, nurse Yeremia and his family to name only a few. There were also special friendships that developed between missionary colleagues during my Singa years. Paula Warner and I spent many happy hours by her fireside reading, talking, praying together. And there were the missionary families with whom I also spent enjoyable times. We shared meals, played games, went on picnics and watched a rare video.

Along the way, Psalm 59:9 in the Living Bible meant a great deal to me and I noted in my journal on January 14, 1968 :

"Oh God my strength! I will sing your praises, for you are my place of safety." This verse speaks volumes to my own heart, as I think not only of physical safety, which does mean a lot in this country in these days. Then there is the more important 'place of safety' just walking in the light of His Word and will, and knowing the peace that comes when 'all is well' between my Lord and me.

Not only did I have a happy term of service but my time in the States was very enjoyable as well. It was always a joy to visit my churches and to report to them what God had been doing in the Congo. Our family times were special, too. I came to the end of my furlough year refreshed and eager to return to my ministry in Africa. Yes, I took the malaria cure and was free of malaria for the year and until the next anopheles, the malaria-carrying mosquito, would bite me in the Congo. Indeed, I saw in so many ways

GOD'S GREAT FAITHFULNESS!!

CHAPTER EIGHT

PIONEERING AT KASHEKE MISSION STATION
(July 1970 - July 1976)

"Let the one who has my word speak it faithfully Is not my word like fire, declares the Lord, and like a hammer that breaks a rock in pieces?"
- Jeremiah 23:28-29 NIV

On July 8, 1970 my plane landed in Entebbe, Uganda where Paula Warner and Judy Gay met me and helped to launch me into my fourth term in the Congo. I spent a few days in Kampala purchasing supplies, taking care of banking, and taking possession of the new Volkswagen Bug that had been ordered for me. I was especially grateful to have the car already in Kampala, for I would need it for the new assignment that awaited me in the Congo. And, of course, we girls could not leave the city without one meal at the Chinese restaurant! After three days I was on my way, accompanied by Lorraine Stondell, a short-termer who had come out to help in the ministry at Ruanguba. Paula and Judy also returned to the Congo on the same day and our little caravan of two cars made the long dusty trip, arriving at Ruanguba, Congo before dark. Two days later I met with the educational committee and the chairman of the field executive committee in Goma. Since I had had experience in the secondary school at Singa the committee asked me to move to Kasheke station to open up a new Cycle d'Orientation (Junior High) for the young people in the southern end of our Congo field.

1970 - 1971

In some ways this was my most challenging assignment thus far. I was excited to have the privilege of being a "pioneer" in starting a new Junior High from the beginning. However, it would take a lot of gymnastics before I would be moved and settled at Kasheke. First, I drove south to Kasheke, four or five hours from Goma where Don and Evelyn Pierce were located. A few days were spent becoming acquainted with the Pierces and the area. Don helped me sign in with the local officials and Evelyn showed me the little house where I would be living and explained that they had plans to add on another room. I noted some challenges in my new housing situation; lots of cracks in the walls, a pipe-less tub and bowl, a flush-less toilet stool, a handle-less door and a door-less cupboard. There were lots of "less" and not much "more." We looked at the sites where the school and a dorm for male students were to be built. It was obvious there was plenty of work to be done by September. I met Celestin, the African pastor, and his wife Celestina. I knew this was where God wanted me to serve and felt sure I would like my new assignment. I was ready to tackle the challenge.

I then returned to Singa where I had served the previous term and where my household goods were stored. I spent two weeks there with the missionaries who gave me many pointers on exactly how to get this new Junior High started. We wanted the Singa and the Kasheke schools to be on the same level. I lined up schedules, books and other supplies. The plan was for me to teach the first group of seventh graders, and then they would move to Singa for the eighth grade. When our Kasheke school would be recognized by the government we would then have our own eighth grade with an African teacher to assist me. While at Singa I made arrangements for missionary colleague, Earl Camp, to move my goods in his truck to Kasheke. I followed in my car and arrived at Kasheke on August tenth. The first load of my household goods had arrived so I set up my bed, found my packed bedding and had the joy of sleeping in my own bed that very first night.

The next weeks were filled with hard work. I hired an African painter to help me paint my little house on the inside and gradually I became more settled. Don Pierce worked hard to get the roof on our classrooms and the boys' dorm on the hill was gradually going up. I loved the challenge of getting ready for my first group of nineteen students. I had one desire as I began my new ministry at Kasheke. I wanted to faithfully speak God's Word to my students, to the women that I hoped to disciple and to all who would come to my home. In order to do this I had to fill my own heart with the Word right from the beginning. Taking time each morning to be quiet with the Lord and His Word when there was so much work to be done was another challenge. I tried to be disciplined early each morning to read the Word and pray before jumping into the manual work of preparing my house and the classroom for our students.

Kasheke is located on Lake Kivu, one hour from the fairly good-sized city of Bukavu at the southern end of Lake Kivu. Even though Kasheke was a rural area, living that close to town was a definite plus. Food, building supplies, gasoline and kerosene for my refrigerator were all more readily available in Bukavu. We had several missionaries serving in Bukavu and they were so good about coming out to Kasheke to give us a hand in preparing for the new school. They also welcomed us to their homes when we drove to town for supplies. I enjoyed the drive to Bukavu from Kasheke on a paved highway and with the view of the lake part of the way.

To give you, my reader, a better picture of Kasheke let me quote from my November 1970 prayer letter. At a quiet spot up on a hill, this is what I wrote:

> "From my nook, where I am enjoying the quietness of a Saturday afternoon following a very busy week, I can look down over the still lake water which is dotted with African canoes, private fishermen seeking food for the family's evening meal. The stillness of the mid-afternoon is broken only by the singing of the birds, barefooted Congolese passing by on the road about 100 feet below where I am sitting, and an occasional truck on its way to the city.
>
> Looking across the corner of the lake I can see many hills. At first glance I can't see many huts, and I begin to wonder if there are many people in this area. A second more careful look reveals scores of large banana groves covering these hillsides. A walk through one of the groves would reveal many little mud huts housing hundreds of Congolese from the Bahavu tribe. On seeing the banana trees one immediately detects the kind of life these people live: selling, buying, and drinking their famous banana beer, and all the sin that goes with it.
>
> To the right of where I am sitting and down in the valley is our little mission station, Kasheke. Opened by Don Pierce in 1955, Kasheke is a center of evangelism in this area. Don makes regular trips with

Congolese Christians to ten different locations where there are groups of believers. One of these is the large island, Idjwi, out in the middle of the lake. Here at Kasheke there is an established church with a Congolese pastor, a primary school run by Congolese teachers (some of them my former students), and a medical dispensary run by a fine Congolese Christian nurse."

A good working schedule was in place as soon as classes started in September. There were classes in the morning and in the afternoons I concentrated on the women. Some days I instructed women individually and other days there were group meetings. The first woman that I worked with individually was Celestina, the wife of the local pastor. Celestina came to my house one day each week for her lesson. She was illiterate but as I led her slowly through the truths of the Gospel of John she responded in a beautiful way. I wrote out a memory verse each week on a card which she took to her home in the village at Kasheke where her ten-year-old daughter helped her memorize it. As God's Word began to penetrate her life I saw real spiritual growth and a desire to share her testimony out in the villages. I taught her a Bible story using flashcards with pictures, which she then would teach to women in a neighboring pagan village. We went out to a number of these villages together.

I was also responsible for organizing a local committee that would help me maintain standards and principles for our new school. I located some Christian African men who agreed to serve on the committee. I spent a great deal of time thinking through what I felt should be guidelines for these principles. The committee dealt with such things as the number of students in a class, limits on students from non-mission churches, discipline problems and housing for African teachers. Africans tended to receive all who wanted to come to our school and there were times when it was difficult to hold to a firm line of quality rather than quantity. But the members of my committee were very conscientious and they stood with me when it came to discipline and other problems related to our school.

Another project of mine was making regular visits to the sixth grades in the area since our new crop of students each fall would come from these sixth grades. I gave short tests in math and French to encourage the teachers to keep the classes up to standard. When I made these visits I also took the opportunity to share a brief Bible lesson with the students. Monthly visits to our five mission stations in the southern end of our field where we had recognized sixth grades gave me the joy of outreach into those more remote areas. Sharing the Word of God in each of these schools brought me great joy and satisfaction.

My co-workers, Don and Evelyn, were due for furlough in May, 1971. Don's brother Bill and his wife Norma joined us at Kasheke where they would minister with me while Don and Ev were gone. Bill, a retired civil engineer, had been in Navigator Bible Studies with Norma and they both were particularly interested in working with individuals. Bill would be able to complete the unfinished carpentry work on the classrooms and he planned to do the addition to my house as well. It was a joy to work with these short term workers who entered into the work with the seriousness of seasoned missionaries. My life was greatly enriched by their love for God's Word and their commitment to doing His will.

Our school year came to a close in June with a final chapel service where one of our African leaders spoke on 2 Corinthians 6:14-18. He emphasized turning away from sin, a timely challenge as many of our students would be returning to their pagan villages with no special spiritual encouragement during the vacation months. They received their grade cards and then we enjoyed an African meal together before they left. Some of them would walk for two days to reach their destinations.

Later in June I helped out at "Camp Kabisi" for four days. This was a camp for young people organized by our missionaries, Bill and Florence Battishill at Kabisi station, located between Kasheke and Bukavu. Young teens came to camp from our stations in that general area. That year there were one hundred three campers in all. I was responsible for twenty-nine girls at the camp. I made a point to speak to each one personally about her relationship with the Lord. Several other missionaries helped out at the camp with teaching, games, food and crafts. Those were four fruitful days when young teens were able to get away from their villages and enjoy fun, teaching from God's Word and meeting other young people.

My vacation that year was a lovely trip with two single missionaries, Mary Yuill and Judy Gay. On my way north to connect with Mary at Ruanguba I stopped in Goma to interview a young man, Edmond, who wanted to come to Kasheke to teach in our school in September. I spent a couple of days at Ruanguba with Mary who was a nurse at the hospital where I had my annual physical exam with one of our missionary doctors. Also while at Ruanguba, I connected with Ancilla, the first African woman I discipled, and we did a review session in the Gospel of John. Finally, Mary and I, in her Volkswagen Van, drove north for two days to meet Judy who was a nurse/teacher at the large medical center at the Brethren Mission at Nyankunde. After several days of relaxing in Judy's home, the three of us made our way toward Kampala, Uganda. On the way we spent two nights at Murchisson Falls where we slept in tents, took a launch trip with crocodiles and hippos all around us, and enjoyed a guided tour to see elephants, lions and rhinos. After that lovely visit in the wild, we enjoyed our annual trip to the city for shopping, dental work, AND eating in our favorite Chinese restaurant.

1971-1972

Back at Kasheke it was time to start the new scholastic year with a fresh class of thirty-four students. Edmond, a high school graduate, did come to teach the class. I turned most of the subjects over to him which freed me to concentrate on a spiritual ministry among the students. I taught the Bible lessons, took charge of scheduling chapel speakers twice a week and spent a lot of time with individual students. It was also a time of adjustment for Edmond and for me. Putting a very scheduled American to work with a more casual, non-scheduled African takes a lot of give and take on both sides. I was the principal of the school and was responsible for its smooth running. There were distressing times for me as I detected, from time to time, an unwillingness on the part of my African teacher to do certain tasks. However, over all, he was a very good teacher and for this I was grateful. There were lessons learned on both sides, I'm sure. It was my practice to confront any potential conflict up front in an effort to keep the lines of communication open. We really had a good year together.

Bill and Norma Pierce were always a constant source of support and encouragement to me. Their twelve-year-old daughter, Joanie, was in our school for missionary children at Ruanguba. She certainly brought a breath of fresh air to Kasheke whenever she came home for vacations. Joanie, with her great love for animals, eventually went to college in the States and became a veterinarian for a while. Later she worked as an air traffic controller in New Mexico.

My home at Kasheke.

Thanks to Bill's carpentry, the addition to my house was completed in October. I was able to enjoy my new living room, complete with a fireplace. I put my desk in one corner of the room which became my study area. The addition included a small storage room as well. With my trusty Singer, I had fun making curtains and re-organizing my new spaces. What had been the kitchen, dining and living room now became a kitchen and dining area with ample space for the many guests who were constantly passing through Kasheke. The house had grown like topsy but it served me well and I was grateful.

My work with the women continued and I discipled from three to four individual women each week. On a regular basis the women and I went out to heathen villages where the women shared their testimonies and I gave a lesson from the Word. I loved this part of my ministry. I was especially

Discipling Honorine.

blessed one day when Honorine, the wife of our Primary School Director whom I had discipled the year before, came to ask if I would review the lessons with her so she could disciple someone else. This was the first indication of reproduction in what I considered to be one of my most important ministries. I recalled the words of a quote I had noted earlier in my journal, "When your fruit bears fruit then you've borne fruit." I longed to see more of that kind of fruit coming forth from my students.

Chapel was held twice weekly at our school. I always tried to get a missionary or an African pastor or leader to speak in chapel. I was often discouraged in my efforts to find men willing to speak in chapel. Eventually, in desperation, I began speaking at one of the chapel services myself. One day I gave a simple Gospel message on "Jesus, the Light of the world," and in contrast, how we walk in darkness: "For you were once darkness, but now you are light in the world. Walk as children of light." (Ephesians 5:8). God blessed the Word and six students accepted Christ that morning. From that point on I did not hesitate to give the

Word in chapel when I could not find a man willing to do it.

We were delighted that second year when official word came from the government of Congo that our school had been approved by them for accreditation. Deighton Douglin, our school inspector, and Michel Ryabahika, our African legal representative, had spent countless hours making the applications and visiting government offices on our behalf. We all felt this was God's blessing on our combined efforts to establish a Christian school with high standards. I recommitted myself to my original goal of having the school completely in African hands with an African principal and all African teachers by the time I would leave on my next furlough. It seemed to be a realistic goal but only with the gracious help of our Lord would we see it accomplished.

When July of 1972 came, I was ready for my annual respite away from Kasheke. I made plans to go to Nairobi, Kenya, driving my car and traveling with E.J. and Tudy Kile. We visited the three capitals of Kigali, Rwanda, Kampala, Uganda, and Nairobi, Kenya on our way to attend graduation for their son Judson from Rift Valley Academy at Kijabe, Kenya. In the past, I had cared for Judd many times when we were all in French study in Brussels, Belgium. I was delighted to be included in this special Kile family event. While we were in Nairobi we saw Joann Kile off for furlough. Joann, the sister of E.J., was the teacher at the school for missionary children at Ruanguba in the Congo. It was fun to be in Nairobi, a much larger city than Kampala, because the shopping was more interesting. We all liked to shop on Baazar Street where we could buy souvenirs, food and beautiful yard goods for making curtains or dresses. It was a good trip and I returned to Kasheke refreshed and ready to plunge into a new school year.

1972-1973

It was about this time that government leaders changed the name of the country from the Congo to Zaire. Along with the name change of the country there were other restrictions and minor changes. For instance, the young men were no longer allowed to wear a western-style necktie and the girls were allowed to wear only their African style dresses. New babies had to be given an African name which meant that no more Bible names were allowed. Our Christians chafed under this name regulation more than all the others for they enjoyed picking out names from the Bible for their children. For the most part, however, our ministry went on pretty much as before.

Semerita and Bernice.

By the time I returned from my Nairobi vacation it was time to start making plans for the new scholastic year at Kasheke. Edmond wanted to enter university and would not be teaching again at Kasheke. Since we were ready to start the eighth grade in September, I needed two new teachers. I made my need known to the central education committee of our mission and also spent a great deal of time praying that the Lord would find me two Christian teachers to fit into our simple situation at Kasheke. One day in late August, Paul Mate, director of the Kasheke Primary School, came to tell me he had an extra teacher for his school and he offered to give me Michel for our Junior High. I interviewed Michel and learned he was a Christian, had graduated from high school, had one year of teaching experience and that he was married with one child. I felt he could fit nicely into our Junior High. I asked permission from the central committee to hire Michel. A few days after that I heard about a young man from way up north in Butembo. Kahindo had just completed his studies at the government school there and was qualified to teach in our Junior High. I worked closely with the local committee and wanted them to interview these two young men and give their approval. It was so important to have qualified teachers who met the government requirements but also I wanted Christian young men who would agree with me on the spiritual standards I had set for our new school. We thanked the Lord for sending us Michel and Kahindo. They were from two different tribes, which was good, for our students represented several different tribes: the Bashi, Bahavu, Wanandi, Watutsi and the Wahutu.

We were off to a good start. "Uncle Bill", as I called Bill Pierce, had completed the office for our school. I was so happy to have a place where I could spread out and from where I could work on the smooth running of our school. I taught Bible, arranged for chapel speakers and did personal interviews with each student. These jobs were all part of my effort to maintain a spiritual influence in our school. Michel and Kahindo fit into their schedules very well with Michel teaching math, since he was stronger in that area. and Kahindo teaching the French classes. The minor courses were divided evenly between them. We had sixty-six students that year in the Junior High. As I continued to visit the sixth grades in the area, efforts were being made to bring these schools up to standard.

"Uncle Bill" Pierce.

With these two fine Congolese teachers working in our school, I had more time to spend in my ministry to women. I was on the committee to plan an area women's conference in the fall and I was asked to be one of the speakers. The "Fruit of the Spirit" was my chosen topic. African women loved the area gatherings when they could meet women from other places. The conference was held in the newly built church in Bukavu in November, 1972. About one hundred women from all of our southern stations met on Friday and Saturday. There was lively singing led by one of the women and messages by Madame Rudia, an African guest from Rwanda. After my message, Celestina from Kasheke gave a Bible story with pictures, making me very proud of her. And, of course, there was always food which the women enjoyed.

The school year continued along fairly well with just enough bumps in the road to keep me on my knees. It seemed as though I was never quite satisfied with the spiritual level of our school and felt it went back to the behavior of our teachers. Drinking was a huge problem in our area and our teachers found it hard to resist the temptation. There was a large brewery in Bukavu where beer was produced and made available to the local population. When teachers began to earn their own money they too often spent it on beer, bringing heartache to me and to their wives and families.

That summer I did not take any long trip away from Kasheke because there was extra work to be done around the station. Houses for teachers needed to be completed and student desks needed to be painted. I had to search for one more teacher for our school and order books and supplies for September. I also wanted to take care of some repairs and extra cleaning in my house. I did manage a week at a Bible Conference across the lake at Kumbya, Rwanda.

Patiently sawing boards.

Missionaries from various missions gathered to enjoy one another, good music and excellent speakers. Kumbya is rather a rustic place with very old cabins where bats fly around freely. There are lovely trees, flowers and the lake is there for those who enjoyed the water for swimming or boating. Good food always makes mealtime around the tables very enjoyable. We surely had good meals at Kumbya. I delighted in time away from my responsibilities when I could share with other missionaries, read and take long walks. I returned to Kasheke refreshed in body, mind and spirit.

1973 - 1974

As I began my fourth year at Kasheke, my goal of having the school in the hands of a qualified African principal was getting closer but not quite there. I was at peace as we began the new year. Kahindo and Michel returned and Kulimushi, one of our own boys and a graduate of our teacher training school in Goma, was sent to teach with us at Kasheke. I was now responsible for three teachers and tried to work out a schedule which would be satisfactory to the teachers and our seventy-four registered students.

As things turned out, this was, without a doubt, my most trying year at Kasheke. Again and again I sensed the attacks of Satan on our work and workers. We were in a very pagan area, surrounded by heathen villages. Beer flowed freely, with a high price to the addicted, their families and to our ministry. Added to that was the allure of a local prostitute who targeted our Protestant teachers. These and many other burdens kept me on my knees, crying out to the Lord daily. Early morning would usually find me at my favorite spot up on the hill overlooking our station, for my private Bible reading and prayer time. The Scriptures were such a blessing to me, challenging my own walk with the Lord and giving me precious promises for those difficult days. Along with the Scriptures, I often took along one or two books by Amy Carmichael, a missionary in India, whose writings had been a great encouragement to me many times before. Amy was a missionary speaking to missionaries and her writings resonated with exhortation, encouragement and love. She helped me to regain perspective when I nearly fainted along the way. From *IF* I read :

"IF in dealing with one who does not respond, I weary of the strain, and slip from under the burden, then I know nothing of Calvary love."

"IF I have not the patience of my Saviour with souls who grow slowly; if I know little of travail (a sharp and painful thing) till Christ be fully formed in them, then I know nothing of Calvary love."

From *His Thoughts said...His Father said...*: No 120:
"There shall be an end" "But still the son felt like a long shore on which all the waves of pain of all the world were beating.

His Father drew near to him and said, There is only one shore long enough for that. Upon My love, that long, long shore, those waves are beating now; but thou canst have fellowship with Me. And I promise thee that there shall be an end; and all tears shall be wiped from off all faces."

The new teacher Kulimushi was such an encouragement to me. Not only was he interested in our students academically but he accepted the burden for their spiritual growth as well. He wanted to become involved in the ministry of the local church and he organized a Sunday School class for the secondary students. Kulimushi also knew the importance of backing up his ministry with his own walk with the Lord. He was sincerely trying to keep his testimony clean and I appreciated that, longing to have more like him working in our school.

We survived the year and I had good cooperation from the teachers during our busy exam week. We had our final chapel with Pastor Sibyola as our speaker. He was the father of one of our eighth graders. The aging Pastor came from the far-away village of Itobolo. He traveled several days on foot then, in a truck, and again on foot in order to arrive at Kasheke in time for our graduation. The blessing that came through this servant of the Lord was worth all the effort that had been made for him to reach Kasheke. One of our teachers who had been dabbling in the things of the world testified to the power of the message to his own heart. During the final week of classes I had asked each of the graduates to write his personal testimony of what the two years at Kasheke had meant in his own life. Following are a few of those testimonies:

> "Since coming to Kasheke I have accepted the Lord as my Savior."
> "I am grateful for Christian teaching received at Kasheke."
> "I have received help from the many memory verses we have learned."

> *"I am grateful for chapel where we can hear the Word of God."*
>
> *"While at Kasheke I have discovered from studying the Word what the conduct of a true Christian should be."*
>
> *"I can now read the Bible for myself and find verses which are helpful to my life."*

We gave out grades and certificates and had a little feast for the graduates. I was relieved when we said "goodbye" to the last student and teacher. I knew in my heart that we could not have all the same teachers for another year. I began praying that God would send us young men qualified both spiritually and academically.

I spent the month of July in Nairobi for my vacation. My memory fails me at this point and my journal is blank on the details. I am sure I went with friends, did the usual shopping and ate Chinese food. I returned to Kasheke eager to take up my duties once again.

1974 - 1975

As odd as it may sound, one of the goals of a missionary is to work himself out of a job. Scripture states it more specifically: "Equip God's people for work in His service." (Ephesians 4:11 NEB) Experience has proven that it is a long and often difficult but very satisfying task. When I was assigned the task of opening up the new school at Kasheke in July, 1970, it was my goal to have the school in African hands by the time I went on furlough. The years flew by and I began to think my goal would never be reached. When I returned from my vacation I learned that our central education committee had chosen Gabriel, a former student of mine from Singa days, to join our staff for the fall of 1974. I was delighted, knowing that he would bring spiritual depth and stability to our ministry in the school. Our local committee had already decided that the wayward teacher of last year could not return and I stood with them in this difficult decision. Instead, God brought to us Lukonge, a graduate of the Kisangani branch of the State University, with two years of teaching experience. He was a second-generation Christian with a humble and willing spirit. He would be our school director, our principal. My plan was to work with Lukonge during the first semester before officially turning the school over to him.

December 1, 1974 was a historic day at Kasheke, when Michel Ryabahika, our African legal repre-

I turned the school over to Gabriel, Kulimushi and Principal Lukonge.

sentative, came to Kasheke to meet with our local school board and to work out some guidelines for the new director and the teachers. The three young men, Lukonge, Kulimushi and Gabriel were called, papers were signed, and the legal representative offered a prayer of dedication. My heart rejoiced in God's faithfulness. At that moment, all the heartaches and trials of the previous years as I worked to reach this goal seemed worth it all.

I worked closely with Lukonge, turning over to him files, books, records and trying to emphasize the standards and principles that I had been working towards for our school. Africans tend to sacrifice quality for quantity and I warned him of yielding to the pressures of the many unqualified students asking for a place in our school. I was pleased with his attitude and could only pray that he would maintain the standard once he was in control.

Shortly after our happy historic day at Kasheke new rulings came from the government regarding all schools. All schools were nationalized as of January 1, 1975. We were required to be in school on Christmas Day. There was to be no further teaching of the Bible in the schools. In the midst of this distressing news, I fell from a chair while washing windows in the school office which resulted in a broken foot and the inevitable cast. This slowed me down considerably but I managed to keep my head and hands operating. I had only three more months to make any kind of an impact at Kasheke and I asked the Lord what I could do in that brief time. The students, teachers and church leaders were as distressed as I over these rulings. I spun into action and organized small Bible studies for our students during out-of-school hours. I felt that scriptural truth reached their hearts in a deeper way than ever before. The primary school teachers asked me to do a study with them and I took them through the book of James with great blessing. Somehow, when one is deprived of something the desire to have that becomes even greater. That seems to be the way of human beings. There were new lessons learned through this experience and I sensed a sincere desire on the part of our students to read and hide the Word of God in their hearts. Before a year had gone by, Bible study was again permitted in the schools.

I made plans for my furlough which was expected to start in April. I packed up my household things and there were many farewell dinners and "good-byes" during the last weeks. I finally left Kasheke and drove up to Ruanguba where I spent some quiet days taking care of final financial reports which needed to be turned over to the mission treasurer before I left. On April 9, 1975 I flew out of Goma, on to Nairobi and Amsterdam and arrived in Chicago on April twelfth.

FURLOUGH - MAY 1975 - JUNE 1976

I had been away from the states six years and the culture shock when I moved back into American life was overwhelming. There were so many changes; more cars on the highway, more lanes in the roads. Would I ever have the courage to drive in the States? Norman Chadbourne from my home church offered me the use of his second car for my deputation travels. I sat in his Ford LTD and wondered how I would ever pilot that huge vehicle out on the busy highway! I had been driving a VW Bug on dirt roads in Zaire. Norman's wife, Shirley, took me out for some lessons and amazingly, I learned to drive the LTD and truly enjoyed its comfort for the year.

As always, I had some wonderful family times before starting on a very busy deputation schedule. Early in May we picked fiddleheads together. Fiddleheads have to be cooked just right and Mother knew how to do it to please all of us. After seeing all my brothers, sisters, nieces and nephews, there was the usual connecting with aunts, uncles and cousins. I had decided that I wanted to take some refresher courses during this furlough. The first of these was at Westminster Theological Seminary in Philadelphia early in June. I took a week's seminar on Counseling with Jay Adams. The instruction, role-plays and fellowship with other students were all of great benefit to me. I stayed with a friend, Dottie, and her mother during that week. While in the area I was able to visit my supporting church in Ambler.

In August I took my parents on a little trip in the LTD to the White Mountains in New Hampshire and on to Cape

Cod and Provincetown. On our return to Maine we stayed in a motel in Massachusetts not too far from the Deighton Douglins. We had breakfast the next morning with Alice and Deighton. This was a nice experience for my folks to meet some of my co-workers from Africa. We followed the coastal route back to Maine and then Route Seven over the Dixmont hills. In September I climbed Borestone Mountain with my brother Charles. Later in September I was again in the Massachusetts area when Alice Douglin invited me to visit the class she was taking at Gordon-Conwell Seminary with Elisabeth Elliot Leitch. This was my first time to meet this lady whose books had made a deep impression on me. In November I had some meetings in the New York City area and I stayed at our mission regional office for a few days. While there I visited the Metropolitan Museum of Art and was delighted to see works by Rubens, Van Dyck, Giovanni, and Jordaens.

 We had our Thanksgiving at my brother Gayland's in Hermon with twenty-five family members present. From Hermon I drove directly to Rockland to connect with Grace Hopkins. The next day Grace and I drove to South Carolina where we both were going to take courses at Columbia Bible College during the short winter term. I took two courses with Dr. Harold Burchett. His courses on New Testament Church Life and Biblical Counseling were a great stimulus for me. I needed that time of stretching in preparation for returning to my work in Zaire. I was lodged in the girls' dormitory and enjoyed being a student again for three weeks.

The rest of my furlough year went by very quickly as I visited my remaining supporting churches and individuals in New England. I put many miles on the LTD and praised God for traveling mercies all along the way. There were more family times before I returned to Zaire. Mother had surgery three weeks before I was due to leave. I was home to cook for Dad and Frankie and at the same time did my packing while Mother was in the hospital. Although very sick for a few days, Mother recovered nicely and even went to the Bangor International Airport to see me off with seventy-five other family and friends on Saturday, June 12, 1976 for my fifth term in Africa.

REFLECTIONS ON MY FOURTH TERM AND FURLOUGH

"A mighty fortress is our God, a bulwark never failing;
Our helper He, amid the flood of mortal ills prevailing.
For still our ancient foe doth seek to work us woe;
His craft and power are great, and, armed with
cruel hate, On earth is not his equal."
— Martin Luther (1483-1546)

The years at Kasheke were the most challenging, the

most trying and the most rewarding of all my years up to that point. I had been given an assignment that caused me to lean upon the Lord for daily help as never before in my life. The Word of God was especially precious to me all during those Kasheke years. There were many opportunities to see God work in the lives of individuals in difficult situations. New lessons in prayer were learned as I was forced to my knees on many occasions to confront the evil in our area. God proved Himself to be a mighty fortress indeed. My reward came when I finally was able to turn the school over to some keen African Christians. Working in the southern area of our field was a new experience where I met Africans from different tribes and I also became better acquainted with our missionaries in that area. My life is richer for the experience of the Kasheke years.

Furlough was especially profitable to be with family again and to see friends in my supporting churches. The stimulation of the refresher courses deepened my burden to do the Lord's work in His way. I was pleased to be able to help out in our family while Mother was in the hospital. Truly this term and furlough was a time of seeing once again

GOD'S GREAT FAITHFULNESS!!

CHAPTER NINE

COUNTRY GIRL MOVES TO THE CITY
(June 1976 - July 1982)

"In quietness and confidence shall be your strength."
- Isaiah 30:15

My furlough year had been very busy and the challenge of the above verse was needed as I entered back into African life. Saying "good-bye" to American family and friends never became easier but the joy of being welcomed by my missionary family and African friends made the separation more tolerable. This time I flew out of Bangor, with stops in Boston, New York, Brussels and Kinshasa. In New York I connected with Phil Bjorklund, a young man from Minnesota going to Zaire to assist our missionaries for a year. Phil was carrying a very long bow and arrow set and I wondered how he would ever get through the Zaire customs. We were on a night flight SABENA 747 jet to Brussels where we had a day of respite before the night flight to Kinshasa. We arrived early in the morning at the Kinshasa airport where a couple of my former students were there to greet me. There was no trouble at customs and we were soon on our way to Goma, bow and arrow set included. It was June 16, 1976 and I was ready to start my fifth term of service.

SPECIAL ONE-YEAR ASSIGNMENT AT SINGA
(1976 - 1977)

I had been asked by the mission leaders on the field to return to Singa on a very special assignment for one year while the Madsens took their furlough in the States. One of our Singa boys, Gatambi, had just graduated from the national university in Kisangani with his degree in education. I had taught Gatambi in Junior High when I had been stationed at Singa in 1967.

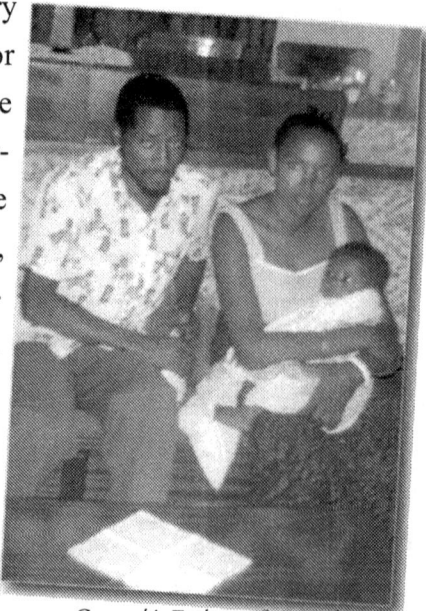

Gatambi, Esther and Migisha.

The Madsens had mentored Gatambi through the years and encouraged him to go on to higher training with the purpose of having him return to Singa and eventually take over the secondary school. Gatambi was a keen Christian, married to Esther and they had one child, Migisha. The Madsens were due for furlough the year I returned from furlough and they wanted Gatambi to become director of the now full-fledged high school at Singa. To do this he would need a missionary to work closely with him for a year and I was given this special privilege. I would be his secretary and also teach part-time at the school. My former student had become my boss — a dream in the heart of any true missionary! I looked forward to the year.

Once the Madsens left for furlough I was able to settle into their house which they had left all set up for me. This was a big help since my own household goods were still stored at Kasheke. Together Gatambi and I faced a big challenge right at the beginning of our year. There was a young man of another faith who was vying with Gatambi for the leadership of the Singa High School. We spent days in government offices, both in Goma and in Bukavu, trying to complete the paperwork for Gatambi to be named director of the school. Lots of prayer and weeks of footwork brought us final victory and we returned to Singa with an official document naming Gatambi as director of the Singa High School, on the condition that I remain at Singa as his mentor for the next year.

There were some profitable days of preparation before classes actually began. We spent a lot of time in a healthy

Pastor Serushago, Singa Church.

exchange of ideas. Gatambi always made an effort to communicate his thoughts and ideas with me and gradually I began to see what my role was to be. I did the secretarial work and taught a few Bible and English classes. This still left me time to spend with the girls in the school as well as the village women. Several women asked for individual time in the Word and I was delighted to do this. I believe God led me to Singa to help strengthen the Singa church. At the time I listed specific ways in which I would attempt to do this throughout the year of service at Singa:

1. I would be technical and spiritual advisor to Gatambi.
2. I would have a spiritual responsibility to the seven teachers and one hundred eighty-eight students in the school.
3. I would have as my special charge the thirty-three girls in the school, twenty-two of whom lived at the mission.
4. I was asked to be class advisor for the fourth year students, a rare opportunity to minister to twenty-five students on a one by one basis.

5. I would maintain a regular schedule with individual women from the church, taking them through the Gospel of John, truth by truth, and helping them to apply the truths to their daily lives.
6. I would also teach a Sunday School class of sixth graders each Sunday.

A dilemma faced me. Which is more important? Should I concentrate on the spiritual training of one hundred eighty-eight high school students, many of whom did not come from Christian homes, or should I sit down with each individual Christian woman and help her to see how she could apply the Word of God to her own life and her family? Which would bring the most lasting spiritual fruit? Since I had been involved in the educational work in Zaire for most of my years in Africa, and at the same time carried on a ministry with individual women, I often pondered these questions. Both ministries were important and had their own value, I'm sure. However, I am still convinced today that God's way of training children is through the home. Deuteronomy chapters six and eleven give clear instructions for parents and the teaching of God's word to their own children in the home. I have been blessed many times in my life by being in homes, both in America and Zaire, where parents have faithfully taught their children the Word of God. The results are always evident. Helping a Zairean mother see this clearly enough so that she would do something about it seemed to be taking years. I did see some encouraging signs among the Singa women and I kept patiently teaching the women, one by one. One special evening I stopped by Jeanne's house where she was sitting by the open fire with her children gathered around her, reading to them from God's Word. As I sat there by the fire with them I was blessed and encouraged to witness that beautiful scene. Then I knew in my heart that the hours spent with individual women were worth it all.

During that year I was back at Singa we missionaries suffered two major losses. Our first loss was Dr. Milton Baker, our beloved Foreign Secretary for many years, who died very suddenly in the States of a massive heart attack. Dr. Baker had been such an encouragement to all of us missionaries on the field. When he came to Zaire to visit periodically he greatly impacted our lives with his high standards for our personal lives and ministry. On one of my furloughs I had heard Dr. Baker speak in Dover, New Hampshire on the theme "Speaking the Truth in Love." Every time I read the verse in Ephesians chapter four, I thank the Lord for that godly man who made such an impression on my own life. Our second loss was one of our Zaire missionaries, Ruth Kreutter, wife of Jim Kreutter and mother of five boys, who died in an auto accident in Kenya. This seemed like such a tragedy to all of us but we rested on the sovereignty of our God. Ruth was an example of loving devotion to her family and of hard working commitment to her missionary service as a nurse. She was truly missed by all of us. Jim stayed in Zaire with his boys until they graduated from high school at Rift Valley Academy in Nairobi. One of his boys, Tim, is now a missionary serving in Uganda. Jim continued to serve in Zaire until retirement.

My year at Singa passed very quickly, and before I knew it, the Christians were having "farewells" for me. I was happy that my little ministries had made an impact for the Gospel in the Singa area. Gatambi had the school well under control with a good core of African teachers helping him. The Singa Sunday School, headed by an African layman, was meeting a spiritual need among the children of the area. Several key women had come to the fore to lead the outreach of the Singa women. My next assignment was to work in the city of Goma.

MOVE TO THE CITY OF GOMA

Sending a country girl off to the city can result in dramatic changes for that girl. I was brought up in the country and ever since coming to Zaire I had served happily on rural mission stations. I loved the simplicity of the rural Africans. However, when I was asked to serve in the city of Goma, I was ready to take up the challenge.

Goma, located at the head of Lake Kivu, had been a favorite vacation spot for wealthy Belgians earlier in the twentieth century. The volcano, Nyiragongo, is ever present with its threats of eruption. There are other volcanoes visible in the distance and two of them are snow-capped from time to time. Goma is within walking distance of Gisenyi, Rwanda. The population of Goma in 1977 was around fifty thousand; by 1992 it had doubled and today the population is between three and four hundred thousand. No longer is Goma that quiet vacation spot so much cherished by the early colonialists.

When I learned that a small African house had been reserved for me, I was delighted. I had always wanted to live in an African section of town where I could more closely identify with the local people. The house had five very small rooms and one bathroom. The foundation was of local stone, the structure was built with cement blocks and the roof was tin. It really was a nice little house, one of several that had been constructed especially for African secondary school teachers. Since the house had been occupied by Africans for the last seven years, there was a lot of work that needed to be done before I could move in. Four boxes of crack filler, seven cans of paint and two cans of cockroach spray were used to give the rooms a new look. Some fresh curtains helped to make it homey and I was soon settled in my own little house and happy. The African director of the Goma primary school, Hategeka, and his wife, Maria, lived next door to me on the hill overlooking a portion of the city of Goma. Hategeka and his lovely Christian family were a special blessing to me as I moved into the all-African neighborhood.

My missionary co-workers in Goma were Deighton and Alice Douglin and Elwin and Lois Pelletier. Deighton was the coordinator of all the educational ministries for our mission in Kivu Province.

The Douglins and Pelletiers.

Alice was a homemaker who took charge of the many guests who came through Goma and had a special ministry to the African teenage girls. Elwin served as field chairman while stationed in Goma and he was a counselor to African pastors in the Goma area. He did evangelistic work in the surrounding villages on the weekends and was often asked to preach in the Goma Baptist Church. Lois had charge of the mission two-way radio communication system, which had to be manned twice daily when contact was made with the other mission stations. These two couples lived in mission housing closer to the lake but well within walking distance from my new house. All of us stationed in Goma served as helpers to the many missionaries who came to Goma for shopping and other business.

My new assignment was to teach Bible in the African high school and to be in charge of the finances in the central office of our field-wide educational work. The Zaire government sent the teachers' salaries to our office and I was responsible for disbursing the funds to the directors of our twenty-five elementary schools and seven secondary schools. This network of schools provided Christian training for thousands of young people all over Kivu Province. Deighton Douglin was in charge of our office and we had African secretaries. I again had a ministry with the women and in the Sunday School. I soon learned that hospitality would be a significant part of my ministry in Goma. In fact, all of our missionaries shared in this special ministry. There was always a steady stream of people coming and going. Missionaries from the rural areas came to Goma for supplies and usually needed a place to spend the night. I had two roll-away beds and a couch which were put to use every week.

Discipling Mrs. Alapa at her house.

Living in the city was not without hazards and challenges. One Sunday evening at about eight p.m. I was returning home with one of our MK's (missionary kid) from our regular missionary gathering at the Douglin home. I had to park my car a little distance from my house. As we walked from the parking area to my house, two bandits accosted us and one of them grabbed my bag which contained my Bible, identity card, driver's license and a bit of money. Later the identity card and my license were turned in at our office. The greatest damage was to my nerves and the incident taught me to be more vigilant at all times.

Remember baby Caroline (chapter six), the daughter of my friend Ancilla? By now she was a young teenager. One day Ancilla and her husband, Toma, came to Goma to ask me if their daughter could live with me for the remainder of the school year and attend school in Goma. So Caroline came to live with me for several months. She helped with house work and was a comfort to me as well. I gave her spiritual guidance while she was in my home. We read the Word together and even read *Pilgrim's Progress*. That was a special time as I had the privilege of impacting my spiritual grandchild.

Two Christian pilots and their families were located in Goma while I was there, Everett and Terry Dirks and Henry and Raija Warkentin. They shared fellowship with our missionary group and both of these couples became good friends of mine. Terry and I met weekly for a period of time to study the book *Knowing God* by J. I. Packer. Raija invited me to spend Christmas with her family on several occasions. I enjoyed the Warkentin's teenage son, Tom, and younger daughter, Tanya. Raija did some work in cultural anthropology with one of the tribes in the Goma area and later wrote her book, *Our Strength is in our Fields*. The Warkentins eventually moved to Canada where Raija is now a professor at Thunder Bay University in Ontario. My life was enriched by having these special friends outside of my missionary co-workers.

I managed to get away for a week of vacation in August that year. My destination was across the border in Rwanda, a Catholic retreat center, Kigufi, on the other side of the lake. The drive there was less than an hour depending on how long it took to pass through both the Zaire customs control as well as the Rwanda border. When the Catholic sisters at Kigufi were not busy with their own people, they would allow other guests to stay in their guest house. They provided lodging and meals for a minimal fee. The setting was ideal for weary missionaries: on the lake, with trees, flowers, a beautifully-kept lawn, as well as peace and quiet away from everyday routine. I hiked over the hills in the area, enjoyed the good food that I did not have to prepare and had time to be quiet and read, meditate and write a few letters.

There was a terrible cholera epidemic in the greater Goma area in the summer of 1977. July and August were our dry months when sickness tended to be more prevalent. Four hundred cases of cholera were reported in Kirotshe, one of the outlying districts, where people died every day. People who neglect cleanliness are more prone to succumb to cholera. We missionaries washed our hands frequently and tried to teach the locals to do the same. The medical people worked overtime trying to save lives. If caught in time, the simple treatment of a solution given intravenously was quite effective.

1978 - 1979

When one is involved in an educational ministry it seems that September always comes around too soon. During the summer months I still worked at the office paying teachers' salaries each month. My ministry to individual women continued, but my Bible classes would not start again until September. One day late in August one of our African leaders, from another town about seventy-five miles away, came to ask if I would consider having his daughter live with me during her senior year in high school. I immediately knew this was something I should do. In less than two months I was to see why God had arranged that I keep Ada in my home. What a great blessing this young girl was to be to me! I can still recall how much fun I had rearranging my house in order to give her a small room of her own. I had not done this for Caroline the previous year since she was to be with me for just a few months before going to live with a relative in Goma.

Before classes began in September I had an overnight guest from Nyankunde, a Brethren Mission two days journey to the north of Goma. Marie-Jeanne had flown in from Kinshasa, the capital, and was waiting for a plane to go north to her station. We had a lovely visit and I even invited some of our missionaries in after supper for home-made strawberry ice-cream. After the missionaries left, Marie-Jeanne and I retired. About ten forty-five we heard a "WHAM"!!! Bandits had thrown a big rock which broke down the kitchen door. We locked ourselves in my bedroom, while they went through the house helping themselves to a water filter, electric tea-kettle, a chest of flatware, record player, blankets and all of Marie-Jeanne's things...the list was long. This was the ultimate experience in my identification with African people. Break-ins, unfortunately, happen all the time in the African villages. I had now experienced first-hand what the villagers go through on a regular basis. I'm afraid it took me longer to regain emotional composure than it does for them. In addition, I felt so badly for my guest Marie-Jeanne, who had lost everything she had with her. Marie-Jeanne went on her plane the next day empty-handed. I presented my list of stolen items to the local officials but I never received anything back. Shortly after the incident, I received a letter from a friend reminding me of the *COST* in keeping to the ideal of identifying with the local people. I realized I was very much a beginner in the lessons of identification.

    One week later Ada arrived to begin her year with me. I was so grateful that she had not been there when the bandits broke into the house. Now I was especially thankful to have her in the house with me. She was a great comfort in the days to come. We had some happy days together as I oriented her to some of my house rules and to my schedule. I knew God had sent her to me.

Ada roasting corn.

September arrived and classes began. I delighted once again to be teaching God's Word to high school students and to my Sunday School class of junior high youngsters on Sunday. A high priority was my personal ministry to young Ada while she lived with me. Time was spent each evening with her exploring the Scriptures. We read through many books of the Bible completely while we were together. On Sunday evenings we read *Pilgrim's Progress*. I had an excellent translation in French of this old John Bunyan classic. Ada's friend Esther, a neighbor and also a student, joined us for this Sunday evening treat.

The educational office was taking more time than I wished and I began to set goals for the future of the office work. By the time I was ready to go on furlough, I wanted to have a trained, responsible African Christian to take over my job as treasurer. Shortly after I began praying about a replacement, I was called urgently to the bank. The bank manager informed me that two of my checks had been forged. One of them was caught in time but the other had been cashed. I was horrified to realize that someone right in our office was guilty. Even more disturbing was my wondering if I could ever find an honest person to take such a responsible position. We, of course, found the culprit and dismissed him. My prayer for the right replacement was even more fervent after that incident.

As the year progressed there were other instances of dishonesty in Goma. My own encounters with dishonesty included missing bed sheets and stolen gasoline. I never had the luxury of a washing machine while I was in Africa. Instead I hired local girls to do my laundry. Much of the time while I was living in the African house on the hill I had African girls living with me and we managed to do our laundry ourselves. The bigger problem was getting the wet laundry dried. Clothes dried rather quickly in the African sun but one had to be vigilant the whole time the clothes were outside on the grass. One day after I had done my laundry and put the clothes out in the sun, I jumped into the car to do a very quick errand. When I returned three sheets had already disappeared. Lesson learned. Shortly after that I discovered that gas had been stolen from my car. Another lesson learned. From then on I left my car in the Douglin's more secure yard and did my errands on foot. Good exercise and great for keeping the cholesterol down!

As the summer break drew near I began making plans to take a short three-month furlough to the States. My folks back in Parkman had sold the farm where their eight children had been brought up. They had purchased a new mobile home which they placed on my sister's land in Dexter. I needed to see their new home while my eighty-one year old Dad was still in it. To leave for three months took a lot of arranging of my work in the office, including the teachers' salaries to be paid each month. My prayers were answered when God led us to one of our African primary school directors who seemed to have a gift for accounting. He worked with me during the pay periods for three months before I had to leave. While I was gone he took over my duties as treasurer and accountant, working under Deighton's supervision. Batende seemed to be the answer to our prayers and possibly could become our future treasurer. I had an especially good year with fifteen students in my Bible class from the senior class. My friends, the Dirks, planned a special evening for us at their home. We had a delicious dinner together and games after the meal. The evening meant a lot to Ada who would soon be graduating with her friends. Since I would have to leave before graduation I was grateful to the Dirks for giving my students the evening together.

SHORT FURLOUGH - JUNE - AUGUST 1979

I planned to fly out of Kigali, a five-hour drive from Goma. Deighton and Alice drove me to Kigali in their vehicle. I recall that we had muffler problems on the way and the muffler finally fell down. Alice, being a nurse, had an ace bandage with her which Deighton used to tie the muffler back up. We arrived safely with no further incident and spent the night with missionaries in Kigali. The next day, June second, I started the long flight to Bangor, Maine and arrived the following day at nine-thirty p.m. Family members were at the airport to meet me and drive me to Dexter. I was delighted to see my folks nicely settled in their new home overlooking a beautiful farm pond. In fact, I am writing this story from that same home twenty-six years later.

On my way to the States.

After driving in rural Africa on single-lane, dirt roads, I needed to practice stateside driving. One of the first practice sessions was a shopping trip with Mom. We borrowed Dad's car and I drove to Bangor where I made three purchases; a pair of walking shoes for Africa, *The Journals of Jim Elliot*, and a piece of material for a new dress. It was a very special three months at home. Every Saturday morning my sister Mary Lou, who lived ten miles away in Dover-Foxcroft, came to see us with doughnuts from the bakery where she worked. On Tuesday mornings I went to Cambridge to pray with my home church ladies. My brother Charles came up from Westbrook several weekends while I was home. I connected with brother Gayland, his wife Clarice and their four children, who invited all of our family down for a cook-out at their place in Hermon. I enjoyed the barbecued hamburger and hotdogs, roasted corn and other goodies that everyone contributed.

Even during a short furlough missionaries were expected to visit as many supporting churches as possible. I set a goal of visiting all of my churches in Maine and quickly found that family members and friends from my home church volunteered each weekend to take me wherever I needed to go. The churches welcomed me and my chauffeur friends and it was a delightful experience on all sides. Only a few times did I have to take the bus. I visited one church in New Hampshire where George and Thelma from my home church drove me and we spent the night. I visited eighteen different churches, seventeen in Maine and one in New Hampshire.

My church contacts were usually made on Sundays, or an occasional Wednesday evening meeting, leaving me most of the weekdays to spend with family. In July I took my sister Bea out for a birthday breakfast and presented her with a New International Version of the

Mom, Dad and I in their new home.

Bible. Mom and I picked raspberries on Page Hill and I had the fun of making a raspberry pie. Our family had an early Thanksgiving dinner in Bangor at our sister Marion's home and we celebrated an early eighty-second birthday for Dad. Every effort was made to see all of my family members, including taking Dad and Mom and my special-needs brother, Frankie, on several day trips. We visited other relatives and one day we had lunch at the Log Cabin in Newport. Shortly before I had to return to Africa we had a big family gathering at my parents' new home, on the lawn next to the farm pond. That day Bea surprised me with a huge early birthday cake in the shape of Africa which was enjoyed by all our family.

The three months of my furlough were filled with positive and happy experiences but, of course, the days slipped by all too quickly. I was so glad I had returned home for those three months. I didn't realize it then but it was the last time I would see my brother Gayland. He died of a massive heart attack while I was in Africa, and my Dad died before I was able to come home again. Besides all of the visiting I had quiet days when I enjoyed reading the *The Journals of Jim Elliot* by Elisabeth Elliot. All too soon it was September sixth and the journey began for my return to Africa. For the first time, my suitcases did not arrive with me in the Congo. They caught up with me two weeks later but one had been opened and a number of items were missing. Still another lesson learned regarding detachment from material things. Africa was becoming a great place to keep learning that lesson!

1979 - 1980

As always, I was happy to be back in Africa but the first few days were usually a series of small and large frustrations. The kerosene refrigerator had to be lit and running smoothly and this could take hours. Water had to be boiled for drinking and the house needed a good general cleaning. While I had been gone a faithful African student had slept at the house for the purpose of guarding it. I was happy to find everything intact when I returned. Then there was the trip to the market to buy a bit of food and while at the market I saw friends I hadn't seen for months. Of course they wanted to have a nice long chat. In Africa you learn that people are more important than projects and you try to give them an appropriate amount of time, even if you are hurrying to complete your market shopping. After a few days things fall back into their familiar routine and it seems as though you have never been away. Ada, who had stayed with friends while I was away, had been given a teaching position as a sixth-grade teacher in the Goma elementary school and would share my home again. She soon joined me to clean and settle her own room. Classes began soon after we were settled. I had five Bible classes at the high school with a total of one hundred seventy-nine students. This was still a great mission field. In addition I continued to teach the junior high Sunday School class. My work in the educational office was on-going, always with the goal of training an African to take over my job. Batende had done a good job in my absence, but he needed to return to Bukavu to take charge of his own school. We continued to pray about our need and his future. All this time Ada and I were also looking for a more secure place to live.

Since I had been in the States when Ada graduated from high school, I wasn't able to have any kind of a party for her. As soon as we both were settled in our fall ministries, I planned a special Sunday dinner and she invited twelve of her friends. We both had fun preparing for this special occasion, cooking two chickens, rice, potatoes, sombe (African greens), bugali (African bread), carrot sticks, juice, doughnuts and peanuts. Her friends came after church and all ate heartily. We sang some of Ada's favorite hymns and Ada shared her testimony of God's faithfulness to her during her high school years. I gave her some carefully chosen verses. Since I longed for the Lord's best in the life of my spiritual daughter, I challenged her with Romans 12:1-2, I John 1:7 and Psalm 91:11.

New Year's Day is a very important day in Zaire and I always loved joining with the African Christians for their early morning service at church. This year we all gathered at six a.m. for singing and testimonies of praise to the Lord for His blessings during the past year. I sat there with about two hundred Africans fighting back the tears as I listened to one testimony after another. To help you understand how those testimonies moved me, here is a sampling:

> A father, whose employment took him away from home much of the time, stood to praise the Lord for his Christian wife and her faithfulness for teaching their children God's Word in the home.
>
> A teen-age boy praised the Lord for taking him through the valley of a long period of illness when his faith wavered.
>
> A widow lady thanked the Lord for taking care of her needs during the past year.
>
> A child stood to thank the Lord for the forgiveness of sin.
>
> An elderly deacon asked the pastor to read Psalm 71:5-8; 17-18. We all rejoiced with him in the Lord's

goodness that allowed him to continue his ministry among us.

A missionary praised the Lord for the privilege of living in their city and serving the Lord with them. When all the testimonies had been given we sang a praise hymn and the service came to a close at nine a.m.

My missionary friend Mary Yuill was over in Gisenyi, just across the border into Rwanda, where she was taking some time out of her nursing at Ruanguba hospital to study the local tribal language, Kinyarwanda. From time to time we enjoyed being together for a weekend at Kigufi, the retreat on the lake, where we relaxed, read books, wrote letters, hiked over the hills, played games and prayed together. A weekend away like that helped us so much to keep a balanced perspective. Another time we went on a safari together out to the distant village of Bitonga. At that time I wrote a rather detailed letter about that trip. I will include it here:

Safari to Bitonga

Since coming to Goma three years ago, I have not had the opportunity to go out to our bush churches as much as I would like. However, one Sunday last month Mary Yuill invited me to go with her to Bitonga. As I review the safari with you, rejoice and bless God with me. We left Goma at six-thirty in Mary's VW bus, taking with us a young men's quartet who were to sing at the church. After an hour's drive, we picked up a guide for the remainder of the trip. We continued on for another five miles or so, then had to leave the car to begin the hard climb. Very shortly we met some teenagers coming from the church. Two of them had been sent to guard the car and the other to carry Mary's accordion to the church.

The climb was beautiful and I had that good feeling that this was the real Africa. We were on a narrow winding path with Africans walking in single file and the accordion on the head of a teen ager. Mary and I mixed in with them, chatting as we climbed. After about thirty minutes we began to see Lake Kivu below and the city of Goma in the distance. Goma, with all its wickedness…I was so glad to be breathing the cleaner country air for a day. Around nine thirty we had our first glimpse of Bitonga. As we came closer, I could hardly believe my eyes. There stood a beautiful church building! I was truly humbled as I thought how the materials for the building had to get there by the same path we had come and all on the heads of the Christians.

Upon entering the village we were greeted by the pastor and his assistant. The tea and bread they served us was very welcome as our early morning breakfast had long since worn off in the climb. We were each handed schedules for the morning service before going to the church which was already filling up with people. The service began promptly at ten. I was deeply impressed with the following:

The organizational ability of the assistant pastor; the three-hour service moved like clock-work.

The spiritual depth of the senior pastor; his message from Haggai 2:12-13 was a great blessing to me.

The display of various spiritual gifts on the part of certain members who took part in the service.

The spirit of hospitality and love shown to us, their guests for the day.

Following the service we enjoyed delicious African food which we ate with the two pastors and their wives. I excused myself early so that I could call on Mukuba, a former student and his family who lived in the area. This meant more climbing, but it was worth the effort as I sat in a broken-down hut with a young man, his wife and two children. Since I had only fifteen minutes to spend with them we opened the Word immediately to John 4:14 and 7:37-38. I wanted to encourage them in their spiritual responsibilities in the home and to their neighbors. They shared with me some of their blessings since their move from Goma. We had a season of prayer together before parting.

Back at Bitonga our group was preparing to leave. With proper African manners half of the villagers accompanied us part way down to the car, and some all the way. We were each given a live chicken! In fact, I had two! One was from Mukuba. Their generosity always overwhelmed me. Walking with the wife of the assistant pastor, I asked her about her program for teaching their five boys the Word of God in their home. Not satisfied with her answer, I eventually had a chance to walk beside her husband. I warned him of the danger of giving so much time to the church work that he would neglect his own family. He thanked me for the warning and I then gave him a few practical suggestions for family devotions.

The descent was almost as hard as the ascent, but we made it by three-thirty. Shortly after five o'clock we were back in Goma, weary but rejoicing that the Lord had led us to serve in Zaire where we could be His lights.

Since the Douglins were leaving for furlough as soon as the school year was completed, and since I would be taking my furlough as soon as they returned, it was decided that I should move into their house for the year. Indeed, the Lord had answered prayer for Ada and me to have a more secure place to live. During the summer break I moved out of the little house on the hill and into the mission house down by the lake. Ada would join me in the fall. I enjoyed spreading out in the much larger house and I had a more secure feeling in the new location. The property had a fence around it and there was an African guard, day and night. It was a very different neighborhood, made up of Caucasian families and the more elite African families. I missed the warm, friendly atmosphere of the all-African community which I had enjoyed for three years, but there were advantages and I hoped there would not be any more missing sheets. My summer ministry was to care for the many guests who were constantly coming and going through the city for shopping, banking and other business, as well as catching flights at the airport. At least once a week I went to the airport to meet the MAF flight that came in from Nairobi with missionary mail and passengers. MAF, the Missionary Aviation Fellowship, is a missionary flight program that assists church and mission work world-wide. Their closest base to us was Nairobi and they made regular flights to Zaire which was a big help to our missionaries. I, of course, still worked at the office paying teachers when the monies came in from the government. The summer weeks went by rapidly. I was busy and happy with more time to spend with people.

1980 - 1981

Ada had spent the summer with her parents in Rutshuru, a village two hours north of Goma, and she returned to Goma at the end of August. I was delighted to have her live with me again for this final year before my furlough. She was asked to take a secretarial position in the educational office which meant she would have to give up teaching. She really loved teaching but after thought and prayer, she decided to accept the position. This was an opportunity for her to broaden her interests and to use her gifts of organization and attention to details.

One day early in September, Muhima, the African pastor of the Goma church, and Dina, one of the women leaders, came to my house to ask me to take charge of the ministry to the church girls. I wanted to do this but needed to wait until I was completely out of the educational office so I could devote more time to the girls. In the meantime, it seemed that Batende, the man who had helped out in the office earlier, was truly the one we had been looking for to be responsible for the educational finances. However, this meant giving up his position as director of an elementary school in the south and moving his family to Goma. This he agreed to do and by September, Batende had found a house to rent in Goma and had moved his family. I worked closely with him on the finances, teaching and guiding him until he felt confident enough to perform the duties on his own. I was so grateful that God had prepared an African replacement for me. Even as I write this story, over twenty years later, Batende is still in that office. He has been a faithful worker and proven himself as a man of great integrity.

As soon as the office duties were no longer my responsibility, I became involved with the girls' work. This meant organizing their

Goma teenage girls.

Sunday afternoon gatherings and often teaching them from God's Word when there was no guest teacher for them. I had from fifteen to twenty teenage girls each Sunday afternoon. We met at the church, sometimes in the home of one of the girls, and on special occasions I invited them to my home by the lake. I also met with them individually to encourage and guide them in their private Bible reading. Elisabeth Elliot sums up what I wanted for our girls:

> "We are called to be women. The fact that I am a woman does not make me a different kind of a Christian, but the fact that I am a Christian does make me a different kind of a woman. For I have accepted God's idea of me, and my whole life is an offering back to Him of all that I am and all He wants me to be."

Part of the blessing of being located in the city of Goma was meeting new people all the time. It was an extra special blessing when new missionaries arrived to work in Zaire. On October 1, Linda Wilms, a newly appointed missionary from Michigan, having completed her French study in Europe, arrived in Goma. Linda stayed in our home by the lake for a few days before going to the station where she would be studying Swahili. During our evening devotions on the first day she was with us, Ada read Joshua 1:7-9 to Linda to encourage her as she began her ministry in Zaire. Linda was blessed and I was very proud of Ada, who was showing signs of real spiritual growth and maturity. I gave a lot of my time and energy to hospitality, for there was no end to the guests who passed through our home. In addition to preparing food and other necessities to make their visits more comfortable, I made it a point to share something from God's Word and to have prayer with each one.

While the Douglins were on furlough I was caring for their dog, Sarge. Much to my distress Sarge became ill and died. This was my first experience trying to bury a dead dog. My outside worker flatly refused to bury the dog for me. I learned some more lessons in African culture and saw what a strong hold some of the old heathen customs still had on my worker. He insisted on getting "dawa kutosha sawishi" (medicine to take away bad luck). In other words, he was asking for money to buy some type of witchcraft medicine that would keep him from encountering any bad luck because he buried the dog. I was finally able to hire someone from another tribe who did not hold to this strong belief and Sarge was properly buried.

Christmas was a happy time in Zaire. The Christians celebrated at church with lots of music, a dramatization of the Christmas story and extra services with guest speakers. They usually had a baptism with large numbers of new believers being baptized, followed by communion service. On Christmas eve day, Ada and I had a hurried lunch before leaving the house to do some quick errands. When we returned an hour later, we were distressed to discover that our house had been broken into. Ada's guitar, her prized possession, was missing and also my cassette recorder and a few other minor items were gone. Just as the afternoon guard came on duty, he rescued my Singer sewing machine from the hands of the thief who was walking out the gate with it. Our sense of security in the new location suddenly deflated and we remembered that Christmas in Zaire is also a time to be especially vigilant and aware of thieves who are lurking on every corner watching for an opportunity to help themselves to treasures. I, of course, was thankful to still have my trusty Singer but felt so badly that Ada had lost her guitar. A few weeks later Ada and I were invited to have dinner at the Dirks and they presented her with a brand new guitar. Ada's joy had no bounds and she hardly let her new treasure out of her hands.

In February word reached me that my Dad, who had been sickly for some time, had passed away at age eighty-two. I was so thankful that I had gone home for those three months. Since my regular furlough was due in mid-July, I decided to finish the school year before going to the States to be with family. I was greatly blessed and comforted when an elderly African pastor came to my home to read Scripture and pray with me after hearing of my Dad's death. There were so many details to complete before I could leave. Final grades had to be dealt with, Ada needed to be settled into another home, my household things had to be removed from the Douglin house and stored somewhere. Then there was the usual round of "Farewells," one of which still stands out in my mind today. Elisabeti, one of our key women leaders, came to my house to escort me to Birere, one of the poorer sections of town, where sixteen women had gathered in Mawazo's home to say "good-bye" to me. They had prepared a very meaningful program which started with the singing of "All the Way My Savior Leads Me" and "Trust and Obey," all in Swahili, of course. Then one of the women read John 14:1-4 and showed us how the Lord said "good-bye" to His disciples. This was followed by words of exhortation and encouragement for me, either with Scripture verses or hymns that each one had chosen especially for me. After a time of prayer, out came the food. My, but there was lots of it: two kinds of potatoes, meat, fish, sombe, vegetables and one bottle of soft drink for me, which I shared with two of the leaders. I was so blessed and humbled by the great love of these simple, godly African women. That evening I noted in my journal:

"Thank-you, Father, for such love and appreciation.

Please, if it is Your will, bring me back to Goma."

The Douglins arrived a few days before I was to leave. My friend, Terry Dirks, invited me to spend some time at their home away from the missionary community to allow me quiet time to work on the financial reports which needed to be turned in before my departure. Finally all was done and I was on my way back to the States, flying from Kigali to Nairobi, to Paris, and landing in Chicago, where I went through the usual medical routine before flying home to

Maine to be with my family.

FURLOUGH - JULY 1981 - JULY 1982

I wanted to live in Cambridge among the people of my home church for this final furlough and was happy to learn that there was a lovely mobile home for rent right in Cambridge village. It was within walking distance of the post office, church, and many of my friends! What a delightful situation for my year-long furlough. Cambridge is only fifteen miles from Dexter where Mom lived, as well as my sister Bea and her husband Skip. Other family members lived throughout central Maine so some good family times were enjoyed through that year. My cousin Alden in Bangor helped me find a second-hand blue Chevette which served me well that furlough. Since Mom did not drive, I was able to take her shopping and out to eat which she especially enjoyed. One of the first things we did together was to visit Dad's grave at the cemetery in Parkman and I helped her order a marker for the grave. We had some great times together continuing to re-build bridges in our relationship that was gradually being healed. I was blessed to be able to have the family together at my home for Thanksgiving that year.

Soon after the Christmas holidays, I had a chance to ride with some friends to South Carolina where I visited Harold and Jane Burchett for a few days. Harold and Jane were my spiritual mentors who taught me how to disciple individuals using the system Harold had written, called *Spiritual Life Studies*. I tried to re-connect with them each time I returned to the States. Harold was teaching courses in the short winter term at Columbia Bible College and I was happy, as well, to visit my alma mater again. From South Carolina I flew to Buffalo, New York to report to a supporting church. January in Buffalo almost always guarantees an adventure! I spoke in the morning service at the Hedstrom Memorial Church and spent the afternoon at the parsonage with Pastor John and Edith Dougherty and their daughter, Karen. Pastor, Karen and I ventured out in the Pastor's car for the evening service where I planned to show my slides and give a more detailed report of my fifth term in Zaire. Edith was not feeling well and decided to stay home. The wind from Lake Erie was blowing hard by the time we arrived at the church, several miles from the parsonage. When we came out of the evening service, we were met with a full scale blizzard. We started for home but only got as far as "Howie's Bar," where the three of us, along with scores of others, had to spend the night. A kind lady loaned blankets to Karen and me. We tried to make ourselves comfy in one of the dining area booths to wait out the blizzard! The storm subsided in the morning, but it took the work crews a long time to clear the roads. We finally made it back home by early afternoon the next day.

With my Buffalo blizzard experience over I went on to

our mission headquarters in Wheaton, Illinois to attend the board meetings and seminars especially prepared for all our furloughed missionaries. There was a special seminar on retirement for those of us facing our final term on the field. These were always refreshing times as we reconnected with the office workers and other missionaries from all over the world. As soon as the meetings were over I flew back to Massachusetts where I was scheduled to take some refresher courses at Gordon-Conwell Seminary in South Hamilton.

My plan was to study at the seminary during the winter term. I boarded nearby in Beverly with Bill and Elvita Minigan and from there, on the weekends, I was able to drive to my supporting churches in the Massachusetts/ New Hampshire area.

I took "Tentmaking Witness at Home and Abroad" with Dr. J. Christy Wilson, Jr, who had served for a number of years as a missionary in Afghanistan. Studying with that godly man, enthusiastic for missions, was truly a rich experience for me. The required reading of eight books included Dr. Wilson's own book, *Today's Tentmakers*. We were required to memorize nearly thirty Scripture verses as part of the course. At the end of the course we had the joy of going to Dr. Wilson's home in New Gloucester where his gracious wife served our class of twenty-four a delicious breakfast. My hard work in the course was rewarded with an "A." As well as taking Dr. Wilson's course for credit, I audited two other helpful and stretching courses; "History of

Modern Missions" with Dr. William Nigel Kerr, and "Jonathan Edwards" with Dr. Richard Lovelace. I enjoyed those days at the seminary. Interacting with a new and vibrant generation of young people who were serious about doing God's will added to my joy of being on that great campus for three months.

About once a month, when I had a free weekend, I was able to go back to Maine to see family and to check on the mobile home. While at the seminary I was involved in a noon-time missions prayer group led by students. Also I attended chapel where there were excellent speakers. On May sixth I packed up my car, went up to the seminary to attend one final chapel where Dr. J. I. Packer, a well-known theologian, was speaking. I then returned to Maine for the remainder of my furlough.

Back in Cambridge in June, I was free to help with the annual Vacation Bible School at church. Pastor Kenneth Monahan and his wife, Cindy, planned an evening school and asked me to teach a class of adults. We studied five famous missionaries: William Carey, David Livingstone, Hudson Taylor, Adoniram Judson, and David Brainerd. Our hearts were challenged by the lives of these dedicated men. It was a great school with children, young people and adults alike, and an overall average attendance for the week of one hundred.

July arrived all too soon and it was time to pack for Africa and spend some final happy times with my family. I flew out of Bangor on July seventh, ready to tackle the unknown challenges of yet another term in Zaire. At the airport Norman Chadbourne, one of our deacons from Cambridge, read Philippians 1:3-8 and Junior Herrick led us in prayer just before I boarded the plane.

REFLECTIONS ON MY FIFTH TERM AND FURLOUGH

"Immortal, invisible, God only wise,
In light inaccessible hid from our eyes,
Most blessed, most glorious, the Ancient of Days,
Almighty, victorious, thy great Name we praise.

Unresting, unhasting, and silent as light,
Nor wanting, nor wasting, thou rulest in might;
Thy justice like mountains high soaring above
Thy clouds, which are fountains of goodness and love.

To all life thou givest, to both great and small;
In all life thou livest, the true life of all;
We blossom and flourish, like leaves on the tree,
Then wither and perish; but naught changeth thee.

Great Father of glory, pure Father of light,
Thine angels adore thee, all veiling their sight;

All laud we would render; O help us to see
'Tis only the splendor of light hideth thee.'"
—*W. Chalmers Smith (1824-1908) Scottish*

The words to the above hymn were sent to me in a letter while I was in my fifth term in Zaire. It was my first introduction to "Immortal, Invisible" but I fell in love with the words and they encouraged me greatly when I wanted to meditate on the greatness of our God.

That first year of my term when I worked with my former student Gatambi at Singa was a very special privilege and I am grateful for that experience. The move to the city of Goma held a brand new series of experiences for me. I had always enjoyed the simple life style of the country folks, their friendliness and their serious hospitality. I found the city folks more sophisticated and harder to reach with the Gospel. However, in spite of my qualms about moving to the city, I came to enjoy the varied ministries and the endless opportunities the Lord gave to me in the city of Goma. The pressures in the city were more pronounced and one always had to be vigilant against the rampant thievery. There were some definite advantages to living in Goma. I could readily obtain supplies without the hassle of a long, tiring, dusty trip from the country station. It was always a joy to see folks as they came through the city. I loved my varied ministry of office work, teaching Bible in the schools, discipling women and hospitality. There were other bonuses to being in Goma, which was right on the lake. We were close to the little retreat center across the lake where we enjoyed going for a weekend.

I was so grateful for the three months that I had in the States when I was able to be with my Dad for the last time. Furlough time always gave me very special family times and I was especially thankful to be able to do things with Mother again. The study time at Gordon-Conwell was much needed and valued before my return to Africa for my final term. Truly, it was a blessed term and furlough, and once again I can say

GREAT IS THY FAITHFULNESS!!

CHAPTER TEN

MY FINAL TERM WITH ITS MEDICAL CHALLENGES
(July 1982 - Sept. 8, 1988)

"Therefore, we do not lose heart. Even though our outward man is perishing, yet the inward man is being renewed day by day." - 2 Cor. 4:16

On July 9, 1982 I landed in Kigali, Rwanda, back home in Africa once again after my furlough. I spent the night with missionary friends in Kigali and the next day they put me on the small Air Rwanda plane which took me to Gisenyi, an hour-long flight which I always endured but never enjoyed. However, seeing Bill and Norma Pierce and Joann Kile at the small Gisenyi airport brought me joy. They drove me across the border to Goma which was to be my home for my sixth term of missionary service in Africa. On my journey back to Africa, spending the night in Brussels, I had written in my diary on July eighth:

"Some meditation on my goals for this next term. I don't want this to be just another term. Reading in Philippians chapter four I longed with Paul that I see 'real fruit that will abound to the accounts' of loving folks who have sent me out."

Rwanda Hills

1982 - 1983

For this term of service I was given a mission house by the lake in the city of Goma. For many years Joann Kile had taught in the school for missionary children at Ruanguaba station and now, for her final term in the Congo, she had been assigned to Goma. She and I would share a house, a very happy arrangement for both of us. Joann had charge of a book depot in Goma and I taught Bible in the high school and continued discipling women. Together we worked to settle into our home. Each of us had a good-sized bedroom/study combination, plus an extra room for guests. My friend, Terry Dirks, offered to buy material and sew curtains for my bedroom. A closed-in backyard meant Joann and I could dry our laundry without fear of thieves! Joann's book depot was also in the enclosed area.

Joann and I, neither of us particularly dog-lovers, talked about the wisdom of having a watch-dog in the city, She heard about some German Shepherd puppies that were available; in fact, the owners were giving them away. We made our need known and one day a little scroungy, sickly, weak puppy was brought to our door. Joann gave him a bath and tick medicine and under her careful nurturing he grew rapidly into a beautiful watchdog whom we called Spunky, because of his limitless energy. Joann and I organized our daily lives so that we would have charge of the kitchen on alternate weeks. We knew that living in Goma meant having lots of guests and it was so good to be able to share the responsibility of food shopping and preparation.

School opened as usual in September and I was soon busy with my Bible classes in the high school and with the church women. I discipled women on a regular basis and did a lot of hut to hut visitation with Elizabeti. She gradually became my closest helper with the women's work, always willing and enjoying home visits with me. Filipo Lukwangomo, an African dentist from the Warega tribe in the Shabunda area southwest of Bukavu, had brought his young bride, Elizabeti, to Goma in the nineteen-fifties where they settled, brought up their family and served faithfully in the Goma church. Filipo is now with the Lord, but Elizabeti remains active in the Goma church and is especially involved in the Goma Widows' Fellowship. I have so many happy memories of ministering together with Elizabeti in hundreds of Goma homes.

All of us who lived in Goma were continually frustrated with the erratic supply of electricity. Often it didn't come on until seven p.m. and then for only two hours. Jo, as we usually called Joann, had brought a small washing machine to our household, so we were often doing our laundry at eight o'clock at night. We were grateful for our bottled-gas stove and our kerosene refrigerator. In spite of frustrations, our ministries were going along well. Jo was happy to be placing Christian literature into the hands of many Africans and I enjoyed my contacts with students and women. I was particularly happy to be working under Gatambi again. He had served faithfully as principal of the Singa high school for several years and was asked to move to the larger high-school in Goma. Once again my former student was my boss. I saw real spiritual growth in Gatambi. This young man with a gift for administration kept the school running smoothly. He did an excellent job leading Tuesday morning chapel at school and preached the Word in such a way that students listened with great interest.

BEING SENT HOME WITH CANCER SOUNDS SO FINAL…BUT GOD

In mid-November I discovered a lump in my right breast. Our mission doctor, Phil Dirksen, did a biopsy immediately and sent it to Nairobi. Three weeks later the pathology report came back: malignant. The word cancer turned my world upside down and the worst part of it was having to return to the States so soon after my return to the Congo. However, I did what I had to do, trusting our kind heavenly Father to take care of the details. He did just that for me. Ten days after receiving the pathology report, I flew out of Kigali and on to Oneonta, New York. Dr. Virgil Polley was a surgeon at Fox Memorial Hospital there. He had traveled to Zaire on several occasions to assist with the medical work at our mission hospital in Ruanguba, so he was like a "family doctor" to many of us. On December twenty-third he performed a modified radical mastectomy. Since Dr. Polley was scheduled to work on Christmas Day, he and Mrs. Polley (Virginia) invited me to eat dinner with them in a quiet spot at the hospital. Several days later the pathology report came back completely clean, which meant that he had successfully removed all traces of the cancer. Dr. Polley told me I could return to Zaire in six or eight weeks and my fears turned to joy and thanksgiving. Physical therapy was scheduled as part of my recuperation. My former pastor, Rev. Burton Murdock, and his wife Sylvia, welcomed me to recuperate in their home in Oneonta where Pastor Murdock was serving as the Director of New York Conservative Baptist Association. Following my time with them, I was able to travel to Maine to complete my recovery with my family. I received loving support from family and friends, flowers, cards, phone calls and transportation; these gestures plus extra time in the Word all served to draw me closer to the Lord during the special season He had brought into my life. Several books were helpful at that time also: *Discipline, the Glad Surrender* by Elisabeth Elliot, *Sometimes Mountains Move* by Dr. C. Everett Koop and Elizabeth Koop, and *Life Together* by Dietrich Bonhoeffer.

In mid-February I returned to Oneonta for a check-up with Dr. Polley and received a clean bill of health. The Polleys invited me to spend the weekend in their spacious and lovely home overlooking the city of Oneonta. I recall the wonderful hike that Virginia and I took in the freshly fallen snow through the woods on that Saturday afternoon. On Sunday we worshiped together in their church. Monday, February fourteenth, was a very significant day when they both took a day off from work and drove me to Binghamton to purchase my first prosthesis. After the purchase I had the joy of treating the Polleys to lunch at a Chinese restaurant. Three days later I began the long journey back to Africa, arriving on February nineteenth. I had been gone for two months. I praised God that the ordeal was over and that I was able to return to my ministry in Zaire. This experience was another indication of God's faithfulness in my life. In no time I was right back into the work that meant so much to me.

In March word came that E.J. Kile, one of our Rwanda missionaries, had a fatal accident with electrical equipment while working on his boat. Our hearts ached for his wife,

Tudy, and for his sister, my housemate, Joann. This kind of loss touched all of us who were a family. Jo felt the loss of her brother deeply for a long time after the accident. We were left short-handed in our work but life had to go on. Teaching, discipling, Sunday School and hospitality filled my days. Soon I was asked if I would consider doing the field treasurer work for one year when Edna Camp left the field for retirement. I wasn't sure that I could handle the extra responsibility and still keep up with my other ministries, but after serious thought and prayer, I decided that I could do the job for a year. There was a rather lengthy period of learning how to handle four accounts of dollars, zaires, Rwandan francs and Kenyan shillings for our thirty-five missionaries. Edna was a patient teacher for a couple of months and when she left on furlough on July first my duties officially began.

That same year I took my vacation over in Rwanda again at the Kumbya Conference. We missionaries had a great week there with four guest speakers, all professors from Denver Seminary: Dr. and Mrs. Robert L. Allen, Dennis Williams, and Jim Cummings. Dr. Allen, the professor of Old Testament at Denver Seminary, had written a three-volume commentary on the Psalms and his commentary on Proverbs was about to come off the press. Before going across the lake to Kumbya these guests had visited several of the Zaire stations to experience the feel of missionary work in that area. At Kumbya Conference the three men took turns speaking in the Bible sessions, bringing great blessing to all of us. Seeing missionaries from other missions was always a treat at Kumbya. The quiet spot by the lake was "just what the doctor ordered" for all of us. I spent quite a bit of time with my dear friend, Tudy Kile, who still grieved the loss of her husband. Tudy and I hiked around the Kumbya area and enjoyed the beauty of God's handiwork.

Our Foreign Secretary, Dick Jacobs, came out from the States to visit our field operations in August. By this time I felt that I was ready to settle on the time of my retirement and we discussed my future plans. We decided that I could retire in 1988 at age sixty-two. Dick told me that since this final term was six years I was entitled to a short furlough half way through the term. I was happy with this plan since I wanted to be involved in some kind of ministry in the States before reaching sixty-five. I was confident that God would direct my steps when that time came and I wanted only His good plan for my later years.

1983 - 1984

Facing the double challenge of a new scholastic year and the added ministry of the treasurer's job, I felt the need for a day away for prayer, meditation and quiet before plunging into the new duties. Alice Douglin had felt the same need, so early in September the two of us went over to

Kigufi, the retreat center in Rwanda, for the day. She did some writing on her very interesting life-story. Alice was born in the Congo, probably in the early nineteen twenties, but she had no clear record of her birth. Her maternal grandfather was an African chief of the Mangbetu tribe and her father was Belgian. Alice was adopted as a child by Harold and Doris Wentworth, missionaries with the Africa Inland Mission. Because of certain regulations, Alice was not allowed to go to the States when the Wentworths went on their regular furlough. She stayed in the home of Dr. and Mrs. Carl Becker at Oicha, where there was a hospital of the Africa Inland Mission. When the Wentworths were not able to return to the Congo for health reasons, Alice spent ten profitable years with the Beckers. Dr. Becker allowed Alice to help with the medical work and he taught her a wealth of medical information which she was able to put into practical use at that time and for many years after. Eventually she did go to the States to be with her adoptive parents and to attend Providence Bible Institute in Rhode Island. While at Providence she met Deighton Douglin whose father had come to the States from Barbados and whose mother was a Black American. Alice and Deighton married, became missionaries with the Conservative Baptist Foreign Mission Society, and were appointed to work in the Congo. Alice and Deighton were co-workers with me for most of our years in the Congo and even today we keep in close contact. They are retired and live in Hamilton, Massachusetts near enough that we do get together at least once a year. While Alice wrote her story, there by the lake on that sunny afternoon, I worked on specific goals for my varied ministries that were coming up and had special prayer for each of them as well. It was a very profitable and restful time, sitting on the lovely lawn overlooking the lake at the retreat center. At the end of that quiet day I returned to the busyness of Goma with a fresh sense of purpose and commitment.

When our world is running smoothly, the Lord often allows tests and trials just to remind us that He is really in control. It was a sad day for me personally when word reached me early in September that my brother Gayland had died very suddenly of a massive heart attack, leaving behind his wife Clarice and four children. Then my housemate Joann received word that her breast biopsy pathology report was malignant. At the same time we learned that two of our choice Zaireans had fallen into sin. All of these trials brought added burden to our already full and complicated lives but God's grace proved once again to be sufficient.

Since Jo had to return to the States for surgery, I decided the time had come to train an African girl to help with the housework. I consulted with the women leaders about my need and asked them to help me find a trustworthy girl. They found Bathseba, a sixteen-year-old Christian girl, who came to work for me. Bathseba washed the dishes, peeled vegetables, went to the market for food, did my laundry, and kept the house clean. This arrangement relieved me of the day-to-day workings of the household and freed me for the work I had come to Zaire to do. Jo returned to the States for her surgery in November and came back to Goma in March.

In October, before Joann's medical problem had surfaced, she and I planned a special day for our African women leaders. We invited fourteen women to our house for a quiet day away from the busy routines in their villages. They enjoyed the day so much, as did we. A light lunch was served and a simple schedule of Bible study was given to each woman. Our goal was for them to have time to reflect and pray together. We did this all together and then sent them to find quiet spots by themselves or two by two. After lunch we went for a walk by the lake. The day was brought to a close when Manasse, an African pastor in Goma, came to minister to us from God's Word. The women loved the special day and begged us to do it again for them.

In November 1983 a group of Campus Crusade young people from Arizona came to Africa to minister in our area. They often joined us for our Sunday afternoon missionary fellowship time. One day in December one of the young men read a Christmas story, "The Two Lambs," to our group. Many years earlier I had used the same story in my work with the mulattoes at Ndoluma and helped the children put on a play based on the story. It became my all-time favorite Christmas story, but sadly, I had lost the actual story. While on furlough from Kasheke the termites ate a trunk full of my books including the one with the story of

"The Two Lambs." I am sorry I cannot give you the publisher. For years I had searched for the story and was ecstatic to find it again! I now had my own copy again and have since given away many more. Following is the story of those two lambs. As you read this tender story, set in the time of Christ's earthly journey, you can perhaps sense why it has meant so much to me.

THE TWO LAMBS

Joshua, son of Asher, hurried as fast as he could, but with such a bundle on his back it was not easy to go very fast. He put his fingers in his ears so he would not hear the rhyme the boys were shouting as they followed him down the street: "Joshua, Joshua, what's in the sack? Joshua, Joshua, what's on your back?"

Tears stung his eyes; his fists doubled up and he bit his lip until a small trickle of blood ran down his chin. He walked faster, for he must not let the boys see him cry.

As they neared the flat-roofed home of Joshua, the boys lowered their voices a bit and one by one dropped back. Joshua entered the courtyard of his home alone. He stopped for a moment and wiped his face on his sleeve.

His mother sat on a stone step at the end of the courtyard. Joshua could tell by the sad look in her eyes that she had heard the teasing of the boys, but not a word was said about it. Her voice was cheery as she called to him, "Welcome, my son. It is good that thou hast hurried home, for thy father and I have planned a surprise for thee."

It was always like this. Mother was always waiting for him, as though she knew how hard it was for a boy with a pack on his back to get along in the big world outside the home. A surprise! For a moment the pack was forgotten.

"Mother, let me guess. I'll need but one guess, I know. You and Father are going to let me go out with him tonight to guard the sheep on the hillside."

"You are right, my son. Tomorrow is thy birthday and thou hast long been begging to go out with thy father. He shall take thee this night."

Asher and his wife had tried hard to get a little extra money together to buy Joshua a birthday gift, but the Romans were so greedy for taxes that there was little left after food was bought and the rent on their little home was paid. Then they had thought of letting him go with his father for the night. "'Tis our birthday present to thee," said Miriam.

"And the best present thou couldst give me, Mother mine," said Joshua.

He was impatient as a young colt to be off. Many times he had dreamed of going to the hillside and spending the whole night with his father, and now his dream was to come true.

"Thou hast given me a goodly lunch, my Miriam," said Asher affectionately.

"Only half of it is thine, Asher. Thy son comes to manhood's estate with this birthday. You will find that a growing son has a big appetite. Close your ears, Joshua, I have a secret to whisper to thy Father." Miriam stood on tiptoe and pulled Asher's head down and whispered in his ear, "I have put a cake in the lunch, a cake of fine ground flour for his birthday. Share it with the other shepherds and make it a festive occasion for the boy."

"Wear thy heavy outer coat, Joshua. The nights are chill, and sometimes the hills are damp with moisture. Be respectful to the shepherds who guard the sheep with thy father. They must never say that Joshua, son of Asher, is an ill-bred lad," said his mother in parting. "Dost thou have thy slingshot, my boy?" asked Asher. "Perhaps thou canst kill a wolf, or a hyena, or maybe a wildcat. It might even be a lion tonight."

"If I kill a lion, I know what I shall do. I shall skin it and take it to Bezalel, the tanner. He will make a rug out of it for Mother. If I kill a lion, the boys won't — " but Joshua did not finish his sentence. In his heart he saw himself a hero in the eyes of the boys of Bethlehem. They might even forget the pack he always carried on his back, the pack he could never take off and one that made the people of Bethlehem speak of him as Asher's hunchbacked son. How Joshua longed for a straight back like other boys.

As they walked down the road side by side, tall, straight, strong Asher and his son with a crooked back, they talked of many things.

Sparrows, swallows and quails, those common birds of Palestine, were to be seen everywhere. Joshua told his father of hunting doves with two of his friends. The boys sold their doves in the market place so they could buy sweets with the money. "I could not sell mine, Father. It was so soft and so helpless. I am making a house for it. I shall give it to Mother. She will love the soft cooing of the dove, won't she?" asked Joshua.

"Thou does love all things that God hast made, my boy. I am glad," said Asher as they began to climb.

"Yes, the great God has made wonderful things and so many of them. But of them all I love one thing more than anything else," confided Joshua.

"More than thy mother and me?" his father asked quickly.

"Thou dost jest, my father. No, I love thee and Mother best of all. I have never told thee before, and thou mayest laugh when I tell thee now. Sometimes at night I awaken and lie thinking that it has come true - that I have something all my own that I want very much. I have wanted it since I was very little, Father."

"Thou hast never told thy mother nor me?" questioned his father.

"No, my father, I have told no one because we have been poor, and I did not want to be greedy," said Joshua.

"What is this, thy heart's desire, my son? Tell me."

"I have always wanted a little lamb for my own, a little lamb that I could carry about with me under my coat. I would love it and take care of it myself," said Joshua.

"Some day, Joshua, thou shalt have a whole flock of sheep and many lambs besides," replied Asher.

"I would rather have just one little lamb now, my father. I would love one little lamb more than I would a whole flock," pleaded the boy as they walked onward.

"Yes, when one is young," said the father, "one little lamb is a great treasure. When a boy becomes a man, a flock does not seem so great a treasure. 'Tis strange, but true. Come, we must hurry."

It was late afternoon when they arrived at the feeding place where other shepherds could be seen tending their flocks. Here in the hills, among rocks, flowing water and green grass, it seemed to Joshua that he had reached paradise.

The sun went down in a blaze of fiery glory; then the night began to settle over the hill. The flocks were gathered close together by their careful shepherds. Fires were kindled to warm the men and boy, and to keep away the wild beasts.

Old Daniel, the chief shepherd, stood by the fire, with his hands locked behind his back. "How wrinkled his face is," thought Joshua, "but how straight he stands." Old Daniel was speaking to him, "We are honored, Joshua, son of Asher, to have thee as a guest among us tonight. These shepherds and I would give thee a gift for thy birthday. But what does a shepherd have to give a lad like thee but a lamb? Mayhap thou wouldst not care for such a gift."

Usually Joshua was quick to speak, but the thought of being given a lamb of his own took him completely by surprise. His father came to his help.

"You will never know, my friends, the joy that you have brought to my son this night. He is too happy to speak. Only today he told me that above everything in the world, outside of having his mother and me, he would like to own a little lamb."

"'Tis not a prize that we offer, Asher. The only newly weaned lamb that we have is the one whose leg was broken and whose side was slashed by the wildcat when it attacked the mother."

Fearful that the gift was going to be taken from him when it was almost his, Joshua jumped up. He tongue was loosed and he cried out, "Sir, I care not that it is not a perfect lamb! As it is, I shall love it, care for it, and give it part of my food. You shall see, sir, it shall be the finest sheep in all Bethlehem - perhaps in all Palestine - after I have it for a while."

"'Tis thine, lad. Do with it as thou dost wish," answered old Daniel.

That night Joshua lay on the slope of the hill with his heavy cloak wrapped tightly about him, for it grew chilly just as his mother had warned it would. Underneath his cloak, nestling close beside him, was the little lamb which had had a broken leg and a wounded side - his very own lamb to do with as he wished! Among all the boys in Palestine that night, there was not a more thankful boy than Joshua, son of Asher. From his heart a great prayer of thanksgiving went up to God as he lay gazing into the starry sky. Soon he fell fast asleep.

It seemed that he had slept only a little while when suddenly he was awakened by loud voices, and, opening his eyes, he saw a blaze of light in the sky. He clutched his lamb, too frightened by what he saw to cry out to his father. There, high above the earth, was a being unlike any he had ever seen - a glorious one in shining clothes, who must have come from the very presence of God. Oh, wonder of wonders, he seemed to be speaking right to Joshua. "Fear not; for, behold, I bring you good tidings of great joy, which shall be to all people. For unto you is born this day in the city of David a Saviour, which is Christ the Lord."

When the glory had faded from the sky, there was great excitement among the shepherds on the hillside. Joshua's father moved quietly but quickly to where Joshua was sitting. He touched him on the shoulder and said, "Arise, my son, we go to Bethlehem to see the Saviour of Israel."

"Hast Messiah come, my father? He for whom all Israel has been waiting?" asked Joshua.

"Come, haste, we shall see, my son," replied Asher as he helped the boy get started.

Faster and faster they walked until it was almost a run for Joshua to keep up with his father and the other shepherds.

The boy was thinking big, deep thoughts. "If Messiah has come, thinkest thou that He would like my little lamb? I shall give it to Him as my gift. It is the best thing that I have." His voice trembled and he felt choked. It would cost him a great deal to part with the little lamb he had just received that night and which he held close to him now.

"Thou art young, my son, but thou knowest that no true Israelite offers in sacrifice a lamb with spot or blemish. Messiah would not be able to accept such a lamb. Let thy heart rest. Remember, thou art not to push thy way in, but allow thine elders the chief place."

It was a very sad-faced, heavy-hearted boy who stepped into the cave where cattle were kept. At first Joshua had trouble seeing because the men were in the way, but he soon found a place where he could peer through. Just then the Baby's mother caught sight of Joshua. She beckoned him to come to her. Joshua turned to his father for permission, and Asher nodded for him to go forward.

"My father says the lambs must be spotless - perfect," stammered the boy.

"There are none truly perfect, dear boy," answered the sweet-faced woman. "They are perfect only as man sees them. Tell me thy name," said Mary in tones so soft and sweet that Joshua lost his fear.

"Joshua," he said quickly.

"My baby's name is Jesus. Your name means the same as His. Do you know what these names mean?" continued Mary.

Just then, as though he wished some attention, the lamb held within Joshua's cloak poked its little woolly head out of the folds with a "Baa-aa." The Baby in the manger stirred in His sleep at the sound. Mary bent down and lifted the precious Little One so that Joshua could see Him. Oh, but He was sweet!

"Thou hast thy little lamb, and I have a little Lamb." There was a faraway look in Mary's eyes as she said it, as if she remembered something. Her lips moved, but what she said could not be heard by the shepherds standing apart. Only Joshua heard, "A Lamb for sin and sinners." "I am sorry," said Joshua, "but I don't have a gift for the Baby. I wanted to give Him my lamb, but my father said it would not do. It is not perfect. It had a broken leg and it had a sore place on its side.'

"My Baby would love such a little lamb. If it is all you have and you want to give it, it will be loved and cared for just as you would do."

It was his own little lamb to do with as he wished. The old shepherd had told him so that very night. It was dear to him, and it was hard to think of parting with it; but he would do it.

Tenderly Joshua took the little lamb from beneath his cloak. He kissed the top of its woolly head, then laid the lamb gently down at the foot of the manger bed. Looking up at Mary he said quickly, for the tears were starting to fall, "It is the best that I have. I am very glad to give my little lamb to thy little Lamb."

"My Son will never forget this gift," said Mary, "and neither will His Father." As she said this she raised her eyes heavenward.

Turning, Joshua walked out into the beautiful night, tears running down his face; but his father soon followed and he was comforted. Down in his heart he felt a great joy and a strange peace he had never felt before. Even the pack on his back seemed lighter.

Years passed by. Joshua now was a grown man and each night found him on the Bethlehem hillside caring for a flock of sheep - all his own. No shepherd loved and cared for his lambs and sheep more tenderly than the hunchback shepherd Joshua. No shepherd loved the great God more than he. Often he would take a lamb from his fold, run his hands over it carefully to be sure it was without spot or blemish, and take it to the temple in Jerusalem to be offered as his offering for sin.

It was on one of these trips to the temple that Joshua noticed a great throng of people. With the lamb in his arms, he edged himself through the crowd and watched with amazement a Man with great kindness and power in His face touch the eyes of a blind man and make him see. The Man's voice was tender and loving and His manner gracious. Suddenly, He raised His head and looked into Joshua's eyes. "Thank you for the little lamb, Joshua."

"Why, I have given Thee no lamb," began Joshua, but the Man was gone. And so was something else. The pack on Joshua's back had disappeared. He stood tall and straight.

That night on the Bethlehem hillside, Joshua from a singing heart talked to the stars and his sleepy sheep. "What the angel said was true. That Baby in the manger was the Messiah of Israel. He is the Saviour of the world. He did not forget my gift. He thanked me for the little lamb I gave Him that night long ago when angels came down to earth. Such a man would I follow to the ends of the earth."

- Aunt Theresa

I always enjoyed sharing the church Christmas activities with the Africans. There was not the commercialism that we experience in the States, rather their Christmas centered around church activities that exalted the Lord Jesus. They often started with a baptism and that year they baptized sixty-one people. A few days after the baptisms I shared a private lesson from John with Ana, one of my African ladies. She related how she and a group from her village had visited in the homes and prayed with fifteen of the folks who had been baptized the previous Sunday. I was so happy with this news and very proud of Ana, who had been burdened to encourage these new babes in the Lord.

Back in October of that year, I had written in my journal "Life is so fleeting. My priority must be the quality of my days, rather than the number of them." I thought about this a lot as the pressures mounted in January and as I tried to balance the responsibilities of mission finances, school work, many guests, discipling of women and visitation. I missed my housemate. Joann did return in mid-March. To give us a little more excitement the volcano, Nyiragongo, erupted again! By now we were quite used to these eruptions and there was no loss of life this time.

All of us missionaries in Goma loved Easter, when we gathered by the lake with other English-speaking people for a sunrise service. After our praise service we cooked our breakfast at the lake over an open fire. Bacon, eggs, home fries and pancakes with a steaming cup of coffee were a special treat for all of us. Later in the morning we attended services held in Swahili and French at the church in town.

The Betts' home where we met for the Sunrise Service.

Early in June of 1984 I took a terrible fall and landed flat on my face. For no apparent reason I began falling from time to time. I noticed that my right leg was not functioning as it should have and I developed a very painful lower backache. After a couple of weeks with no relief I flew to Nyankunde Medical Center to visit a doctor and have tests. Dr. Ruth Dix found nothing seriously wrong and prescribed complete rest and exercises. Back home I decided to get away from the pressures of Goma and went up to Ruanguba to be with my friend Elfreida. I stayed with her for a month and the only mission work I continued to do was the finances. Despite good rest my back continued to hurt badly. I also noticed that I experienced a loss of sensation in my right leg. On my return to Goma after a month, I was still unable to enter into my full schedule for the remainder of the summer. I was grateful that Joann was in good health and kept our household running. I personally was more than a little discouraged to be facing another medical challenge which forced me to cut back on the ministries

I loved.

1984 - 1985

As we entered the fall and another busy school year, I knew something had to change. There were good days and bad days with my back but most of the time it simply hurt. I was unable to carry on with my regular responsibilities outside of the home. The Douglins were on furlough, leaving Joann to shoulder much of the Goma burden herself. She was due for retirement in early spring and needed to wind down her own affairs. I could be most helpful to her by taking over our kitchen and leaving the other responsibilities to her. That arrangement was practical for both of us and with the help of Anita, our new African girl worker, I managed to keep food on the table. I had already turned the mission finances over to Marilyn Neil, just back from her own furlough. She had been the field treasurer before and so was familiar with the procedure. I did teach my Bible classes and that was about all I was able to do among the Africans. I thought that my ministry to the women would come to a standstill but I was wrong. They started ministering to me and as they did this, they grew by leaps and bounds. Most afternoons I was flat on my back on my bed. They came to see me, bringing carefully chosen Scripture verses to encourage me. They often sang a hymn and then prayed for me. Every week several small groups of women came to encourage me. They were a very precious bonus to an otherwise trying time. I often thought of the first Scripture verse I memorized as a new believer from Romans 8:28:

"And we know that all things work together for good to those who love God, to those who are the called according to His purpose."

Surely the Lord was working out His good purposes for me and for His African believers during this next season of medical testing.

In an attempt to bring relief to my hurting back, I tried hot packs, cold packs, aspirin, exercises, all of which brought only temporary relief. In consultation with our medical people and mission leaders, we decided that if relief didn't come, I would need to go to the States as soon as the Douglins returned in March. I would then take the short furlough already talked about and get medical help as well. I made every effort to hang on until that time. The Psalms were a great comfort to me. A friend loaned me David Watson's *Fear No Evil,* which was a special blessing. In his chapter "Overcoming Suffering" I found this nugget: "It is not what we do, but who we are that matters most in life; and it is not what we endure, but the way we endure it that counts. We can overcome evil with good." I really tried not to make a big deal about my hurting back, despite the fact that it hurt badly and seriously hampered my ministry. In January Ann Johnson, a physical therapist, arrived. She was a new missionary and I became her first patient. After working with me at length, we both realized that exercising was not enough.

Since this would be Joann's final Christmas in Zaire, I wanted to make it extra special for her. We invited her sister-in-law, Tudy Kile and the Kile clan, all six of them who worked in Rwanda, to spend Christmas with us. We had a festive time with our guests and enjoyed the usual church activities, knowing Joann would soon leave Zaire.

Christmas in the Congo.

Soon after the Christmas activities ended, Joann began serious sorting and packing. Her plans were to leave in February. Feeling the need to have a proper farewell for her, her nephew, Mark, and I spun into action. First of all we wanted to surprise her. We invited her family and missionaries with whom she had worked closely over the years. We planned the meal with each guest contributing a dish. I was in charge of making place cards and decorations. Mark planned the program. The event was a big surprise for her and everyone enjoyed a delightful evening reminiscing over Joann's many years of service in Africa.

I knew that we must include the Africans in some

farewells for Joann. One evening we invited two African couples, special friends of hers, to have dinner with us.

One of Joann's farewells.

Another day we invited the African church women to come to our house for a farewell luncheon. Over thirty women came to say "good-bye" to her. They brought special verses, then sang "God Be with You" and "Where Jesus is 'tis Heaven," all in Swahili, of course. I was so proud of the women who took charge of our little program. There was yet one more group, our African workers, who did not want to be left out. I planned a special meal for them and invited our house girl, garden boy and night watchman to eat with us. Following the simple meal of chicken, rice, potatoes and corn, Pascal, our night guard, had special prayer for Jo after reading to her from Hebrews 6:9-15:

"But, beloved, we are confident of better things concerning you, yes, things that accompany salvation, though we speak in this manner. For God is not unjust to forget your work and labor of love which You have

shown toward His name, in that you have ministered to the saints, and do minister. And we desire that each one of you show the same diligence to the full assurance of hope until the end, that you do not become sluggish, but imitate those who through faith and patience inherit the promises. For when God made a promise to Abraham, because He could swear by no one greater, He swore by Himself, saying, "Surely blessing I will bless you, and multiplying I will multiply you." And so, after he had patiently endured, he obtained the promise."

Joann was blessed and felt as though she had been properly "farewelled" from all angles. On February 25, 1985 she left Africa, having served for over thirty years, to begin retirement in Minneapolis, Minnesota.

The Douglins arrived back in Zaire on March seventh and I was greatly relieved to see them. I began packing for my trip to the States. Permission had been granted for a short furlough which would, no doubt, need to be extended into another medical leave for me and my back. I had always wanted to take the direct flight from Amsterdam to Los Angeles and this time I did. The trip started in Goma with stops in Nairobi and Amsterdam before landing in Los Angeles. I spent a restful week in Santa Ana, California, with missionary friends, Elwin and Lois Pelletier. There was a weekend with the Campus Crusade young people in Phoenix before flying to Oneonta, New York where I was scheduled for medical check-ups.

It was a medical adventure, this rather circuitous route which took me from Oneonta, to Carlisle, Massachusetts and finally to Boston. Many helpful medical personnel, an unbelievable number of tests and various diagnoses finally resulted in locating the ugly spinal meningioma in the upper cervical. Nationally-known neurosurgeon, John Shillito, removed the benign tumor at Brigham and Women's Hospital in Boston. So many friends stood with me at that time. My good friend, Marguerite Gay, in Nashua courageously drove me into Boston three times, my sister Bea in Maine organized a prayer chain during surgery, others prayed, sent cards and telephoned me. One card that I kept as a special momento is pictured above.

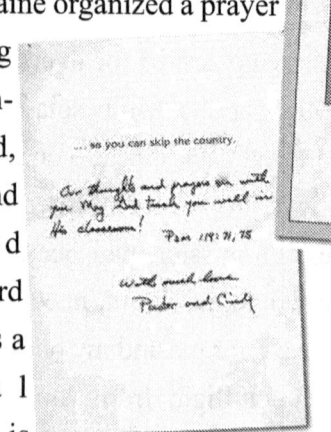

A card from Pastor and Cindy Monahan.

The long days at Brigham and Women's were memorable. My first roommate was a ninety-six-year-old blind black lady, who delighted in having me read Psalm twenty-three to her. The hospital chapel was a lovely quiet room where I went many times for prayer and meditation.

Chaplain Diane Phillips was a charming lady who was especially kind to me and prayed for me before the complicated surgery. I was blessed to be able to leave a witness with a number of people at the hospital, including patients, workers, and medical staff. After the surgery, I felt immediate relief in my back and legs and could not praise my heavenly Father enough. My special praise verse was Psalm 32:7 (NIV) "You are my hiding place; you will protect me from trouble and surround me with songs of deliverance." I was delivered from the deadly tumor and the terrible pain I had endured for so many months and I had new hope that I would be able to return to Zaire.

Marguerite and her daughter Carol picked me up at the hospital and drove me to Nashua, New Hampshire, about an hour from Boston, for a few days of recuperation. My sister Bea connected with me there and together we rode with friends to New Brunswick, New Jersey to attend the National Conservative Baptist meetings, a first for me. I enjoyed the wonderful speakers and saw so many friends. Rest was the order for the remainder of the summer. I visited with family in Maine, spent a week at Rumney, New Hampshire with Marguerite, and a weekend in Toronto with dear friends, Pastor and Mrs. Harold Burchett. Back in Boston, I checked with my doctor and received a clean bill of health. I could return to Africa in early October! Can you imagine, dear reader, the joy I had in my heart to be able to return to my adopted land and carry on with the ministry

God had given to me?

On October 4, 1985 Skip and Bea drove Mom and me to Bangor where we ate lobster rolls in a quaint little restaurant near the airport. Over fifty friends and family members gathered at the airport to see me off. The evening was foggy and rainy, making my plane late in taking off. I finally arrived in Boston and checked in at SABENA. This was my first time to fly directly out of Boston across the Atlantic and I was delighted not to have to go to New York for my overseas flight. While relaxing in the lovely SABENA waiting area, shortly after nine p.m., to my amazement and delight there appeared Jon and Bonnie Burchett and their three little girls, Kimberly, Heidi and Holly. Jon, the eldest son of my friends Harold and Jane Burchett, had driven up from Rhode Island with his little family to say "good-bye" to "Aunt Bunny." They brought me a bouquet of three carnations, pink, red and white, plus yellow daisies and asters which traveled with me all the way to Zaire and gave me joy for a whole week. Jon and his family also shared with me carefully chosen verses from 2 Thessalonians 2:16-17; 3:16:

"Now may our Lord Jesus Christ Himself, and our God and Father, who has loved us and given us everlasting consolation and good hope by grace, comfort your hearts and establish you in every good word and work.
Now may the Lord of peace Himself give you peace always in every way. The Lord be with you all."

Our hour-long visit was not only a complete surprise but a great benediction as I flew off for my final years in Zaire.

1985 - 1987

With ecstatic joy and sincere thankfulness, I stepped out onto African soil again, my return yet another indication of God's faithfulness in my life. I could not wait to walk to the African village to see all my friends. Then of course, I needed to get my house in shape. Anita helped me do a thorough cleaning. I also planted several rose bushes which did very well in the African climate and in due time I had a fresh rose for my house most of the time. At that time I was reading through Second Timothy and was blessed yet again to see the standard that God had set for His workers. At the same time I was praying about my own ministry for my final three years in Goma. Reading through the book of Acts just before returning to Zaire, two words stood out to me, "encourage" and "strengthen." I wanted my ministry at all levels to do just that for the African brethren. I knew I needed to pour myself into people and make the most of every opportunity to witness to those who did not yet know the Lord and to encourage and strengthen the believers.

As I went through the routine of greeting individuals and groups, strongly expected in the African culture, I began to see a wonderful new ministry opening up to me in the little prayer chapels that surrounded the city of Goma. Capable African teachers would now be teaching Bible in the schools so I was relieved of that particular ministry, but I would still disciple individual women, teach the Junior High Sunday School class, have charge of the Book Depot, and do hospitality in my home. I want to share some highlights from each of these ministries with you, the reader, as indications of God's blessing upon my final three years of ministry in Africa, the richest years of all.

GOMA PRAYER CHAPELS

Goma Baptist Church was located in the center of Goma and there were five prayer chapels in key locations on the outskirts of town. Instead of coming all the way in to the central church for early morning prayers, the African Christians would gather at the chapel closest to them. Before my medical leave I had worked with women in some of these chapels so I was familiar with the chapel locations and the leaders of each group. The chapel leaders were chosen by the central church, thus closely linking the chapels and the central church. Immediately on my return to Zaire I visited each of these prayer chapels, greeting the people again. I sensed two things during my visits: first, that my presence at the early morning services was a great encouragement to the believers and secondly, I realized the need of more solid teaching from the Scriptures on the part of the chapel leader. One day I asked a leader if I could bring a brief devotional the next time I visited. The response was very positive and I began a regular routine of visiting and teaching the Word in each prayer chapel.

The five chapels were called: KINGI, VIRUNGA, MAPENDO, KATINDO, and MABANGA, indicating the section of the city where each chapel was located. KINGI was about a twenty minute walk from my house. The group there had started in the home of a dedicated, simple and illiterate African woman. They soon outgrew Susanna's living room in her small hut with its mud walls, grass roof, small living/ kitchen area and tiny bedroom. She asked the Lord to provide her with a larger hut. He answered her trusting prayer and they soon outgrew the larger room. Then they met in her front yard while a proper chapel building was being constructed. I can still recall their joy when they were finally able to meet in their new chapel, constructed of cement blocks with a metal roofing.

Kingi Prayer Chapel.

VIRUNGA was located in a fast growing area of the

city of Goma. I used my car to reach them, a fifteen-minute drive over a very rough, unpaved road. That group was composed of many Wanande people, all energetic and enthusiastic, with a desire to become a full-fledged church one day. MAPENDO was the closest to my house, a twelve-minute walk. They were meeting in the home of their leader, a sincere group who wanted to go forward in their walk with the Lord.

Getting to KATINDO meant driving in my car for fifteen minutes and then hiking over sharp lava rock for another fifteen minutes. Their little chapel sat on a hill where we could see the sun come up over the horizon. Mateso, their capable leader, worked at the Goma airport. I had discipled his wife, Mbula Mena, before my second medical leave. Together they served the Lord ministering to the people in their growing prayer chapel.

MABANGA's group was a ten-minute drive away and a fifteen-minute walk, also over lava rock. I recall the beginnings of that group. A single faithful African lady, Sarah, had held the group together in her hut until they finally built their own permanent chapel building.

My goal was to meet with each group once a month. I prepared a teaching from the Scriptures, using the same message for each group. I taught them how the Bible instructs fathers to train their children and I spent quite a few lessons on the fruit of the Spirit from Galatians, chapter five. I tried to select subjects from the Bible that were close to their daily lives. Since I am by nature a morning person I loved that early morning ministry. I was always encouraged to see the early morning enthusiasm of the African Christians as they met together to hear God's Word and to pray at the beginning of their day. Even though it wasn't always convenient to get up and going by five-thirty a.m., especially when I had a house full of people, the effort was well rewarded. There were times when I would sneak out and return by seven a.m. in order to prepare breakfast for my guests who never even missed me! The believers gathered at their prayer chapels from six to six-thirty a.m. as they, too, had to dash off to their work places.

MINISTRY TO WOMEN

Although Africa is pretty much a man's world, the women bear much of the burden of physical labor. The traditional African woman bears many children, works in the family garden, gathers and carries wood for the kitchen, carries water for the family use, all in addition to the regular duties of cooking, cleaning, laundry, and clothing the children. Their villages are often located on a hill with the source of water way down in the valley. Fetching enough water for a family of eight or ten is a major burden for the women. As soon as children are old enough they are required to help with this task. The women gather wood from wherever and do their cooking over an open wood fire.

Cleaning is a simple procedure done with a little handmade broom. They sweep out the mud floor of their huts on a daily basis. For the most part their huts are neat and orderly. The women work very hard with very little appreciation shown to them. Many of them have not had the opportunity to go to school but most of them desire to be able to read so they can read the Bible.

From the beginning I had been eager to encourage the women, especially in their Christian experience. Discipling women, one by one, was a rewarding ministry where I spent an hour each week for twelve weeks, taking each woman through the truths of the Gospel of John. There were some very special encounters. Ana, married to an unbeliever, had an unusual desire to understand the Scriptures and to grow in her walk with the Lord. Week after week I met with her in her terribly run-down hut, with rats running around as if they belonged there. The consistent and regular meeting together studying God's Word paid off in spiritual fruit as I saw real growth and understanding in her life. She asked me to pray for her

Reading the Word with Anastasia

husband and eventually he started going to church and tried to give up his drinking habit. He also made a serious effort to renovate their living quarters.

During my final three years in Goma I had the privilege of personally meeting with nearly thirty different individual women to help strengthen them in their Christian walk. I went to their homes for these sessions, having learned the hard way that I could control the timing better by going to them instead of waiting for them to come to me. I heard their stories of financial stress, physical problems in the family, unfaithful husbands, wayward children, and of God's loving faithfulness through the hard times in their lives. I sought to encourage them with principles and promises from the Word of God and received the greater blessing in return.

Each Thursday the women of the Goma Baptist Church gathered at the church in the afternoon for a time of praise, prayer and study. These meetings were led by the women themselves, several women among them capable of leading their own meetings. I tried to attend their meetings just to be an encouragement to them and about once a month they asked me to be their speaker. I gave them practical teaching from God's Word that would help them in their daily lives. Having observed their lack of teaching their own children in the ways of the Lord, I often took them to the Scripture passages that had special teaching for training children. They always thanked me for the encouragement I gave them for their children. Even now that I am far away from them, whenever I write to one of the women, I always say "usisahau kufundisha watoto" (don't forget to teach your children).

Once or twice a year I invited the women leaders from all of the prayer chapels around the city of Goma to come to my house for a mini day - retreat. Around twenty women were invited to come to the retreat, two women leaders from each prayer chapel and several key women from the central church in Goma. I asked them to come without their small children so that they would give full attention to the teaching and be able to enjoy the day. There was an exception for nursing mothers. I turned my good-sized living room into a "chapel" where they could sit comfortably and feel the cool lake breezes. A full program was organized for them: worship, study of God's Word, testimonies, and prayer in small groups out on the lawn. The lawn with green grass was a special treat for them as most of their little villages had only dirt yards. We ate our simple lunch out on the porch with a treat of salted peanuts to finish the meal. Then we walked down closer to the lake to give them a chance to see the boats on the water. At the final session an African Pastor spoke to them. Those times meant so much to the ladies who loved being in a quieter, cleaner section of town for even one full day. The greater blessing was mine, to see their joy and response to the effort that had been made for them.

I carried on a continuing ministry of visitation in their

homes. Elizabeti, the wife of the African dentist, was my faithful co-worker as we made weekly calls. She kept abreast of the urgent needs of the women and took me where she felt we could help meet those needs. One time we would visit a woman who was not well physically, another time we would pray with a mother who had a wayward child. We often met with and encouraged a woman who was wayward in her walk with the Lord and there were always unbelievers to whom we gave the clear message of the Gospel. We did this on foot and Elizabeti led me into every nook and cranny of the city of Goma!

I truly loved my ministry to the women. There were discouraging times when it seemed as though our teaching was not being received, but for the most part I was encouraged and blessed by the response of those simple women when I saw the spiritual impact that was made in their lives. There were times when a woman would, in turn, impact her husband. Very often after we made a call in one of the homes, the husband would appear in church the following Sunday. The African Pastor saw these results and he often thanked me for working with the women.

HOSPITALITY

Africa is known for its hospitable people who offer a warm welcome and selfless generosity. They shared a hot or cold drink and food from their table even when I knew they couldn't afford it or they were depriving their children in order to share with me. That is the African way and they do it out of genuine love for their guests. One of the beautiful African customs is hand-washing. If you are to be served food that has to be eaten with the fingers, the African hostess will bring a basin of warm water and soap and she will pour water over your hands and offer you a towel to dry your hands. Missionaries in Africa soon learn that one of the keys to becoming one with the African people is to practice the same generous hospitality. In Goma I learned that I needed to have a hospitable spirit to live and serve the African people in that urban area. Two old African proverbs say it best:

"A house without guests is without blessing."

"Guests are a blessing to the house that welcomes them."

Hundreds of people passed through my home during the eleven years that I served in Goma. Most of my guests were fellow missionaries who came to the city for shopping and other business. Hospitality was a favorite focus of my ministry and I tried to put into practice all I had learned from the Africans. In Africa, joy and personal sacrifice are the standards for receiving guests.

LITERATURE

When Joann left to retire she placed her Book Depot in my charge. This involved ordering Bibles from the London

Bible Society, as well as ordering other books from a variety of places. I ordered French hymnals from Europe, Swahili hymnals and other booklets and tracts from a neighboring mission at Nyankunde. Besides keeping the depot supplied, I had to fill orders that missionaries gave me for their stations. The financial angle of this project took time. This was a very important ministry I had inherited because of my location. It really needed someone to give more time to it than I had and one of my goals was to find another missionary who would take over the whole Book Depot project. After a two year struggle with the Book Depot, Terry Evernden, a missionary at Ruanguba, felt led to take charge. We worked together on inventory and I showed her how the system worked, turning the book finances over to her. She then moved the Book Depot to Ruanguba station where she and her husband Jim were serving.

SUNDAY SCHOOL

Wherever I was assigned in Zaire, I always tried to be directly involved in the local church in some way. I had a special love for the Sunday School, and since most of the African Sunday Schools were not all that well organized and always needed teachers, I tried to use my gifts of teaching and organization to give a boost to this area of ministry. During my years at Goma I taught the junior high young people. We studied a number of complete books from the

Bible and also various topics that were relevant to their needs, including knowing God's will, assurance of salvation, living for Christ in a pagan culture and trusting God for material needs. The junior high young people were very responsive and open to God's Word. My Sunday morning ministry in the Sunday School gave me a great deal of pleasure.

COMFORTING THE BEREAVED

While this was not a scheduled ministry for a missionary, I soon learned it was very important to the Africans. I tried to have a small part in what they called the "kilio." When a person died in Africa the body needed to be buried immediately. There was no system of embalming and the heat of Africa demanded immediate burial. The church leaders sent a church choir to the home of the bereaved to bring comfort with Christian hymns. Friends and relatives came to spend the night in the home in order to offer care and support. In two or three days, the Pastor would indicate that the "kilio" was over and the whole church would gather at the home of the family early in the morning. Gifts of food were brought for the family and the Pastor shared a message from the Word. This special time, about six a.m., was when I gathered with them for this part of their sorrowing and I always brought a gift of food for the family. Those times allowed me to bond with the Africans in a new way. There were some weeks when there would be several deaths, making this special ministry a priority for the week. I learned much about comforting others from the Africans.

EXTRACURRICULAR ACTIVITIES

The volcano Nyiragongo, with its height of eleven thousand two hundred ninety-two feet, not too distant from the city of Goma, erupted in the summer of 1986, always a bittersweet event. With each new eruption there was a certain amount of destruction. If it was a major eruption whole villages could be destroyed and always crops were ruined. Usually there was not a great loss of lives as people could flee ahead of the lava flow. At the same time it is a spectacular sight with the glow of the erupting volcano lighting up the sky at night and the red hot lava flowing like a river down the side of the mountain. We missionaries would often drive to a higher spot where we could have a good view. When Nyiragongo was not active people could climb to the top. Once, when friends

At the summit of Mt. Nyiragongo.

came to visit from the States and arranged a climb, I decided to tag along. I tried to prepare myself ahead of time with extra walking and climbing hills. At the age of sixty-one I was not at all sure I could make it to the top but I wanted to try. It was one of the very few occasions when I wore slacks in Zaire. I had good walking shoes and a walking stick to help me along the way. We all carried extra jackets for it would be cold at the summit. An African guide went with us and we reached the top in about six hours. The panoramic view from the top was spectacular! We looked down into the open crater, an awesome sight in itself. It was a great moment for me to have reached the summit. Returning to the foot was almost harder than the climb and the African guide helped me out with a few piggy-back rides.

That same year, 1986, we saw Halley's Comet in our area for several weeks during March and April. That, too, was an awesome sight which we could see with the naked eye. This was a first for me and each evening I had to go outside and have a look at the beautiful comet with its long tail.

One Saturday in August a small group of us went to see the gorillas in the wild. We spent the night at Ruanguba, our mission station to the north of Goma. Early the next morning we drove for about an hour down through an area called the Jomba. We then hiked for forty minutes to a central post manned by government employees where an African guide led us further into the forest. About thirty minutes later we found the family of gorillas, a big silverback named Marcel with two of his eight wives and several little ones. They did not seem to mind our presence and we took pictures freely. Another awesome sight, to behold more of God's creatures. We watched them for over an hour as they munched on bamboo shoots and other forest herbs and played with each other. Then we hiked back to our Land Rover for the dusty return trip to Goma.

Marcel, the Silverback gorilla.

During those final three years in Goma I was able to get away twice for a real vacation. A trip to Mombasa, on the east coast of Africa, was always an adventure. First we flew from Goma to Nairobi on the small one-engine MAF plane and then from Nairobi we took the all-night train to Mombasa. Once we were settled in the hotel and could look out on the gorgeous Indian Ocean and walk in the soft sand of the well-kept beach, we forgot the burdens of the Congo and the hassles of the trip and simply enjoyed the peace and quiet of that delightful spot. There were comfortable lawn chairs on the beach and early each morning the guests would go out to the beach and stake out a place for the day. Not being a swimmer I enjoyed my books and my handwork and took long walks on the beach collecting little butterfly shells. Those days in Mombasa were like balm for the soul and prepared me to return to the rigors of life and ministry in the Congo.

PACKING AND FAREWELL

I was scheduled to leave Zaire in March of 1988. This would give me six months in the States to make a final visit to each of my supporting churches by my September birthday, when I would turn sixty-two. The schedule for retirement was set up by our Mission Board and all missionaries were expected to follow their regulations. However, during the Christmas activities of 1987, in the midst of the festivities, busy with guests and enjoying my final Christmas in Africa, I sensed that something was wrong. I saw the mission doctor a couple of days later and he discovered a lump in my left breast. Since I was so close to leaving for the States, he chose not to do a biopsy but asked me to leave a month earlier than planned. This added time constraint meant even more careful planning of my remaining days and hours. I wanted to do my packing first and then spend time with my African and missionary friends. Since my house would be used as a guest house after I left, my furniture could stay in place. I only needed to take care of my personal belongings. Everything that I would take with me was placed into the big guest room and my friend Tudy Kile came across the border from Rwanda and packed my two footlockers. She was the best packer I knew and I was so

Tudy packing my footlockers.

grateful for her help.

The round of farewells commenced, a sad, sweet time for me. I wanted to make one last visit to each of the prayer chapels, to share a final word of encouragement with them. Sessions that I had started with individual women in the Gospel of John were to be completed. Since I was on the Finance Committee I needed to attend one more meeting at Ruanguba. While there, the Ruanguba missionaries prepared an elegant dinner and farewell for me. Surprise!! My last day there I was invited to speak to the nursing staff at the early morning devotional time for the hospital. This was a special privilege for me and I spoke to them from Psalm seventy-eight and one of the nurses prayed for me. Then one of the doctors whisked me to the helicopter pad and fifteen minutes later I was back home in Goma! Amazing! This was my first ride in a helicopter and I enjoyed being able to see the countryside from a much closer perspective than can be seen from an airplane. The latest in technology and transportation had finally arrived in our area just as I was leaving.

Gatambi, the high school principal, and his family invited me to their home for a private farewell, a special time with my former student. In the afternoons, Elizabeti and I visited as many homes as we could in order for me to say "good-bye." One day I invited the five women leaders of the women's ministry at the central church in for a final lunch and I gave them each a little souvenir. Finally, I invited my three African workers to have lunch with me. I gave each of them one of my old suitcases and they were delighted to possess a suitcase for the first time in their lives. The final Saturday morning in Africa I had to clean out the kitchen. No more entertaining. That afternoon the church leaders and wives had a feast with me as the guest of honor. There was goat meat, rice, two kinds of potatoes, cabbage cooked the African way which I dearly love, carrot sticks and Sprite, a soft drink. It was a delight being with all these special people with whom I had worked for the past eleven years.

The biggest farewell of all took place on Sunday, January 31, the day before I was to leave Zaire behind forever. My special friend, Tudy, came over from Rwanda to be with me the whole day. After teaching my final Sunday School lesson on Mephibosheth, we attended the Swahili worship service. The adult choir, the young people's choir and the children's choir all sang special songs for me. There were testimonials, verses and gifts of African handiwork.

The church leaders asked Gatambi to bring the message that morning. That meant so much to me to have my former student bring God's Word for my final day in Zaire. At one point they asked me to give a word. My thoughts for them came from Mark 10:29-30:

"There is no one who has left house or brothers or sisters or father or mother or wife or children or lands for my sake and the gospel's, who shall not receive a hundredfold now in this time — houses and brothers and sisters and mothers and children and lands, with persecutions — and in the age to come, eternal life."

Even though I had left my own family to come to Africa and serve in their country, I had literally received a hundredfold in joy and blessing. They had become like family to me, my African family, with fathers, mothers, brothers, sisters, and children. I thanked them for giving me the privilege of teaching God's Word and for teaching me so much in return — their language, culture and love for the Lord Jesus. I would miss them very much but it was God's time for me to return to my country. It was an emotional moment for me but I managed to hold back the tears until later when I was alone at home.

The Pastor then presented me with a letter from the church leaders and he read it aloud to us all. The letter thanked me for five specific things:

1. For attending prayer meeting with them every Wednesday.
2. For going to the prayer chapels early in the morning in the cold, even when I had to walk.
3. For going from house to house to teach individual women.
4. For attending the grieving process with the family of a deceased one and for bringing gifts like everyone else.
5. For helping financially when they built the Kingi chapel.

They included verses from I Corinthians 15:58 and Colossians 2:5 in their letter, which was written in beautiful Swahili, signed by the Goma church leaders and with a proper church seal. I was very humbled by their letter, for to me, I was only doing what I saw as my duty as a servant of the Lord.

That last afternoon more than one hundred women came by my house to say their personal "good-byes." Tudy, who stayed with me the entire day, helped me give each one a little souvenir from my personal things — such as a piece of jewelry, or cloth or a booklet. That evening there was the usual English Bible study with missionaries and other English speakers. We watched a Dr. Charles Stanley video and heard his excellent message. Then I was presented with the most fantastic book which had been assembled by an English friend, Deborah Betts. She had included photographs, drawings, and testimonials from so many of my friends, all to be enjoyed long after I had left Africa behind.

This was followed by an elegant ham dinner and a dessert cake especially decorated for me.

The next day I said "good-bye" to Zaire and traveled to Gisenyi where I spent several quiet days with Tudy. I needed this time to take care of last-minute financial reports and correspondence. Later in the week Tudy drove me to Kigali. We left early in the morning, watched the sun come up over the Rwandan hills with the volcanoes in the background, a sight that I had never tired of seeing. That evening I flew out on Air France, a journey from Kigali to Paris and finally Chicago. I went directly to our mission headquarters in Wheaton. A mammogram was scheduled the next day and the suspected malignant tumor was found. Then came the usual round of medical check-ups and more mission business at various offices. Four days later the surgery was scheduled at Central du Page Hospital in Wheaton for the modified radical mastectomy. Our African director, Dick Jacobs and his wife, Ruth, were so kind to me and welcomed me into their home for my recovery. It was the year of the winter Olympics in Calgary and I enjoyed watching the competitions on the television. One day Dick and Ruth drove me out to Trinity Seminary, where Basolene, a former student of mine from Africa, was working on his doctorate. The Jacobs and I had a delightful visit with Basolene, his wife Kavira, whom I had discipled in Zaire, and their four children. Before leaving Wheaton I was invited to have lunch with Esther Ker and her mother, next-door neighbors of the Jacobs. After lunch, Mother Whitaker, Esther's mother, gave me Jeremiah 29:11:

> *"For I know the thoughts that I think toward you, says the LORD, thoughts of peace and not of evil, to give you a future and a hope."*

This special verse became mine during those dark cancer days. I stayed with the Jacobs for nearly three weeks during the successful recovery period. The Olympics helped the time to pass more quickly. When I checked in with my doctor for the final time, he prescribed Tamoxifen, an oral cancer treatment and said I could travel home to Maine the first week in March.

GOODBYES TO MY SUPPORTING CHURCHES

On March eleventh I returned to Maine to be with my family. It was indeed a very dark period in my life. Where would the cancer go? Would I have a ministry? These were only two of the questions occupying my thoughts. I clung to my verse in Jeremiah, a gentle reminder that God had my life in His control. I stayed with Mom in her mobile home, slowly gaining my strength back from the surgery and all the while praying for clear direction in the days to come. One day, later in March, I received a phone call from Dr. Bruce Ker, one of our mission leaders from Wheaton, Illinois. He was calling from South Portland, Maine and told me that Dr. Carl Grathwohl, President of New England Bible College in South Portland, was looking for a missions instructor. He had suggested my name to the president and asked if that was okay with me. At that moment, light flooded into my dark tunnel and I began to see my way through and out of the dark days. Truly God was in control and even had blessings for me far beyond my imagination. I told Dr. Ker that it was more than okay.

While I waited for the details for my next assignment to be worked out, I located a small furnished apartment in Dexter and settled down to begin visiting my supporting churches. Cousin Alden helped me find a used Buick Century for my travel needs. I was able to visit most of my supporting churches and see family members as well. By the time September arrived I was ready for the next step in my life.

REFLECTIONS ON MY FINAL TERM IN ZAIRE

"To God be the glory, great things He hath done,
So loved He the world that He gave us His Son,
Who yielded His life an atonement for sin,
And opened the Life-gate that all may go in.

> *Great things He hath taught us, great things*
> *He hath done,*
> *And great our rejoicing thro' Jesus the Son;*
> *But purer, and higher, and greater will be*
> *Our wonder, our transport, when Jesus we see.*
>
> *Chorus:*
> *Praise the Lord, praise the Lord, Let the earth hear*
> *His voice!*
> *Praise the Lord, Praise the Lord, Let the people*
> *rejoice!*
> *Oh come to the Father, thro' Jesus the Son.*
> *And give Him the glory, great things He hath*
> *done."*
>
> *Fanny Crosby (1820-1915)*

Now I look back on those last six years in Africa with amazement and thankfulness to my heavenly Father for His grace and love for me. Each of the three medical challenges was an interruption to my ministry and each was a particular trial at the time. But God helped me to bounce back after each one. Many people prayed for me and I believe that God answered those prayers and allowed me to complete my time in Africa with joy and blessing. In many ways my final term was the richest of all. I felt closer to my missionary co-workers and to the African believers than ever before. I saw more fruit for my labors during that final term than in any other. Former students were now taking places of leadership in churches, in schools and in their country. Women were growing in their spiritual walks and they were eagerly reaching out to other women.

All the farewells and kind words of both Africans and missionaries were quite overwhelming. To me, I only followed the pattern that God had given me before I ever left the States the first time. I was seriously doing what I believed to be my duty. And I was doing it knowing that I had the help and strength of my heavenly Father.

GREAT IS HIS FAITHFULNESS!!

CHAPTER ELEVEN

THE BONUS YEARS AT NEW ENGLAND BIBLE COLLEGE
(September 1988 - May 2003)

"For I know the thoughts that I think toward you, says the LORD, thoughts of peace and not of evil, to give you a future and a hope." - Jeremiah 29:11

The lights flashed and the bells rang as I stepped into an apartment at 289 Mitchell Road in Cape Elizabeth, Maine. I knew this was the place that God had reserved for me. The month-long search for an apartment had come to an end. The lady next door, I learned later, had been praying for some time for a Christian neighbor. In due time I became acquainted with Elaine Bean and we were neighbors and friends for the next fifteen years. I had fun settling into the split-level apartment, with living room, kitchen and dining area on the lower level and a spacious room upstairs that I divided into a bedroom and study area. I placed my desk in

My apartment in Cape Elizabeth.

front of the large picture window that looked out on the lawn and trees. A bathroom, walk-in closet, large clothes closet and another storage closet completed the upper level. I was now living in much smaller quarters than I ever had in Africa but with many more conveniences - carpeted floors, dependable hot and cold water supply, laundry facilities in the complex and electricity functioning most, instead of some, of the time. And, of course, I had the Maine snow to deal with! I missed Africa but knew I would get used to Cape Elizabeth and the new life that was ahead of me.

Driving in the greater Portland area presented a new and traumatic challenge for me. For over thirty years I had driven on dirt roads with only one lane going each way. Eventually I learned the one-way streets and in which lane I needed to be. My pastor's wife, Cindy Monahan, took me out driving on several occasions and patiently helped me learn city-driving. My home was conveniently located, only a fifteen-minute walk from the ocean. I was just two miles from the church and Bible College in South Portland where I would be teaching for the next fifteen years.

Teaching on the college level was a completely new experience for me. In the Congo I had taught elementary school and worked my way up the line to junior high and finally to high school. I was so grateful to my mission board who insisted back in 1952 that I complete the work for my Master's degree. With the Lord's sovereign control, I was now qualified to teach at New England Bible College. I learned from other instructors how to prepare a syllabus and learned early that a word processor would be a necessity in my new career. The new challenge excited me.

New England Bible College had been founded in 1980. However, its roots were in Glen Cove Bible College, founded in 1959. NEBC's heritage includes many of Glen Cove's resources as well as the State of Maine's legislative approval to continue Glen Cove's degree-granting privileges. The Rev. Jack Christensen, then pastor of First Baptist Church of Portland, was appointed as the first president of NEBC and classes began in January 1980 in the facility of the First Baptist Church. NEBC was founded to serve Conservative Baptist churches and others of similar doctrine partnering to equip their people for the Lord's service. The college identified three areas of vocational specialization in which to serve the Lord — pastoral studies, missions and Christian education — as well as courses in preparation for advanced seminary studies.

In 1984 Edward Hales became the college's second president. That same year NEBC moved to larger facilities at First Baptist Church of South Portland, where it remains today. Dr. Carl Grathwohl became the third president in 1987 and was the first to serve on a full-time basis. He concentrated on providing good, solid pastoral training for the conservative churches of Maine. In 1992 Dr. Grathwohl became the first chancellor of the college, a position which he held until his death later that year.

Rev. William E. Inman was named the fourth president in 1992. Under his leadership NEBC began to offer BA and BS degrees, replacing the Bachelor of Religious Education program. The curriculum underwent revision and plans were laid for several new majors: the first, in missions was launched in 2001. Rev. Inman completed his ministry as president in 2002. Dr. Jack Christensen is presently serving as the Interim President. Today the school averages from forty-five to fifty students each semester under the instruction of three full-time and nine part-time faculty. The school rejoices in its rich heritage and presses forward toward the shared goal of reaching the world for Christ. I was delighted and privileged to become a part of this young college and very thankful to the Lord for having led me there and given me new hope in my own life and ministry.

MY FIFTEEN YEARS IN THE PORTLAND AREA

In order to help you, my reader, see how much I appreciated the new location and ministry God had given to me, I want to share with you snippets of my various involvements during the fifteen years I lived and ministered in the Portland area. Each picture that I give you will be another evidence of God's continued faithfulness in my life. I am always learning the wonderful truth that our heavenly Father does care for the smallest of details in the lives of His children.

First Baptist Church of South Portland, Maine

Being part of a local church family has always been very important to me and to be involved in the church, using my spiritual gifts, is a high priority in my life. I hoped to settle in a local church as soon as possible. The First Baptist Church in South Portland, Maine had been one of my faithful supporting churches all the time I was in Africa. Since I now lived only two miles from that church, I decided to join that congregation. I transferred my membership from Cambridge Baptist Church to First Baptist Church in South Portland where Rev. Kenneth Monahan was the pastor. Pastor Monahan had been my pastor in Cambridge, Maine while I was serving my final term in Africa. Missionaries usually keep their membership in a home church while serving in a foreign field. Pastor Monahan and his wife Cindy were both very helpful to me as I settled in the Portland area. They had four children: Erin, Kenney, Sarah and Timothy. I stayed at the parsonage with the children while their parents went on a two-week missions trip to Honduras in March of 1989. That was a time of bonding with the children, especially with Timothy, the youngest who was not yet in school. I took him to the children's library, we walked on the beach, ate at MacDonalds and did other fun things. Of course, these children are now grown, either graduated from or attending Philadelphia Biblical University and all married to great Christian spouses and serving the Lord in various ministries.

As I left Africa I carried a particular burden with me. Wherever I would locate, I needed to be part of a regular prayer group that prayed especially for missionaries. There was no such group in the South Portland Baptist Church, but I found a lady, Lucy Penney, who was willing to meet with me every week to pray for the twenty-five missionary units supported by our church. In time, two other ladies joined us, Gladys Irish and Annie Weatherbie. The Wednesday ten a.m. prayer time soon became a highlight of my week. This was a focused and serious group, each lady with her notebook where she kept the latest prayer letter from each missionary so she could pray specifically for their current needs. Gradually others joined and our little group grew. Although one by one the Lord called these ladies home, He always raised up others to take their places. Every Easter I placed a lily at church in memory of the ladies from our prayer group who had left us to go to their heavenly home.

Discipling women was always a passion of mine and very soon after my arrival in South Portland Pastor Monahan gave me my first opportunity. I took this lady through the truths of the Gospel of John, just as I had done with the African women I had discipled, but this time in English. This became an on-going ministry for me in my home church. I remember so well the day our youth pastor, David Spencer, telephoned to ask if I would consider discipling one of the teen girls in his youth group. While we were still talking on the telephone, Luke 2:52 was pressed on my heart and I could hardly wait to prepare an outline that I would follow with teens. I wrote my own guide and had the privilege of discipling a number of teen girls in our church including Fleur, an exchange student from Germany.

The senior ladies' Sunday School class was another ministry I enjoyed very much for a number of years, in addition to the Wednesday evening home Bible study that I led for nearly ten years. Some of the same ladies were in both groups. During that time, we explored in depth most of the sixty-six books of the Bible.

I served and chaired the Missions Committee of our church. The first task the committee faced when I became a member was to prepare a missions policy for our church. We spent months on this laborious task, researching policies from other churches and eventually finalizing our own missions policy. I knew it was vital for the committee members to personally become better acquainted with each of our missionaries and I set a plan in motion to make this happen. As the missionaries visited our church on their furloughs, we set aside time for them to meet with the committee to exchange ideas and prayer. We usually did this around a meal where one committee member would invite the missionary for the main meal and the other members would join them for dessert. We questioned the missionaries as to their goals in ministry, their more personal problems that they might not feel free to share in a public meeting, their financial needs and anything else they wanted to share. We also gave them the opportunity to ask us any questions. We always encouraged them to give us specific prayer needs and we prayed with them. These were rich times for both the committee members and the missionaries.

When Pastor Monahan moved to Dover, New Hampshire in June of 1995, I was asked, along with six other members of the church, to serve on the Pulpit Committee to search for a new pastor. Our committee met for nearly a year before we finally agreed to present David Spencer, then serving as our interim pastor, as a candidate for senior pastor. David had also served as our youth pastor for eight years prior to becoming the interim pastor. Two weeks later the church voted to call David and Cindy Spencer. The Spencers moved into the parsonage rather quickly. Their twin girls, Sarah and Hannah, were born sev-

Dave, Cindy, Sarah and Hannah Spencer.

eral days later on June 4, 1996. The Spencers served our church faithfully for the next six years before moving on to Concord, New Hampshire where they are still serving in the First Baptist Church of Concord.

Being a part of First Baptist Church of South Portland for fifteen years was an enriching experience for me. I was given many opportunities to use my spiritual gifts which helped me to grow in the Lord and I felt I helped others to grow as well. I developed lasting friendships among the church family and some of these friends have already braved the two-hour drive from Portland to visit me at my new location in rural Dexter.

Ministry at New England Bible College

I had moved to the Portland area on faith. Dr. Carl Grathwohl had invited me to teach one missions course at New England Bible College, with no indication that I would teach other courses in the future. Nevertheless, it seemed right for me to move to the area. My first course was

"Missionary Principles and Practices," a junior/senior course, and as the name indicates we studied certain principles of missionary work and how the principles could be carried out in practical ways in real-life situations on the mission field. I trembled inwardly at the thought of teaching on the college level. My first class was four young men: Phil Andrukaitis, Russ Cotnoir, Ron Sargent and Robin Twombly. I don't know how they really felt about having this single lady missionary as their instructor but they were gentlemen and kind to me in every way. They were thinkers and we enjoyed some lively discussions in our classroom about missionary work around the world. We took one field trip that semester to the inner city of Boston to see first-hand the ministries of missionaries Ralph and Judy Kee and Paul and Jan Bothwell. My students gained fresh insights into the variety of opportunities, as well as difficulties, that come with a ministry in the inner city.

My first class, Robin, Russ, Ron and Phil.

During that first semester I still visited my supporting churches on the weekends to give my final report on Africa to each of my churches and to express my appreciation for their faithful support over the years. The mission leaders gave me a few extra assignments along the way. One was to be the missionary speaker for a group of Conservative Baptist women at Monadnock, New Hampshire. At the same women's conference, Cynthia Heald, author of the best-selling Bible study, *Becoming a Woman of Excellence* and an internationally known women's speaker, was the Bible teacher. Cynthia's topic at this conference was "The Excellent Woman" and I spoke on "Spiritual Lessons Learned through Physical Battles." God used those days together with Cynthia to bond our hearts. That was the beginning of a very special friendship that endures today. Cynthia and her husband Jack, missionaries with the Navigators, live in Arizona which means we don't see each other very often. However, during the time that I lived in the Portland area I heard her speak on several occasions when we had time to be together.

David Christensen, the Academic Dean of the Bible College, telephoned me one summer day in 1989 to ask if I would teach "Personal and Group Bible Study" to the freshmen in the fall. I was a little hesitant at first, thinking that I could do a better job on a missions course but I agreed to teach the class. This newest challenge excited me and I began reading Psalm 119 to prepare my own heart for teaching this important course. Psalm 119, with almost every verse referring to the Word of God in one way or another, encouraged me as I meditated and filled my heart with the truths of the effect that God's Word can have in our lives. For example, verse eighteen says, *"Open my eyes, that I may see wondrous things from Your law"* and this became my prayer as I worked on the syllabus for this new course. The course involved teaching principles of personal Bible study and gave the students themselves the opportunity to teach group Bible lessons. In the fall, well into the semester, my new friend, Cynthia Heald and her mother, Eunice Hall, came to Maine where Cynthia would speak at a Conservative Baptist women's retreat at the Ramada Inn in Bangor. They flew to Portland so they could spend a few days with me and then I had the fun of driving them to Bangor, following the coastal route all the way to Bar Harbor. Since Cynthia was an expert in Bible study, I wanted to share her with my class. I turned one of my class periods over to her and she spoke to my students and their friends who had been invited to come for that special occasion. Cynthia's keen knowledge of the Word of God, her warm, loving manner and her homey and personal illustrations made her input a spiritual treat for all of us that day. I found that I loved teaching the course because I could see immediate progress in the students' ability to handle the study of the Bible once they began applying the principles taught to them. I assure you that the teacher learned right along with them!

When the regular instructor for "Ministry to Women"

moved out of the area, I was offered my third course, which soon became my favorite. My goal was to help develop godly women who would, in turn, produce more godly women. I introduced the women students to some of my favorite women mentors, among them Amy Carmichael, Mrs. Howard Taylor, Elisabeth Elliot, Cynthia Heald, Margaret Clarkson, Edith Dean and Ruth Tucker. The women read books by the above authors and our class texts were *Let me be a Woman* by Elisabeth Elliot, *The Measure of a Woman* by Gene Getz, and *Becoming a Woman of Excellence* by Cynthia Heald. They were required to write papers on a variety of subjects including "Masculinity and Femininity," "Biblical Self-esteem," "Solitude and Simplicity" and they wrote a longer paper on a woman in the Bible. They were required to interview an older godly woman and write their reflections. From time to time, I invited a panel of local church women to discuss specific topics, particularly those having to do with the Christian home. This became a popular phase in the course. After a few years, the college began inviting women from the area churches to take the course with the younger college students. The response was good and their presence added a new dimension to our class.

A fourth course was dumped unceremoniously into my lap because none of the other instructors wanted to teach "Cultural Anthropology." Oh, of course, they wouldn't admit this, for they reasoned that since I had lived in another culture I was a natural for the course. At any rate, I was sufficiently challenged by the course to thoroughly prepare and determined to create an interesting course for the students. The course was an introduction to cultural anthropology, with special emphasis on its missionary implications. It was designed to help the student understand other people and their cultures for the purpose of accurately distinguishing between the changeless Christian message and the variables that might affect the cross-cultural communication and application of that message. My lessons were enhanced by sharing experiences from my life in Africa. In the early 1990's, people from several ethnic backgrounds, Russian, Cambodian, and African, were moving into the Portland area. I wanted my students of anthropology to experience these different ethnic groups. Every month I arranged a special "other cultural experience" by either taking my students to visit these people or bringing some of them into the classroom as our guests. One time we visited in an African home where we were served an African meal of rice, potatoes and chicken. We also visited a Jewish synagogue. Another time several Cambodian young people came to our class to interact with my students. Our text for the semester, *Cultural Anthropology: A Christian Perspective* by Grunlan and Mayers, was very helpful. The students read and reported on books that gave good insights into other cultures. *Peace Child,* by Don Richardson, was a favorite. As it turned out, I thoroughly enjoyed this course and my own life was enriched by all the contacts we made with the ethnic groups. There were always opportunities along the way to share our faith.

My greatest challenge while at the Bible College was to create a new missions course. I worked an entire year on "Unreached Peoples," which became my fifth course. I introduced the students to the "10/40 window," the area from ten degrees to forty degrees north of the equator stretching from West Africa to Japan where so many peoples of the world have not yet heard the Gospel of Jesus Christ. They were encouraged to concentrate on that area and to choose a people group for research, prayer and possible ministry. A major paper was required by the end of the semester on their researched people. Most of the semester was spent doing the research. The students wrote letters, used e-mail, the internet and the phone to gather information. I stood by to encourage and help in any way I could. I felt satisfied that the experience broadened their vision of the great number of people still without the Gospel and increased their burden to minister to the unreached peoples in our world. A copy of each of the research papers was kept on file at the college for the benefit of future students.

The sixth and final course given to me was "Spiritual Life." This course kept me on my knees. It was a practical course, designed to help the student grow in relationship with Jesus Christ. We explored the role of the church and spiritual gifts. Bible study, Scripture memorization, prayer, witness to the unsaved, a personal mission statement, and disciplined use of time were all involved in this course. A.T. Pierson's book, *George Müller of Bristol*, helped me prepare my own heart. Among other books, the students were required to read *Celebration of Discipline* by Richard Foster, *Pursuit of Holiness* by Jerry Bridges, and *The Spirit of the Disciplines* by Dallas Willard. These authors were living when I taught the course and I felt that they had significant insights to offer on the matter of the spiritual life. This course was a heart-searching and heart-stretching experience, one that I never really felt worthy to teach.

At the close of each semester, I always planned a celebration for students in my classes. I invited them to my home where they could see my African memorabilia and enjoy a light meal or goodies, depending on the time of day. I prayed regularly for the students I taught and tried to be available to them when they needed help with their lessons or just needed to talk.

The college library was another of my responsibilities during my last years at the college. Karen Chagnon, a volunteer (bless those volunteers!), placed all nine thousand volumes into the library computer and I was her helper for this major project. The student workers in the library were also my responsibility. A very long time and many hours later, I felt I understood the Library of Congress catalogue system!

I delighted in my years of ministry at New England

Bible College. I was happiest when I was busy with some project in the cool lower level facility of our small but powerful institution. I was stretched and blessed as I interacted with fellow faculty and staff. I knew I was where God meant me to be and doing what He had chosen for me to do. Truly, my faith-move to the area in August, 1988 was abundantly rewarded. God gave me "a future and a hope."

Family

Washing dishes three times a day in the old slate sink on the farm in Parkman for our growing family, now seen in perspective, was worth it all. In Africa for over thirty years, I had missed out on many significant family events but God then brought me back to Maine where I still had time left to enjoy my family. By this time our father and two brothers had passed away but our mother, four sisters and two brothers still lived in Maine. There were plenty of nieces and nephews scattered around, too. When I located in Cape Elizabeth, my youngest brother, Charles, lived in Augusta and worked for Central Maine Power. Sister Beatrice and her husband, Skip Patterson, lived in Dexter and worked for Dexter Shoe. Baby sister Mary Lou and her husband, Wayne Redmond, a construction worker and heavy equipment operator, lived in Dover-Foxcroft. Sister Marion Russell lived in the Bangor area close to her daughter, Debra. Our special-needs brother, Franklin, lived in Monson and later in

Sister luncheon at Marion's - Bernice, Mary Lou, Bea and Marion

Harmony. I had two aunts, Aunt Esther Harrington in Albion and Aunt Lizzie Cooley in Mercer. In just a little over a two hours' time I could drive to any of these relatives and I made an effort to see them as often as possible.

Gradually each family member came to see where I lived. I loved showing them the interesting sights along the great Atlantic, a fifteen-minute walk from my house. I was present for the weddings of my two nieces and some of my nephews. Because I lived closest to Charles, he and I were able to do things together. We enjoyed musical concerts and eating out (Charles often picked up the tab in those days!). We usually spent Christmas together, first at his home then at mine. His church in Augusta did an impressive "Living Christmas Tree" each year, and I tried to reserve time for that in my schedule. Charles also played his trumpet in a community band during the summer months and I enjoyed taking my friends to hear his band play on the library lawn in Boothbay.

I made it a point to give priority to our mother and as often as possible with my busy schedule, I drove to Dexter to see her. Since she didn't drive, it was important that we take her out for rides. She loved to visit her favorite restaurants where her special scallops were on the menu. When our father was still alive they had loved to drive to the White Mountains in New Hampshire. My first summer in Cape Elizabeth I planned a little trip to New Hampshire and Vermont with Mother, Aunt Esther and her friend Maud. We had a lovely drive across New Hampshire and into Vermont and stayed in the Yankee Traveler Motel in St. Johnsbury, Vermont. We drove to Montpelier to see the gorgeous gold-domed capitol building. The next morning we enjoyed French toast with pure Vermont maple syrup and visited the Maple Grove Candy factory. Then we drove back to New Hampshire, down through Franconia Notch where we saw the "Old Man of the Mountain" and the White Mountains in all their glory. We lunched near Lake Winnipesaukee. Our original plan had been to drive back to Maine, spend one night at my house, and see some of the sights in the Portland area. Our plans changed when Mother slipped on the grass in front of my house and broke a bone in her ankle. The next day I drove her back to Dexter. A cast was put on her leg and I cared for her until she felt stable and secure in her mobile home.

Sadly, in October of 1990 Mother had a stroke which put her into the hospital. From the hospital she was sent to the Rehabilitation Center in Portland where she stayed for six weeks. I lived close enough to Portland to visit her every day. Thirteen family members gathered at the center to celebrate Thanksgiving with Mother. On Christmas Day Charles and I brought her to my house for dinner. On December twenty-ninth she was released from the center and I drove her to Dexter and cared for her in her home for two weeks. When it was time to return to my classes, Mother moved to sister Bea's house, where she lived for the next year. Hired ladies stayed with her while Bea went to work during the day. This arrangement wasn't always satisfactory and eventually Bea took a leave of absence from her work to care for Mother. During my Christmas break I stayed with Mother while Bea and Skip took a two-week break in Florida.

In February 1992 there was an opening in the Dexter Nursing Home and Mother became a resident there. After the original difficult adjustment Mother gradually became acquainted with the nurses, workers and other residents and felt more at home. She was in a wheel chair and I learned how to

Mother at the nursing home. Bernice, Mother, Elsie and Ruth.

transfer her to my car. I tried to go to Dexter as often as possible to see her, take her out to eat and visit her friends. If I was there on a Sunday, she liked for me to attend "church" with her. Different area pastors ministered in the nursing home on Sunday afternoons. She was in the nursing home for five years and passed away on September 26, 1997 at age ninety-two. There was a memorial service at Mother's church, the First Baptist Church in Dexter and the burial was next to Dad in the family plot in Parkman. Mother was a hard-working individual, loyal to her husband and her children, active in her church and a volunteer at the Dexter museum. She was very strong in times of family tragedy - when our father had to spend a year in the sanatorium and when she lost two of her sons in early deaths.

After Mother's death my trips to Dexter were less frequent, but I continued to see my brothers and sisters from time to time. Every summer I spent a week or so with family. There were regular check-ups with Dr. Fernow, who was monitoring my health while I was on tamoxifen. Since Dr. Fernow was in Dover-Foxcroft, this gave me an opportunity to visit with family when I saw her. In May, 1996 she took me off the tamoxifen I had taken for eight years, the usual time period for that drug to be effective.

It was always delightful when family came to see me in Cape Elizabeth. Charles came from time to time for special occasions. He enjoyed the musical concerts at the Merrill Auditorium in the summer. Bea and Skip visited for a day or two almost every summer. Marion and her daughter Debra came to see me several times and Debra spent the night with me occasionally. Once Marion came on the bus to see a special art display of the paintings of Frederic Edwin Church of the Hudson River School. We enjoyed his paintings at the Portland Museum of Art and had lunch at DiMillo's Floating Restaurant in the Old Port of Portland. For the twenty-first century celebration on July twenty-eighth, tall ships called "OP SAIL 2000" gathered in the harbor. Bea, Skip, and Mary Lou spent two memorable days with me and we all enjoyed the parade of tall ships as well as visits on board several of them. These are just a few of the many good times we siblings enjoyed together as adults now that we were all here in Maine. I thank the Lord often for each family member who is uniquely special to me.

Culture in the Portland Area

Having lived for over thirty years in Africa where we amused ourselves with a climb to the crest of a volcano, a trip through the park to see elephants and lions, or with games of Scrabble and Skip-Bo in the evenings, I anticipated a different kind of culture when I moved to Cape Elizabeth. I loved the greater Portland area with the ocean, beaches, and lighthouses in close proximity to my new home. When guests came we visited the ocean, the Longfellow House on Congress Street or the Portland

Museum of Art. Every Tuesday evening during the summer, we were privileged to enjoy the Kotzschmar organ concerts at City Hall where organists from all over the world came to perform. The organ had been built by the Austin Organ Company and given to the city of Portland in 1912 by Cyrus Hermann Kotzschmar Curtis. It contains over six thousand six hundred pipes and is one of only two restored municipal organs remaining in the United States. The Portland Symphony Orchestra played regular concerts throughout the year and on rare occasions there would be an opera. There was a great shopping mall, book stores galore, and public libraries where one could order any book on interlibrary loan. The Cumberland County Civic Center hosted larger events including ice skating and a variety of shows. Favorite eating places were DiMillo's, the Olive Garden, the Village Café and Newick's. Excellent medical care was available at the Maine Medical Center. Portland is truly a place for broadening one's horizons. I am so very grateful for my fifteen happy years in that area where I could enjoy American culture again. I will always miss Africa but I am so thankful for the years to reconnect with my roots in America.

My Return Visit to Zaire

My return trip to Zaire after four years of absence was one of the most rewarding things I have ever done. For some time I had been thinking about going back to Zaire for a visit. This is very important to the Africans, and since they had sent me off with cancer in 1988 never expecting to see me again, I wanted to show them in person what God had done for me. I had a free semester at the college in the spring of 1992 and decided to return to Zaire in March for a six-week visit. I traveled with Judy Kee, a former Zaire missionary and personal friend from Boston, who also wanted to return to visit the area where she had worked. While in Zaire I stayed with missionary friends Paul and Faye Hurlburt, in the city of Goma where I had ministered for eleven years. In fact, they lived in the same house I had occupied and they offered me my old bedroom which was a special treat. Alice and Deighton Douglin were in their final term before retirement and they invited me to their home often for meals. Alice is the greatest cook of gourmet African food - mushrooms, ndizi (fried bananas), chicken wamba (chicken cooked with palm nuts), samaki (tilapia fish), and other African ethnic foods. I was very comfortable and at ease as I settled down to make contacts with my African friends.

There were two goals that I wanted to accomplish during my visit to Africa. First, I wanted to visit each of the prayer chapels which had become such a vital part of my life during my final years in Goma. Second, I wanted to visit as many homes as possible of the women whom I had lovingly discipled. I went to work immediately for I knew the six-week visit would pass all too quickly.

The heart-beat of the Goma work is in the prayer chapels where people meet at six a.m. for praise, prayer and fellowship. I was greatly blessed and encouraged as I visited the eight centers for early morning prayer. Believers of all ages - men, women, young people and children - delighted to gather and lift up their voices in praise to their heavenly Father whom they trusted to see them through the political and economic disasters that engulfed them at that time. Young people were vitally involved in the morning gatherings with their small choirs and the typical African drum. On Sunday morning each chapel held Sunday School for the children before going to worship at the central church.

One of these chapels, VIRUNGA, had become an organized church with its own pastor and elders and they had already spawned a prayer chapel, KIBWE, out on the edge of town where the hike over the lava rock was quite a challenge. I visited the latest new chapel of the Goma church, called BETHEL, where they were still meeting in a home but had plans for building as the Lord would enable them. In each of the eight chapels I was asked to share the Word of God. I shared with them some thoughts which I believe the Lord had given to me for them from Hebrews 12:1-11. Verse eleven speaks of "nevertheless afterward" and I reminded them of my season of physical "chastening" back in 1982-1983 and of my joy and praise to the Lord for having restored my health. He had even brought me into a new season of peace and fruitfulness. I sought to encourage them to trust our same loving Father through their seasons of difficulties.

Visits in over fifty homes was a rich and rewarding experience. I listened to women tell me about their walk with the Lord, their involvement in the life of the local church and their children. I made these visits on foot with Elizabeti, my former faithful helper. We heard stories of joy and growth, burdens of wayward husbands or children, concerns for the future of their country, but stories always with a confidence and a deep sense of trust in the Lord, who alone gave them hope.

Elizabeti, my faithful helper.

I was asked to speak to women's groups on five different occasions and to a group of forty teen-aged girls who were still willing to listen to an older woman. One evening I was the honored guest in the home of Pastor Mutima, the pastor of the central church in Goma, who had included the church elders for a lovely African meal of rice, beans, sweet potatoes, and a delicious beef meat with sauce. This was their way of telling me they truly appreciated that I had returned to visit them. I enjoyed a very special visit with my friend Ancilla who traveled the long distance from Rutshuru to Goma to see me. One of my earlier home visits was with Simon and his wife Laokadia. Simon, a former student of mine, was now the legal representative for the association of churches in that area. Simon gave testimony to the wonderful support his wife was to him and Laokadia told me details of each of their nine children. I was able to visit Ruanguba station, one of my former places of ministry, for a day and a half. While there I made five home visits and took part in the missionary "farewell" for the Douglins who would soon be leaving Zaire for retirement. The six weeks were packed full and I was so blessed to see my African friends again and encouraged to see growth from the seeds that the Lord had earlier allowed me and others to plant.

God's Provision for my Financial Needs

When I returned to the States following my trip to Zaire I faced some financial needs and began looking for a little side job that would provide some pocket money. I found a Saturday morning cleaning job in the home of Mrs. Norwood, an elderly lady living alone in South Portland. I worked a year for her before she went into a nursing home. For a short period of time I did an evening shift caring for Mrs. Philbrick. For several months I stayed one afternoon a week with Mother Russell while her daughter Charlotte did errands.

When I had no work for a while I placed an ad on the CVS bulletin board outside their store. Mrs. Vogler saw the ad and called me. She was looking for a cleaning lady for two or three hours on Fridays. This fit nicely into my teaching schedule and I began working for her in March 1994. Her body was riddled with arthritis and she needed a lot of help in her home. She was a very thoughtful, kind person and I thoroughly enjoyed working for her for the next four years. During that same period another lady, Anita, needed some cleaning done and I was able to fit her need into my schedule for one day a week for the next year. Mrs. Vogler eventually moved closer to her daughter in Pennsylvania. At the same time New England Bible College was able to give a raise in pay to the adjunct instructors and I no longer needed the extra work. I will be forever grateful for these ladies whom God brought into my life to help meet my needs.

Visits with Friends in Florida

I did not have a second semester class my first year at New England Bible College. When my friend Shirley Chadbourne, who lived in St. Petersburg, Florida invited me to visit her in February 1989 I jumped at the opportunity to see Florida for the first time. I was excited to pick oranges and grapefruit off the trees and I enjoyed eating the luscious fruit while relaxing in Shirley's Florida Room. I planned my trip to coincide with the annual missionary conference at Shirley's home church, Northside Baptist Church in St. Petersburg, where I met missionaries from all over the world. Shirley, ever hospitable, had several of the missionaries in her home for meals, which added to my joy. At the conference, I recall my thrill when I met Rachel Saint, sister of Philip Saint, one of the five missionary men killed on January 8, 1956 by the Auca (Waodani) Indians in Ecuador. That first Florida experience enriched my life and ministry as I was privileged not only to hear the reports of the missionaries at the conference, but to meet so many of Shirley's friends. Although I had no desire to live in Florida, I enjoyed a winter get-away every couple of years. The weeks away seemed to shorten our long Maine winter. I visited Shirley a number of times and one year I visited my friend Marguerite Gay who lived in Palm Bay on the east coast of Florida. For many years I had been a welcome guest in Marguerite's home in Nashua, New Hampshire. How delightful it was for me to be able to see her lovely new home and meet her many friends in Florida. As I am writing this in 2005, both of these friends have sold their Florida homes and are living in Maine to be closer to their families. We talk often on the phone and I see them from time to time and we always give thanks for the many happy memories.

Rumney Bible Conference
The New England Fellowship of Evangelicals, head-

quartered at Rumney, New Hampshire, parents several ministries: a Bible Conference for adults located on the conference grounds at Rumney, White Mountain Ranch for teens located a few miles up in the hills from the conference grounds, and a Snow Camp for teens. My earliest memories of Rumney Bible Conference go back to my college years in the 1940's. Dr. J. Elwin Wright was, at that time, the executive director of the New England Fellowship. My first summer there I was the counselor in charge of the conference grounds' dormitory for their working girls. For the next two summers I was a senior counselor and Bible teacher at Camp Cathedral Pines which was the girls' camp hidden away on a hill behind the conference grounds. There was also a boys' camp, Pineridge, located on the other side of the hill.

Before leaving for my first term in Africa, I had visited my best friend's parents at their cottage in Rumney. Ed and Lois Beaumont made sure that every furlough I had at least one visit back at Rumney, a place that does get into one's blood. There were excellent Bible teachers morning and evening with great Christian music in the evenings and special concerts on the weekends. After the Lord took the Beaumonts, I continued to spend time with Arthur and Marguerite Gay in their simple cottage at Rumney Bible Conference. During my years at New England Bible College, Marguerite, by then a widow, invited me to spend a week with her in her lovely renovated cottage at RBC.

Each year I studied the brochure very carefully and decided which speaker I wanted to minister to me for a whole week. For fifteen years I looked forward to my annual week of vacation with Marguerite when I could smell the ever-fragrant, sharp aroma of the pine trees, enjoy my early morning walks, have private prayer time in the little chapel, and listen to the fabulous music and guest speakers at the Tabernacle. All of this was topped off by super fellowship with my very special friend. Even after I retired to Dexter, I had two more summers with Marguerite at Rumney before her Homegoing on August 8, 2005. Now her cottage has been sold and her family and friends are grateful for pleasant memories where God met His people and impacted our lives for greater devotion to Him.

The Birthday Girls

Celebrating birthdays with family or friends makes the day have so much more meaning, as well as being just plain fun! Gradually I became acquainted with other single ladies from churches in the Portland area. Elaine Sawyer, a former missionary to Haiti, was active in the Payson Park Evangelical Free Church, Charlotte Russell was very involved in the life of the First Baptist Church of Portland and Marion Soule, a lovely widow lady, was from my church in South Portland. As the years went by, these three women became very special friends and we began to celebrate our birthdays together. The birthday person chose the location where we would eat and celebrate. We shared so many fun times together, including walking the Freedom Trail in Boston, visiting Heritage, New Hampshire, eating lobster on Cabbage Island, riding on the boat, "Romance," to Bailey's Island and eating lunch at Cook's Restaurant. At "The Balsams" in Dixfield Notch, New Hampshire we enjoyed lunch in the gorgeous dining room where there was a sumptuous buffet lunch with plenty of chocolate desserts for Charlotte. There were visits to the Farnsworth Museum in Rockland, lunches at the Samoset and a visit to the State House in Augusta where we sat in the Chamber of the House of Representatives for a while and then enjoyed lunch at the Senator. These are only a few of the places where we shared fifty or more birthdays together while I lived in Cape Elizabeth. I remain grateful for these special friends who enriched my life during the years we were together.

Birthday Girls at The Senator.

Seven days after my birthday, on September eighth, Elaine Bean, my next-door neighbor in Cape Elizabeth, had her birthday. Every year she and I celebrated our two birthdays together by going to Newick's Restaurant in South Portland where they offered a free dinner for the birthday person. Often Elaine's sister Gertrude and her husband Frank Ham, invited Elaine and me out for a special birthday meal around the time of our birthdays. In addition, we all enjoyed a baked bean supper on the first Saturday of each month during the winter with Frank and Gertrude. Karen Chagnon, the library volunteer at NEBC, shared my birthday and we got together every year for a free breakfast at the International House of Pancakes in Portland. When I turned seventy-five, my friends at the college threw a big birthday party for me at the home of teaching colleagues Pete and Caryn Hasbrouck.

Sylvia Bradfield Mitchell, another of my neighbors, became another good friend and prayer partner. We also tried to coordinate our schedules to have time to celebrate birthdays. She has since moved to New York City where she is a chaplain and founder of "on the Way Ministries," a Chaplaincy in Transportation.

A Trip to Prince Edward Island and Nova Scotia

It had long been a special dream of mine to go to Canada and visit Prince Edward Island and Nova Scotia, but after spending over thirty years in Africa and all my furloughs filled with visiting my supporting churches there never seemed to be a good time to take the trip. However, in

2000 Charlotte and Marion, two of the birthday girls, and I met with Charlotte's cousin, Jean Cummings, who lived in New Brunswick, and we made the marvelous eleven day trip together. We crossed the nine mile Confederation Bridge from Tormentine, New Brunswick to Prince Edward Island where we spent two nights. The first night we stayed in a lovely cottage at "Kindred Spirits," very close to Green Gables, where we learned about the background for the book *Anne of Green Gables* by Lucy Maud Montgomery. We then visited Charlottetown where we saw the awesome "Anne of Green Gables" musical. We found a lovely bed and breakfast out in the country on a horse farm where we spent our second night on the island. My friends could have left me on the island, for I had fallen in love with the place! Reluctantly we moved on, taking a seventy-five minute ride on the ferry over to Caribou, Nova Scotia.

Jean drove ever-so-carefully the full length of the Cabot Trail and we enjoyed the breathtaking scenery all along the way. We visited the very interesting and educational Alexander Graham Bell Museum at Baddeck. Nearly a whole day was spent at the Louisbourg Fortress, a restored

In Canada. Charlotte, Jean, Marion and Bernice

French fortress and fortified village depicting the culture and customs of the eighteenth century. We saw soldiers re-enact the firing of the cannons, visited the museum, and ate our lunch in a small restaurant typical of the period. For lunch there was delicious pea soup and dark bread served in tin dishes by a lovely waitress in period costume.

We journeyed on to Kentville and Grand Pré in the heart of the beautiful Annapolis Valley. We saw the statue of "Evangeline," a living memory to the world-famous poet from Portland, Maine, Henry Wadsworth Longfellow. We visited the Church of St. Charles, a replica of the original church which now houses a museum dedicated to the Acadians, including the heroine Evangeline, who were deported from Nova Scotia beginning in 1755. On our way to Halifax, we visited Peggy's Cove to see the memorial to those lost in the terrible plane crash of SwissAir 111 on September 2, 1998. Peggy's Cove is a picturesque fishing village which is popular with tourists. There was a unique lighthouse/post office where I mailed a postcard to myself! A bagpiper delighted us with her music while we explored the unusual rock formations in the cove.

A most special memory of our trip was our early morning devotion time together. We followed the Scripture readings and comments in *Daily Bread*, read from our own Bibles and discussed the passage. In prayer together, we shared some of our personal concerns. These times of prayer and fellowship helped bond us further together in Christian love.

The climax of our trip was the visit to Halifax, where we spent the night at the Citadel Halifax Hotel and went to the famous "TATOO" performance in the huge Metro Centre in downtown Halifax. The show began at seven thirty in the evening. We were enthralled with the many Canadian bands, bagpipes from Scotland, the Brussels Royal Air Force, bikes from the Netherlands, Paris Police gymnasts, the Royal Canadian Mounted Police and more, in a show that lasted until eleven p.m. In all ways it was truly an unforgettable experience.

The day after the "TATOO" show, we made our way back to New Brunswick and to Jean's cottage on Skiff Lake. Before returning to Maine the next morning, Jean's Canadian Indian neighbor gave us a ride in his classy new boat. We then crossed the border back into the United States and that night were back home in our own beds. A trip is always fun but one never fails to be grateful to arrive back home safely. We had driven two thousand three hundred miles of unforgettable adventure. We were all thankful to our heavenly Father for giving us protection, fellowship and fun all the way.

African Style Hospitality in America

The Scriptures teach us to be hospitable and I learned how to do it from the Africans, whose warm and generous spirits were living models to me. Returning to Maine where people are more reserved and much less hospitable than the Africans, I went through a period of culture shock in reverse. Once I was settled at my apartment in Cape Elizabeth I wanted to share hospitality - African style. My first house guests were George and Thelma Burns from my former home church in Cambridge, Maine. George had been a friend for many years and Thelma was one of my most faithful prayer warriors during my years in Africa. We had a delightful weekend together as I showed them some of the sights along the coast of Cape Elizabeth: Two Lights, Crescent Beach, Higgins Beach, and Portland Head Light. Thelma, a great lover of Skip-Bo, a family card game, brought her game with her so we could enjoy it together in the evenings. They later sent me a game of Skip-Bo as a hostess gift. I still have it and enjoy playing the game with my friends.

Over the years many missionaries and pastors came to visit me including Paul and Cathy Erskine from Brazil, Ted and Barbara Ekholm from Standish, Maine, Paul and Ruth Pretiz from Costa Rica, Dave, Glenda and Dan Rogers from Zaire, Don and Peg Penney from Senegal, Ralph and Judy Kee from Boston, Ralph and Polly Brown from Pakistan, Burt and Sylvia Murdock from Colorado, Harold and Jane Burchett from Virginia, Pastor Quentin and Sylvia Johnson from Thomaston, Maine, Paula Warner from California, Mark Kile from Minnesota, and Susan Hay from Zaire and

Uganda. Some came for a meal and others for overnight. Each visit brought warmth and blessing to me and my home and allowed me to practice my African hospitality skills.

In an effort to become better acquainted with our church leaders in South Portland, I invited several families to share a meal with me. I tried to vary the meals using both African and American foods. I was particularly interested in inviting the college students from our church family. I felt strongly that our students from the Bible College needed to see the importance of practicing hospitality. Each guest in my home signed my guest book. During my fifteen years in Cape Elizabeth, I filled up three guest books with a total of one thousand four hundred ninety-eight names! What a lot of blessings to me and my home. True hospitality is a two-way street; you give a lot in time and effort to prepare for guests but the blessings in return far exceed that time and effort. When invited to a student wedding my standard gift was a nice guest book and I was confident that they understood the purpose of my gift.

From Snowdrifts to Sand Dunes - Prayer Walking in North Africa

When I heard that Andy and Nancy Spohrer, Conservative Baptist mission representatives in New England, were leading a Prayer Walk to North Africa, I knew that I needed to go with them. I invited Bea and Skip to join me and before I could blink they were filling out their passport applications! I was so delighted that at last family members would be able to share a bit of Africa with me. The tour was scheduled for March fifth through the thirteenth of 2001 with eighteen tourists in our group. Five of us from Maine, including Mark Hartley and Bruce Stevens, were delayed because of a very bad snow storm that had dropped two feet of snow in the Portland area. We five finally connected with each other and with Holly Reed, Andy Spohrer's secretary who served as our guide, at Logan Airport in Boston and we flew to London together. Since we had missed the rest of our group and the flight to North Africa, we spent a long and sleepless night on hard, uncomfortable benches in Heathrow Airport. The next morning arrangements were made for us to transfer our airline tickets to another airline which flew out of Gatwick Airport, one hour away from Heathrow. With only one hour to catch the plane, a very kind taxi driver whisked us to Gatwick in one of the famous black English taxis. Gracious people helped us all along the way and the pilot kindly delayed the flight for thirty minutes. Such scrambling and scurrying you never saw until we were all finally aboard the plane. We were a happy and grateful group of six who flew across Europe and the Mediterranean Sea to land safely in North Africa three hours later. At our landing point we were met by a gracious tour representative who presented each passenger with a welcome bottle of water! A bus took us south to meet the rest of our tour group. The countryside was lovely with olive trees everywhere and shepherds watching their small herds of sheep. What a happy reunion two hours later, when our group of eighteen was all together for the first time - pastors, lay people and students from all over New England.

    Early the next morning we were on a small bus headed south toward the Sahara Desert with a Christian guide who had lived in the area over twenty years. Our guide gave knowledgeable and interesting commentary on the area and people as we rode along. We visited an ancient Roman amphitheater where gladiators fought and many early Christians met a martyr's death during the wave of Roman persecution that swept across North Africa in the third century. Out of that persecution the church triumphed and grew for a time, producing such leaders as Tertullian, known as the "father of Latin theology" and Cyprian, a bishop in North Africa. While standing on the spot where the Christians had died, we prayed quietly that God would once again build His church in that land. We walked through an oasis to see date palms and fig trees. Later we were in a hilly area where people called troglodytes lived in dug-out caves, which in the heat of the African climate are very practical and cool. We enjoyed an African lunch in a cave-restaurant, where we were served brik, fried dough with an egg inside, couscous, the national food of North Africa, meat, vegetables, and macaroons for dessert. After lunch we had the joy of visiting a private cave home where we met father, mother and two children. They welcomed us into their home with typical African hospitality. Even though we were not allowed to share the Good News with them, we prayed silently for this lovely family.

As we approached the edge of the great Sahara Desert, we began to see sand dunes and camels. To experience the sand dunes more closely a camel ride was necessary. Before mounting the camels each of us put on the typical long flowing robe and a cloth wound around our heads. Young African boys led us up into the dunes, caravan-style. While it was great fun and an unforgettable experience it was not the most comfortable ride. Personally, I was hanging on for dear life! At one point we all dismounted and walked in the soft, warm sand and noted how easily one could get disoriented

On a Prayer Walk in North Africa.

and lost among the high sand dunes. As we rode our camels back to the bus we had another opportunity to pray quietly for those people who eke out an existence in such an arid area. We prayed they would be allowed to hear about the One who is the Water of Life.

After a good night of rest at a hotel in the area, we started the return trip back to our original hotel. On the way, we spent time in a museum where we were introduced to the multi-layered history of the area, from the Phoenicians through the Roman, Arab-Islamic, and French influences. At another interesting stop we saw well-preserved Roman arches and the ruins of ancient Roman temples. As we stood around one ancient mosaic baptistery, we asked our Father once again to raise up some true believers in that land, baptized believers who would establish a church and be shining lights in the midst of the darkness and oppression. Of course we saw Islamic mosques everywhere and the minarets from which the summons to prayer is cried by the muezzin five times a day.

On Sunday morning we walked for thirty minutes to the edge of the old city to worship in the home of our Christian guide. He and his family lived in a second-floor apartment where they had permission for expatriates to come for worship. However, nationals were forbidden to attend the Christian services. The group of forty people who were packed into two small rooms and the hallway of the apartment consisted of British, Dutch, Korean, American and French-speaking Africans from other parts of Africa. Scripture was read in several languages, communion was served, a children's story was given and there was a beautiful message on unity from Ephesians. As we sang the closing hymn, "Bind Us Together, Lord," we sensed we were worshiping the living God with a oneness of spirit that cannot be described in mere words. Following the worship service, our group of eighteen was divided into small groups and sent in different directions for prayer walking. My group walked for an hour through the narrow streets of the old city. It was a moving experience to lift up these very spiritually needy people to the Father.

Our final days in Africa included time for shopping and more prayer walking around the city. Most evenings we met in one of our hotel rooms with our guide who gave us information on Islamic beliefs and, of course, there was more prayer together. The delightful days came to an end all too quickly and we were soon flying back toward London and on to Boston and Portland, where Frank and Gertrude Ham were right on hand to meet us. There was much rejoicing as we sat around the table at the Village Café to enjoy the evening meal together and we shared with them what we had experienced in North Africa. By the way, the very high snowbanks were still there and we dreamed of the warmth of the great sand dunes!

Christian Classic Book Club

"The man who doesn't read good books has no advantage over the man who can't read them."
Mark Twain (1835 - 1910)

"Man's mind, once stretched by a new idea, never regains its original dimensions."
Oliver Wendell Holmes (1809 - 1894)

In October 1994 my friend, Karen Chagnon, invited me to visit the Christian Classic Book Club in Portland. I met the leader, Ginny Kurtz, who told me that the purpose of the club was "to gain knowledge and wisdom in fellowship with like-minded women who desire to live their lives as lived before the face of God." Ginny also referred me to Proverbs 8:10-11 which further highlighted the goals of the group, "Receive my instruction, and not silver, and knowledge rather than choice gold; for wisdom is better than rubies, and all the things one may desire cannot be compared with her." The club members read the Christian classics, a book per month, and met once a month to discuss the book with one of the ladies leading the discussion. The women in the group came from a variety of churches around Portland. I liked what I saw, a comfortable setting for expanding my horizons and I gradually became involved in the monthly discussions. We read the works of John

Bunyan, Augustine of Hippo, A.W. Tozer, C.S. Lewis, G.K. Chesterton, Jonathan Edwards, Amy Carmichael and Corrie Ten Boom. My turn to lead the discussion stretched me even further. Ginny also led another club group in the evening for women who worked and were not able to meet in the daytime. In June she invited the two groups to come together at her lovely home by the water in Cape Elizabeth. We shared the evening meal and then enjoyed a guest who led the discussion on the book we had read for that month. We all enjoyed the special fellowship where we could become acquainted with the ladies in both groups. During the summer months we read books of our own choice and the regular club meetings resumed in September.

For the remainder of my years in Cape Elizabeth, the monthly book club was part of my routine. God used it in my life to stretch my heart and my mind, to make me more familiar with the Christian classics, to give me a greater appreciation for Christian authors, and to give me new friends along the way. As the time approached for me to leave the area, I felt a burden to start a Christian Classic Book Club in my new location.

Other Significant Highlights during my years in Cape Elizabeth

Deighton and Alice Douglin - Most of our Zaire missionaries came from the midwest and beyond. However, Alice and Deighton, with whom I had worked closely in

Africa, settled for retirement in Hamilton, Massachusetts. From my home in Cape Elizabeth it was a comfortable two-hour drive to Hamilton and I made an effort to see the Douglins several times a year. They filled a real need in my life to stay connected with the missionary family. Since they lived very close to Gordon-Conwell Seminary, we went to special events together. Occasionally I spent Friday night with them in order to attend the Saturday Ockenga Seminars, events which featured outstanding men and women speakers. Favorite speakers included Haddon Robinson, Elisabeth Elliot and Ravi Zacharias. Each time I visited with the Douglins we shared news of Zaire and always had special prayer for our mutual friends. Now that I live two hours further from Deighton and Alice we are not able to see each other as often. How I miss our times together.

David and Cindy Spencer - For almost fifteen years the Spencers have been a vital part of my life. David was Youth Pastor and then the Pastor of First Baptist Church in South Portland. I had discipled Cindy before her children were born. The three of us shared meals together from time to time. We enjoyed Chinese food and

Sarah, Moriah and Hannah with "Auntie Bunny."

always played a game or two of Skip-Bo. David liked to think he was the Skip-Bo champion. As their three girls came along, I often baby sat to allow the parents some free time. I enjoyed being "Auntie Bunny" to Sarah, Hannah and Moriah. One of the special bonuses in our friendship was becoming acquainted with both sets of their parents. Dave's parents, Bill and Myrna Spencer, lived in Massachusetts and came up to Maine quite often. Cindy's parents, Ron and Barbara Fitzgerald, lived in New Hampshire and came often to see those grandchildren, too. Eventually I was able to visit the elder Spencers and the Fitzgeralds in their respective homes, worship in their churches and meet some of their friends. My life was greatly enriched by these two sets of grandparents who graciously shared those precious granddaughters with me.

Elisabeth Elliot Gren - For many years I had admired Elisabeth Elliot from a distance and read and collected all of her books. I listened to her daily radio program, "Gateway to Joy," and went to hear her speak when she was in the area. It had all started back on my second Atlantic crossing when I read her magnificent book, *Shadow of the Almighty*, where she gives the life and testament of her late husband Jim Elliot. Through her writings and her talks Elisabeth has impacted my thinking more than any other person I know. One day my friend Ginny Kurtz called to invite me to their home for dinner, saying that Elisabeth and Lars Gren would be there! I was ecstatic to have the privilege of a closer contact with this very famous lady. Ginny included me several more times when they entertained the Grens and gradually I became better acquainted with Elisabeth and her Norwegian husband Lars. In August 2002 when I was invited to have dinner at the Kurtz home with the Grens, I summoned the courage to ask Elisabeth if she would consider speaking to my small class of women at the Bible College. I already had plans for retirement and I knew that this was the last time I would be teaching the class. I was delighted when the Grens agreed to come and minister to my class. There were nine women in the class that semester and I told them they could each invite one person to come with them for the special class and that all were sworn to secrecy! What a marvelous evening we had! Elisabeth spoke to us on "Servanthood" and her husband, Lars, brought a good supply of her books which the students purchased and Elisabeth autographed. After the class I invited the Grens and the Kurtzes to my house for homemade apple pie and ice cream. The evening was one which I will never forget.

Bernice and Elisabeth.

Conservative Baptist National Meetings

Attending the national meetings is always a special treat for me where I can see old and new friends and listen to excellent speakers. I had been able to attend only once during my years as a missionary. The year I retired it was required that I attend in order to meet the Board one more time, to share my testimony and to receive my retirement plaque. In 1988, the year of my retirement, the meetings were held in Minneapolis. I flew out early to spend a few days with my friend and co-worker, Joann Kile, before the meetings began. The Conservative Baptist Foreign Missionary Society luncheon, with over two hundred people in attendance, was a highlight as was the evening when we retirees were recognized and presented with our plaques. Another very special evening was the recognition of the new missionaries who had been appointed to serve in various countries around the world.

The following year, 1989, the meetings were held closer to Maine. Springfield, Massachusetts was an easy drive for me so I made the effort to attend. It was fun staying in the Sheraton Tara with many of my missionary and other friends. I found a new friend, Ann Irish, who walked with me early every morning. The speakers were excellent and the CBFMS luncheon and evening session when the retirees were honored were both blessings. Joann, my former housemate from Goma, Zaire, was also present and I invited her to come back to Maine with me. We spent six days together and I showed her the interesting sights of our area and we drove to see my family in central Maine before she flew back to Minneapolis.

In 1993 I ventured across the country to Portland, Oregon for the Conservative Baptist national meetings. I flew out early to Tacoma, Washington to attend the wedding of Victor Madsen and Carmel Ragsdale, both children of missionary parents from Africa. Following the wedding I spent several days with Dick and Louise Madsen in their home in Tacoma. They took me to worship at their home church where I met many of their friends. We did the North West Trek where I saw grey wolf, elk, bison, pronghorn antelope, moose, mountain goats, deer and Mt. Rainier in all her glory. A few days were spent in Portland with Linda Willms and Heidi Madsen, both of whom had been coworkers in Zaire. After breakfast one morning Linda showed me many of the rare trees in their area including the coast redwood, a grand sequoia, and the world's largest Sitka spruce. In 1973, that Sitka was seven hundred years old, two hundred thirteen feet tall and fifty-two and one half feet in circumference. Linda is the editor for Timber Press, a company which prints books on trees, flowers and plants of all kinds. It was such a delightful morning seeing and learning about the flora of the great Northwest. The majestic Columbia River, separating Oregon from Washington, and the lovely Multnomah Falls were also included in that morning with Linda.

The national meetings were held at the Red Lion Hotel in Portland, Oregon, where over two thousand people gathered for the fiftieth anniversary celebration of Conservative Baptists. On Sunday morning we worshiped in a church of our choice in the area and in the afternoon we all gathered at the great Oregon Convention Center for a special celebration. We heard a choir made up of many churches in the Portland area, a concert by popular Christian soloist Steve Green, and a heart-stretching message by Charles Colson, former presidential aide to Richard Nixon and founder of Prison Fellowship, an international ministry. For the next three days we enjoyed messages by Ajith Fernando, a pastor from Sri Lanka, seminars, special luncheons, and reunions of missionaries by country. There were forty-four Zaire missionaries present. There was the Fiftieth Anniversary Banquet where Dr. Warren Webster, the retiring General Director of Conservative Baptist Foreign Mission Society, was honored. The new Director, Hans Finzel from Wheaton, Illinois, gave a stirring message on "A Vision for the Future." I was so grateful to have been a part of those wonderful meetings where I could see so many of my friends and help celebrate the fifty years of our great mission society.

The fourth time I attended the annual meetings was in 1996 at Valley Forge, Pennsylvania. I contacted Herb and Doris Rambukir who lived in Oneonta, New York and was able to drive with them to Valley Forge. Gladys Jones, a fellow retired missionary from Japan, would also be riding with the Rambukirs. On my way to Oneonta I stopped for two nights in Massachusetts to visit with Ralph and Polly Brown. They had lined up several speaking engagements for me. In Oneonta I stayed for two days with Rev. John and Edith Dougherty, dear friends from a Buffalo supporting church. I enjoyed a delightful breakfast and morning with Dr. Virgil and Virginia Polley, who had been so kind to me when I had flown home from Africa in 1982 for my breast cancer surgery. The next day we were off for Valley Forge, Herb, Doris. Gladys and I, representing Argentina, Japan and Zaire. What a great time of missionary fellowship we enjoyed along the way to Pennsylvania!

The meetings of 1996 were held at the Sheraton in Valley Forge and as always there were excellent speakers. Dr. Leith Anderson was the keynote speaker and the music was led masterfully by Richard Farmer, a young black musician. Jean Hendricks spoke at the ladies' luncheon. The special joy for me personally was seeing so many of our missionary family. We had time to do a bit of sight seeing around Valley Forge. My favorite stops were the statue of Washington at Prayer, the Washington Memorial Chapel and the well-kept Washington's headquarters with its old rail fence.

On my way back to the Brown home in Massachusetts, I stopped in Williamstown in the Berkshires where I had lunch at a delightful inn. At the campus of Williams College I saw the famous Haystack Monument, dedicated to the first missionaries who went out to India from the United States. I took pictures of the monument for my students who would be taking my missions course in the fall. After a restful night at the Browns I made my way back to Maine, so grateful for yet another opportunity to attend the national Conservative Baptist meetings. My horizons had been stretched and broadened and that would help me be a better teacher in the year that followed.

Community Service

A month of jury duty in June of 1999 was another new experience for me but something I had always wanted to do. My eyes were opened to a new and interesting phase of American life that I had not before understood. I was called to serve on two different and very intriguing civil cases. Driving to the Portland Court House meant crossing the Casco Bridge in the morning early, in order to find free parking on Commercial Street. I did my Bible reading and prayer time in the car while waiting for time to pass and then hiked to the Court House. That way I saved daily parking fees and was able, with the stipend received for jury duty, to buy a desk chair to remind me of that memorable experience.

In the year 2000 I applied to be a census worker. After

four days of intensive training I began the very difficult procedure of trying to find willing people at home to fill out their census forms. I worked hard during the month of May. I met some very kind and willing people and also had a few doors slammed in my face. Overall it was a wonderful experience. There was a great supervisor and co-workers who made the task more enjoyable. The job made it financially possible for me to take a trip to Canada with my friends later that summer.

Farewells

Monday morning chapel was always a favorite time for me at the Bible College and I tried to be there on time every week. However, on May 5, 2003, the final chapel of the school year, I was running late and walked right into a trap! Students and faculty were already singing Isaac Watt's "When I Survey the Wondrous Cross." Stan Olsen was leading the worship and Dominique Bourgoin was playing the piano. Dean Susan Schriver stood to inform me that this was a

Farewell roses at NEBC.

farewell chapel in my honor and asked me to turn around and look to the back of the room. There, to my utter amazement and joy, were roses of all colors, dozens of them! It was a well-sprung trap! I was completely surprised, overjoyed and speechless. There was a beautifully decorated cake with the words "We will miss you, Miss Foss," chocolate-dipped strawberries and many other goodies. Before indulging, however, a number of the students gave testimonials. This was only the first of a series of farewells for me to enjoy before sadly leaving the place of ministry that I had come to love so much.

A week later the Christian Classic Book Club that I had participated in for several years held another farewell for me. We met at Ginny's home on the ocean for our discussion of *One Day in the Life of Ivan Denisovich* by Alexander Solzhenitsyn. This was followed by a delicious luncheon, and the ladies presented me with a gift subscription to *World* magazine which I appreciated so much. It was beginning to dawn on me that I was soon to leave the Portland area, my home, my church, the Bible College faculty and students and all my friends who had been a part of my life for the past fifteen happy years.

Our Bible College graduation on May sixteenth was a special time for Don Fisher and Davis Harriman, two gentlemen who were to receive their degrees. Each of these men had worked long and hard to reach that place in their lives. Rev. Walter Holder, our guest speaker for the evening, brought a very challenging message for our graduates on "Servanthood." Rev. Robert Bell, the chairman of the board, overwhelmed me when he presented me with a plaque giving me the status of "Professor Emeritus," a box full of farewell cards from my friends, and a check to help me update my aging Buick. Pastor Quentin Johnson and Sylvia were there and stood with me on the platform while Pastor Johnson had prayer for me. The biggest surprise of all was having my sister Bea and her husband Skip, brother Charles and baby sister Mary Lou all present for the happy occasion.

The Sunday following graduation my church held a dinner in my honor. During the farewell ceremony the church elders had special prayer for me and commissioned me for my new assignment in Dexter. There was a beautiful cake with the inscription "We love you, Bunny - Psalm 121." Psalm 121, the Traveler's Psalm, has become a sort of signature for me. I have had it on my license plate since 1988, when I first came home from Africa. I was presented with a lighthouse tray which I treasure to this day and another gift of money for my car. I am so grateful to the Lord who allowed me to be a part of the First Baptist Church of South Portland for those fifteen years where I grew and had the opportunity to serve the Lord. Actually, the church had been a vital part of my life for over fifty years since they were one of my supporting churches during my thirty-six years in Africa.

On Wednesday evening our Bible study group had

another dinner for me in Carolyn's home with more "goodbye" gifts. This time they gave me personal cosmetics. The next day Larry and Bob Bell drove me to Augusta to look at newer used cars. We found a beige 2000 Buick Century with only twenty thousand miles and, yet again, God had provided for me. There was one more farewell when the ladies of the Overseas Missionary Fellowship prayer group took me out to the Great Wall Restaurant for Chinese food which I dearly love. Two days later Leon Olds drove a Budget rental truck with my household goods to Dexter. His wife Orabelle followed in their car and I drove mine. Thus ended this supremely happy fifteen-year era in my life, and I began a new and unknown adventure, with the Lord always as my faithful Guide.

TESTIMONIALS FROM MY STUDENTS

One Sunday morning in the summer of 2005, Dr. David Lambertson, from Cumberland, Maine, brought the morning message to First Free Baptist Church in Dexter. Later, over lunch, I shared with him the outline of my years at New England Bible College and asked for his suggestions on my book, since we had worked together for most of that time at the college. His only suggestion was that I enhance my story with some testimonials from my former students. It sounded like a great idea, but I was hesitant to ask the students myself. Pastor Robert Bell graciously came to my rescue and contacted the students for me. I am grateful, overwhelmed and humbled as I share the following with you:

> *Phil Andrukaitis*, first of the "original four" in the missions course at NEBC, now pastor of First Baptist Church in South Portland, Maine.

> *"You impacted me with your life of devotion and your prayers. You are a model of a godly woman devoted to God and serving the Body of Christ. I believe you stretched me more than I stretched you."*

> *Daniel Coffin*, my student in "Personal and Group Bible Study," now pastor of a church in Sebasco Estates, Maine.

> *"I saw her deep love of the Bible. It was so touching and genuine that it has changed my outlook toward God's Word. Her respect and sincere love for all her students was a tremendous encouragement during those years at college."*

> *Nate Colson*, my student in "Cultural Anthropology," now pastor of the Turner Baptist Church in Turner, Maine.

> *"Her personal experiences from the mission field coupled*

with her sincere love of the subject made her class thoroughly enjoyable. She returned from a prayer walk in North Africa with souvenirs for each student, a copper plate with our names engraved in Arabic and a carved spoon made of olive wood. I learned from her example that cultural anthropology was not just an academic exercise, but was personally her way of life, serving Christ and people as a missionary."

Russ Cotnoir, second of the original four in the missions class, now pastor of Fayette Baptist Church in Fayette, Maine.

"One thing you modeled for me was your encouragement to become a 'faithful finisher.' You have instilled a great part of that pursuit in me through your faithful example. Thank you for being a strong 'finisher' and a faithful follower. I am eternally grateful for your ministry in my life."

Pam Davis, my student in "Ministry to Women," a homemaker, teacher, and worker in the First Baptist Church of South Portland.

"Older women are 'to be reverent in the way they live' and 'teach what is good.' These words frame for me her life. What I treasure most was her attitude toward the Word of God. Her eyes lit up as we talked together

about verses we had memorized or studied. 'What nuggets did you discover?' she was always quick to ask, delighting in the precious truths she knew the diligent study of God's Word would yield. She did indeed 'teach what is good' and I am grateful for the benefit of her godly example."

Don Fisher, my student in "Cultural Anthropology" from Wiscasset, Maine, now a missionary appointee to serve in Ethiopia.

"Though she taught much in the classroom, I am beginning to realize that my greatest lessons to be gleaned from her are watching her life. Thank-you, Miss Foss."

Joeline Inman, my student in "Ministry to Women," a pastor's wife, serving in the Cambridge Baptist Church in Cambridge, Maine.

"Bunny has been an inspiration to me for many years. While she was serving the Lord as a missionary in Africa and I was a student at Providence-Barrington Bible College, I received many notes of encouragement from her. I have had the privilege of sitting under her teaching at New England Bible College as well as in Sunday School classes. She has been used of God…many people have grown through her discipling and as a result of her praying."

Margo Lambertson, my student in "Personal and Group Bible Study," the wife of a college professor, mother of four adult children and an education technician in the Middle School at the Collaborative School in New Gloucester, Maine.

"Classes with you were a delight and a joy for me. You helped me to meditate on Scripture and think through what the messages of certain passages were and how to apply them to my life. Your gift of hospitality was very evident. I felt the support of your prayers and thank you for them."

Becca Loring, my student in "Ministry to Women." She is a worker in a new church plant in Portland, Maine.

"It was not until I met Miss Foss that I truly began to wrestle with, understand and embrace my God-given design and beauty as a woman. By her godly example, honest teaching style, and compassionate mentorship Miss Foss spoke into my life the truths, realities and joys of being a woman after the heart of God. Not only does the Lord bless her work, I know that when the man I marry finds me, he will want to thank her for all she has taught me."

Ron Sargent, third of the original four in the missions

class. He is pastor of the Hollis Center Baptist Church in Hollis, Maine.

"I consider it a great blessing from God to have been ministered to by Miss Foss in the first year of her second career at the New England Bible College in the Fall of 1988. I was impacted by her commitment to the Lord in having served 36 years in Africa and her example remains a motivation to me to this day. She gave her whole life to the Lord."

Wendy Sargent, a homemaker and wife of Pastor Sargent in Hollis Center, Maine. I discipled Wendy privately.

"Miss Foss impacted me in the area of hospitality. She encouraged me to be more open to hospitality in my home, remembering the importance of fellowship. She also impressed on me the importance of Scripture in all circumstances of life, whether it be visiting someone in need or in my own personal walk. She exemplified being content in whatever circumstances God placed her. I am thankful that God allowed her to be part of my life.

Hugh Staley, a worker in North Africa.

"She introduced me to a life-impacting book, Teaching to

Change Lives by Howard Hendricks. I, in turn, gave a copy to the head of the English department in North Africa where I was teaching.

Nancy Staley, a former student and worker in North Africa.

"I observed her love for the Lord and enjoyment of the Word. She taught me the inductive method of Bible study. I have used this method in my own ministry in the States and abroad."

Karen Twombly, my student in "Unreached Peoples" class, I also spent time personally with her as we studied Amy Carmichael's book *Kohila* together. Karen is now a full time wife and mother in Hollis Center, Maine.

"I will always appreciate Bunny Foss for reaching out to me and patiently teaching me what it meant to follow Jesus Christ wholeheartedly. She had tirelessly reached out to those around her with love and uncompromising faith."

Robin Twombly, the fourth of the original four in the missions class. Robin serves in his local church in Hollis Center, Maine.

"Being one of Bunny's students I have been inspired by how God used her life. I have been touched by her words and blessed by her friendship."

Jean Warman, from Topsham, Maine was my student in "Ministry to Women." She is a homemaker, teacher and worker in her church in Brunswick, Maine.

"Bunny is a disciplined follower of Jesus Christ, a woman of prayer and wisdom. Her care for each one of us in the class made an impact on me. She prayed daily for each of us, and showed by example, as well as in text how true femininity manifests itself in the life of a godly woman. Bunny surprised us with a visit and presentation by Elisabeth Elliot Gren and her husband Lars. I thank God for the privilege of taking her class."

REFLECTIONS ON THE BONUS YEARS

"And can it be that I should gain an interest in the Saviour's blood? Died He for me, who caused His pain? For me, who Him to death pursued? Amazing love! How can it be that Thou, my God, shouldst die for me?

'Tis mystery all! Th'Immortal dies: Who can explore His strange design? In vain the first-born seraph tries to

strange design? In vain the first-born seraph tries to sound the depths of love divine. 'Tis mercy all! Let earth adore, let angel minds inquire no more.

He left His Father's throne above, so free, so infinite His grace, Emptied Himself of all but love, and bled for Adam's helpless race, 'Tis mercy all, immense and free; for, O my God, it found out me!

Long my imprisoned spirit lay fast bound in sin and nature's night; Thine eye diffused a quick'ning ray, I woke, the dungeon flamed with light; My chains fell off, my heart was free, I rose, went forth, and followed Thee.

No condemnation now I dread; Jesus, and all in Him, is mine! Alive in Him, my living Head, and clothed in righteousness divine, Bold I approach th'eternal throne, and claim the crown, through Christ, my own."

— *Charles Wesley (1707-1788)*

The New England Bible College hymn sums up much of what I learned as I walked through those wonderful fifteen years with faculty, students and the Lord. In 1988, when I heard the word "cancer" for the second time, I thought that was the beginning of the end for me. However, God restored my health and gave me those marvelous bonus

South Portland. They were years of learning and being stretched by my co-workers at the college, my students, the church family at First Baptist and the many new friends and experiences I enjoyed in the greater Portland area.

Having been so far away from family for over thirty years, I was very pleased to be back in Maine where I could see my family more often and be able to enjoy special family times of graduations, retirement parties, open houses and weddings. Even though I learned to appreciate the African drum in a worship service in Africa and unique African art of many varieties, I was delighted to be able to visit American art museums and attend classical music concerts while living in the Portland area. I was privileged to see other parts of our world during the years that I was a missionary, but there was so much of our own United States I had never seen and was delighted with the number of trips I took with friends during my years in Cape Elizabeth. Truly, they were bonus years in every sense of the word, a gracious gift from the loving hands of my heavenly Father and once again I shout,

GREAT IS THY FAITHFULNESS!!

CHAPTER TWELVE

GOD'S FAITHFULNESS CONTINUES
(2003 - to the present)

"And the LORD, He is the One who goes before you. He will be with you, He will not leave you nor forsake you; do not fear nor be dismayed." - Deuteronomy 31:8

With the above promise in my heart, on May 28, 2003 I returned to Dexter to begin a new phase in my life, moving into the mobile home located behind my sister's home. My siblings and their spouses had worked hard to prepare my new home for me, including new windows and fresh, light-colored paint to

My new home.

brighten the dark-paneled walls. There was new kitchen flooring, new beige carpeting in the living room and rose carpeting for my bedroom. To move into a clean and spotless home was a delight. As I settled in, I sorted out items for a yard sale that my sister Bea was planning for June. I had really tried to keep my possessions and "stuff" to a minimum. When one moves to a new location there are always many details to think about; telephone, computer, e-mail, an oil company, bank, grocery store, post office, garage, flowers to plant - the list is endless. Little by little, things fell into place and I began to feel at home. I purchased or made curtains for all the windows. My brother, Charles, took care of my electrical needs and helped me hang my pictures. My brother-in-law, Skip, helped me with numerous other details including putting shelves in my bedroom closet, setting up the work table for my computer and printer and assembling bookcases for my collection of missionary biographies. We placed a white bookcase in my bedroom for my treasured collections: a complete set of books by Elisabeth Elliot and almost a complete collection of Amy Carmichael's works.

View of the pond from my house.

One of my goals when I moved back to the Dexter area

was to become better acquainted with my family members. Sadly, on my second day in Dexter I attended the burial of Beth Stuart, the wife of my cousin Alden. I spent that day with Alden and his three boys and their families, some of whom I had not seen in many years. Later there was the funeral in Kingfield for Uncle Elwood. On a happier note, a few weeks later there was cousin Jessica Goss's wedding in Skowhegan and in June my nephew Derek Foss's graduation party in Carmel. I was grateful to be able to reconnect with family members so soon after my arrival.

There were special events in the Portland area that I did not want to miss. The first of these was the fiftieth wedding anniversary celebration for Jack and Edna Christensen at Galilee Baptist Church in Gorham, Maine. Jack was the interim president of New England Bible College where I had been privileged to work with him during my last years at the college.

Jack and Edna Christensen.

Later in June I returned to Cape Elizabeth for the end-of-the-season celebration for the Christian Classic Book Clubs. I stayed with Dick and Ginny Kurtz, the book club leader, in their gorgeous home by the ocean. Both morning and evening clubs gathered there for an evening meal and a discussion of Milton's *Paradise Lost*, led by

Bonnie Helms. I stayed with the Kurtzes for two more days so I could attend the wedding of one of my former students in South Portland. Mark Labacz and Sara Ryder were married in a lovely church wedding at the First Baptist Church in South Portland.

Cambridge Baptist Church had been my home church during all the years I was in Africa and, although Cambridge is fifteen miles from my home, I felt led to reconnect with my church family there. I transferred my membership from South Portland Baptist Church back to Cambridge Baptist Church. I wanted to become involved where I was needed and where I could use my gifts.

In June all of the Fosses gathered in Parkman with the McKusicks at their farm across the road from the old Foss farm. The McKusick twins, Victor and his wife Anne, and Vincent and his wife Nancy, came as well as some of their nephews and spouses. All of my siblings were present and we enjoyed sitting on the McKusick lawn, looking down on our old farm and the great view of Harlow Pond across the way. We had a delightful time reminiscing on yesteryears while we enjoyed a delicious outdoor barbeque prepared by the nephews.

Early in July I spent a week with my friend Shirley Chadbourne at her daughter's camp on Lake Ambajejus in Millinocket. We have enjoyed a week together at camp almost every summer since my return from Africa. With Mt. Katahdin in full view, a week at camp with a special friend is pure delight.

As with all of my homes, I wanted my new home to be dedicated to the Lord. One Friday evening in July I invited Pastor Harold Wheeler to lead a private dedication. Gathered in my living room were Mary Lou Wheeler, my sister Bea, her husband Skip and their son Jeff. Pastor Wheeler shared some appropriate verses which he had chosen from the Psalms and led us in a beautiful prayer of dedication. My home was to be a place where Christ is honored and where guests feel welcome. The following Sunday afternoon I hosted an Open House for my family and friends. I enjoyed giving each group a little tour of my home while my siblings served light refreshments on the lawn on that hot July afternoon. Forty-seven people signed my guest book that day and then I felt I was truly a resident of Dexter. As I settled into my new home, my friends from Portland came to visit me. Some came for a brief visit while others arrived to spend a night or two.

Dedication of my home.

In August I spent a week with my friend Marguerite Gay at her cottage in Rumney, New Hampshire, the place where I loved to go each summer for spiritual and physical refreshment. The week there is always a spiritual treat for me, to hear the teaching of superb speakers, to enjoy great music and to reconnect with old friends. Marguerite and I enjoyed many hours of lively discussion, talking about books, mutual missionary friends, family and even politics. While we prepared most of our meals in her cottage, from time to time we enjoyed eating at the conference dining hall where we connected with Christian people from all over New England.

Charlotte Russell, Elaine Sawyer and Marion Soule, the "birthday girls" from South Portland came to see me in September. We drove to beautiful Moosehead Lake for our annual birthday luncheon and enjoyed a delicious meal at Kelley's Landing.

By September, ministry opportunities came my way. I began teaching the book of I Corinthians for the ladies' Sunday School class in my home church in Cambridge. The ladies from the United Baptist Church of Old Town asked me to speak at their annual women's retreat in Camden/Rockland. We stayed at the Country Inn in Camden and had our main sessions at the First Baptist Church in Rockland. We shared a delightful weekend together and I was blessed to see the ladies' keen enthusiasm for the Lord. My message to them was "The Steadfast Woman," with my text taken from Psalm 51:10 "Create in me a clean heart, O God, and renew a steadfast spirit within me." I challenged them to be steadfast in their personal lives, in their homes, in their churches and in their suffering.

Ministry opportunities continued to come my way when a small group in my sister's church in Dexter asked me to lead them through *The Purpose Driven Life* by Rick Warren. We grew together as we explored this study each Monday evening for ten weeks. I was busy and content as I prepared for my Sunday School class and the Monday evening lessons. Guests still trickled by to visit me in my new location and I enjoyed reconnecting with each one. It was fun for me to prepare our family Thanksgiving at my new home. There were six of us at the table and after our meal, we all went to the local nursing home to visit with a friend. A long, leisurely walk ended our day together.

When I settled in Dexter, I felt called to contribute in some way to the community. In December I was sworn in as a member of the Dexter Library Board and I served for over a year in that capacity. Also high on my priority list was starting a missionary prayer group. By January of 2004 I had found a core group of ladies who shared my burden to pray for missionaries. Eventually the group grew to seven ladies from several different churches who met monthly to pray for the missionaries supported by our churches.

The biggest project for my retirement was to write my memoirs and in February of 2004 I began the first chapter. I kept at the project, writing a little bit each month. In the early spring of 2004, I returned to Portland for the annual

Christian Education Conference which is held at the First Baptist Church on Canco Road. It was a time to encourage and support my friend Patty Shepardson who coordinated the conference. It also afforded me time to see a number of my former students from NEBC.

Another of my goals for retirement was to start a Christian Classic Book Club with the purpose of encouraging people to read good Christian books. By April I had found five interested people and we inaugurated the club by reading *Mary Bunyan* by Sallie Rochester Ford, the story of the blind daughter of the famous author John Bunyan. The following month we read Bunyan's *Pilgrim's Progress*. We still meet once a month to discuss the chosen book of the month. My life has been impacted and enriched by reading and discussing the great authors of the past: Augustine of Hippo, C.S. Lewis, G.K. Chesterton, Jonathan Edwards, Brother Lawrence and Charles Haddon Spurgeon, to mention a few.

Christian Classic Book Club. Pamela, Benita, Bernice, Pastor Lew and Barbara Bell. Guests: Ginny and Dick Kurtz.

It is always a special blessing when missionaries can gather together for reports and fellowship. There was such a reunion in May of 2004 in South Hamilton, Massachusetts.

Twenty-one of us Conservative Baptist retired missionaries from New England met for lunch at Gordon-Conwell Seminary. What a great time of fellowship we enjoyed! There were missionaries from Argentina, Brazil, China, the Democratic Republic of the Congo, Indonesia, Pakistan, and Taiwan. After lunch we each shared where we were currently located and what we were doing. We were keenly interested in how the Christian church was growing in the various countries.

My first year in my new location ended on a happy, positive note. I was so blessed to be closer to my family and thankful for the good health that allowed me to continue with some ministry opportunities in my retirement. I was especially thankful for the missionary prayer group which met monthly, for the joy of teaching the Sunday School class in my church, for the monthly book club and for the Bible study I had been asked to teach in Dexter. I was indeed very happy and sensed, as always, that God had come before me in a wonderful way. Indeed He was showing me His continued faithfulness in many surprising details.

SUMMER 2004

That summer was unusually busy but delightful as I entered into family events, entertained a number of guests and made several trips to see my friends. The family events included niece Nicole's graduation from high school, nephew Jerry's return from Iraq, a Vacation Bible School closing program for grand nephew and niece, Jacob and Hillary, and a trip to Castine for niece Ryan's lovely wedding by the water. Sixty years is a long time not to see a friend and when Donna Welts Wagoner, a good friend from my elementary and high school years now living in Iowa, came to Maine to visit family, she spent a whole day with me. We had a great time catching up on the years.

The five ladies who completed the study on *The Purpose Driven Life* met at my house for the final session. Each one gave her personal testimony, we watched some video clips from a tape by author Rick Warren and we prayed with and for each other. A meal together topped off our evening. My Sunday School class ladies celebrated the end of our three-month study by meeting at a restaurant for breakfast and fellowship. They presented me with a lovely hanging ivy plant which still graces my living room.

On my annual trek to Rumney, New Hampshire to visit Marguerite Gay, I stopped off in Cornish, Maine to spend the night with my friends, Harlan and Patty Shepardson. The next day I had lunch with other Cornish friends, Arthur and Althea Folsom. Dr. Woodrow Kroll was the speaker that week at Rumney and we feasted on the Word with him twice a day. My friend Marguerite was having increasing difficulty breathing because of her pulmonary fibrosis, so instead of enjoying our usual walk to the tabernacle each evening we drove to the services. It was still a delightful week together. However, I began to wonder if this would be our final summer together. On the second Sunday at Rumney, I drove to Concord to spend the day with my former pastor and his family, Dave and Cindy Spencer. I attended their church, heard Dave preach that Sunday, was introduced to some some of their friends and finally met at their condo where Cindy served us a delicious meal. After dinner I joined Cindy and their girls, Sarah, Hannah and Moriah, at the pool. Late that afternoon found me back at Rumney where I spent another day with Marguerite before returning to Maine.

Child Evangelism Fellowship (CEF) is an international ministry that reaches out to children all over the world. Jeanette Linsey, director for the Central Maine chapter, has been a friend for many years. Every summer the CEF workers in the Dover-Foxcroft area meet for prayer once a month. Jeanette invited me to meet with her group and three times that summer I met with them and became better acquainted with their workers and needs.

Late in July the First Baptist Church of Portland hosted a farewell service for Pastor Arthur Gay and his wife Joann. My life had been greatly enriched by this dedicated couple. Although I had been connected with the Gay family for many years, it wasn't until Arthur and Joann moved to Portland that I had the privilege of truly knowing them. Joann and I were in the same book club for several years and our hearts had bonded right from the beginning. To be pres-

Arthur and Joann Gay.

ent for that farewell celebration was important to me. At the Sunday morning worship service the Lord was uplifted, followed by a time to honor and appreciate Art and Jo. Lunch at their church gave each person an opportunity to personally say "good-bye." After the farewell service Art and Jo moved to Chicago, where Arthur serves on the boards of several mission agencies and Jo enjoys being closer to grandchildren living in the area.

When Larry and Audrey Bell from my church in South Portland celebrated their fiftieth wedding anniversary, I had another excuse to visit friends in the Portland area. I love to celebrate with a couple who have set the great example of staying together for fifty years. The Bell children honored their parents with a lovely meal and fellowship at Verillo's restaurant.

Soon I had another opportunity to spend a few days with my friend Shirley at her daughter's camp where we enjoyed Lake Ambajejus with

Shirley at camp.

its full view of Mt. Katahdin in the distance. The days were filled with chatter, books, games and relaxation. I was once again grateful for an especially happy summer enjoyed with so many friends.

Today, when students from the Bible College in South Portland make their way to Dexter to see me, we always celebrate. Becca, a former student, and her friend Megan arrived one Saturday morning in August and we drove to Greenville where we enjoyed a picnic lunch by Moosehead Lake. After lunch we drove to Rockwood and from there rode on a small launch to the peninsula where Mt. Kineo is located. There is so much history connected with this famous mountain. In the early part of the nineteenth century there were many railways in Maine. Tourists came from all over the country to spend time in the Mount Kineo House, the large hotel on the peninsula. Today this landmark has been abandoned. We had fun walking around and gazing at the unusual little mountain. The next day Becca and Megan went with me to the Cambridge church where they sang a beautiful duet a cappella. After lunch at my house they returned to Portland.

By this time, we had been without a pastor in Cambridge for over a year and were overjoyed when the pulpit committee presented the Rev. William Inman as a candidate. He was quickly called by the congregation to be our new pastor. It didn't take Pastor Inman and his wife Joeline long to bring new life and enthusiasm into the parsonage. They scrubbed, cleaned, papered and painted until we hardly recognized the tired old parsonage. I had worked closely with the Inmans for a number of years at New England Bible College and was especially happy to be ministered to by them in Cambridge.

While I was still teaching at the Bible college, a student named Judy Ahlquist took my "Ministry to Women" course. One day, after I had moved to Dexter, Judy, now a full-time working lady, called to share how excited she was to have become a part of the women's ministry team at her local church, Galilee Baptist in Gorham, Maine. I felt led to invite Judy and her team to my house for a one-day mini-retreat and a date was set for later in August. I looked forward to having these lady leaders come and study with me for a whole day! I planned a Bible study for the morning session, a simple lunch, and an afternoon study, with times of sharing and prayer in between. Judy and three other ladies arrived about nine in the morning and we shared snacks and a took time to become acquainted. A Bible study on "A Quiet Spirit" came next, followed by their prayer burdens and prayer time. Our luncheon menu was homemade mushroom soup and mandarin chicken salad. My sister Bea brought a peach upside-down cake and joined us for the dessert. Then she shared her own personal testimony with the ladies. We all enjoyed a short break and relaxed on the freshly mown lawn by our small pond. For the afternoon session, I taught them some spiritual lessons from the life of

Retreat ladies at lunch. Judy, Hazel, Sherry and Kaye.

Amy Carmichael, a famous Irish missionary to India from the late nineteenth to the mid-twentieth century. We read some of her poetry and I presented each lady with one of her booklets. Our mini-retreat ended with a time of prayer for each other. I was so happy with the response of these ladies that I thought I would like to host further retreats with teams from other churches.

FALL 2004

Early in September, the three birthday girls from South Portland came to visit me on a Friday afternoon and stayed until Sunday afternoon. We celebrated Elaine's and my birthday with another trip to Moosehead Lake. On the way we stopped in Monson to visit Daryl Witmer, Executive Director of the AIIA Institute (a contemporary construct of the ancient Athenian Areopagus) where the practice and promotion of Christian apologetics is taught. We all enjoyed the visit with Daryl and his lovely wife Mary and we saw the beautiful old church building they had recently acquired for their study center. In Greenville we visited the Moosehead Marine Museum and learned more about the "Golden Age of Mt. Kineo" when wealthy tourists poured into the area for the summer. We then boarded the boat, "Mt. Katahdin," for a delightful three-hour ride, including a picnic lunch, around the lake. Following the boat trip we drove to Rockwood to find a clearer look at Mt. Kineo. My friends went to church with me on Sunday morning and then we drove to Scotty's restaurant in Newport where they treated me to lunch before their return to South Portland.

Friends come and go but most evenings I am here alone. I don't watch much television, but I am a huge "Jeopardy" fan. I was particularly interested when the now-famous Ken Jennings began winning every night. I followed the games very closely all fall until November thirtieth when Nancy Zerg toppled Ken, who had already won over two and one half million dollars and had been on the show forty-seven times. I try to learn something new each time I watch.

My sister Mary Lou had discovered a quaint little restaurant in Sebec Village not too far from her home. She took me there for a delicious birthday lunch where we ate on the porch, enjoyed the gift shop and took a walk around the park by Sebec Lake. The little restaurant has now become a favorite spot to take our friends for lunch.

When I moved back to central Maine I not only missed

my friends in the Portland area but also friends I would see from time to time as they passed through Portland. So when Debbie Rowe, a New England Bible College board member, invited me to go with her in October of 2004 to Schroon Lake, New York, to attend the New England Conservative Baptist annual meetings, I gladly accepted. It pleased me so much to have the opportunity to attend these meetings, to see Schroon Lake for the first time and to be able to reconnect with many of my New England friends. We enjoyed the trip to New York accompanied by Debbie's pastor, Roger Nauss, and Pastor Nate Colson, a former student of mine. The fall foliage was spectacular during that first week in October and we became "leaf peepers." Haddon Robinson, Distinguished Professor of Preaching at Gordon-Conwell Seminary, and his son Torrey, pastor at Terrytown, New York, were the featured speakers, and as always, were excellent communicators. I felt richly blessed during all of the sessions, seeing so many friends, missionaries, pastors and wives, and meeting some new friends as well. Being at Schroon Lake was a wonderful experience for me and I remain grateful to Debbie for inviting me.

Earlier in the summer, when I had been in the hospital for a procedure, I discovered that my anesthetist, Karen Dow, was a Bible-believing Christian. We became friends and when she learned that I had been a missionary in Africa, she invited me to speak to a group of ladies at her Methodist church in Corinth. She asked me to share my faith journey with Christ and, of course, my years in the Congo. I enjoyed sharing my story with those ladies, showing them some of my African curios and photographs. God blessed our time together.

Later that October, Susan Hay, a missionary friend from my Congo days on home assignment from Uganda, came to spend two days and nights with me. It is always a special treat when my missionary friends make the extra effort to come to Dexter to visit. Naturally, Susan and I celebrated her visit by driving to Greenville to see Moosehead Lake and to Rockwood for a good look at Mt. Kineo! We lunched at Kelley's Landing and hoped to see at least one moose on the return trip but no such luck. I wanted Susan to leave with something special for her ministry in Africa. When I had lived in Cape Elizabeth, it had been part of my daily routine to walk every morning and many days I found coins on the ground. I had placed the coins and sometimes bills into a container which came with me to Dexter. With Susan's visit I knew the time had come to count my loot and give it to her for ministry back in Africa. Together we counted forty-two dollars and ninety-five cents worth of rusty and dirty pennies, nickels, dimes, quarters and several dollar bills. "Pennies from heaven" on their way to work in Africa!

Early in November 2004 my sister Bea and I attended a concert by the Bangor Symphony Orchestra at the University of Maine in Orono. There we met my former pastor and his wife, Quentin and Sylvia Johnson. We sat together to enjoy the program of the gorgeous music of Bach, Grieg, Haydn and Liszt. I had, from time to time, attended classical concerts in Portland and especially appreciated attending this one in Orono. During all my years in Africa I did not have the opportunity to hear classical music. Instead, I learned to appreciate and enjoy the African drum and the lovely choirs, adult, youth and children, at the church services.

My niece Debra invited our family to her home in Bangor for an early Thanksgiving because her brother David, who lives in New Jersey, was to be in Maine at that time. Debra and her husband Jeff Courtney and their three loving boys welcomed us into their home. Grandmother Marion and all of my other siblings were present. There was fun and laughter and lots of picture-taking. On Thanksgiving Day itself a smaller group of us ate together with Bea and Skip in Dexter. I invited Jeanette Linsey, my Child Evangelism Fellowship worker friend, to join us and Skip invited a man from their church who had no one with whom to share the

Bernice, Bea, Marion, Mary Lou, Charles and Frankie.

holiday. It was a time of real thanksgiving for each of us as we reflected on our family, friends, home and good health.

Early one Saturday afternoon in December my brother Charles took Skip, Bea, and me to Thomaston to enjoy a presentation of "The Spirit of Christmas," composed by Barfoot and Goss. Over forty singers were under the direction of Robert Wyllie from the Thomaston Baptist Church. It was a performance by the Living Christmas Tree where the singers formed on stage to represent a Christmas tree. The beautiful music was a delight to hear, so professionally done by the Living Christmas Tree Choir. As always I enjoyed chatting with a number of friends and we ate a delicious meal in a Rockland restaurant before the two-hour return trip to Dexter.

When the faculty of New England Bible College invited me to join them for their annual Christmas party in Portland, I jumped at the chance to be with my former co-workers once again. I drove to Portland in time to have lunch at "Canco by the Woods" with my friend Marguerite Gay. Her daughter Judy had come from Boston that same day and the three of us enjoyed sweet and sour pork together in the lovely dining room. Marguerite was on part-time oxygen by then, something she had dreaded since her diagnosis of pulmonary fibrosis. Despite this, I found her courageous, with a great attitude and positive outlook on life. After lunch we had prayer together in her room; I did not realize that I would not see her again on this earth. I then drove across the winding Casco Bay Bridge to South Portland where I spent the night with Pete and Caryn Hasbrouck and their two children, David and Julia. The Hasbroucks are former missionaries to Ecuador and we worked together at the Bible College for a number of years. We enjoyed the evening at the spacious condo of interim president, Jack and Edna Christensen, where twelve friends had gathered for their annual Christmas party. After a delicious holiday meal, we played games, exchanged gifts and were happy and blessed to enjoy a relaxed time together.

Back in Dexter I closed out the year by having some of my church family over to share meals. One group I invited was the college young people who came to my house for fellowship and pizza. The final week before Christmas I made Christmas cookies and stollen breads to share with family and friends. My friend Jeanette spent Christmas Eve with me and brother Charles came for Christmas Day. Although I missed the simplicity of Christmas in Africa, I did some of the same things there that I do here. Friends were invited for meals and I made Christmas goodies to share. One of the big differences is the African focus on church activities during the Christmas season. Africans plan big conferences where hundreds of people are baptized, followed by a communion service. They often have one evening of Christmas plays, produced with all the props, including live animals, a bright star, appropriate costumes, and a real live baby, of course. Throughout the weekend there are special services with lots of music sung by the various church choirs. On the other hand, it is nice to be able to be with my family at Christmas time. That wonderful year came to an end and the unknowns of the new year began with a trip to South Portland to spend New Year's Eve with Charlotte, Marion, Elaine, Ginny and Jeanette. The get-together for the six of us had become an annual event when I lived in Cape Elizabeth and I wanted to continue as long as I could manage the two-hour drive to reach them.

As the 2005 year was under way with snow and cold, I spent many profitable hours preparing for a women's retreat and Bible study, my responsibilities for early in the new year. The ladies at Galilee Church in Gorham had asked me to speak to them for their one-day retreat in April. I was pleased with my choice of an in-depth study on Mary and Martha and I was really looking forward to the retreat. In addition, a group of Dexter ladies had asked me to lead a Bible study on *Becoming a Woman of Prayer*, by Cynthia Heald. The Bible study began in January with ten ladies from different churches in the area. I delighted in the privilege of teaching and learning with this group. As a culmination of our Bible studies we all looked forward to a day of retreat that Cynthia was scheduled to lead in October in Waldoboro, Maine. Maine temperatures began dropping below zero with regularity and I was content to stay warm inside and began to move forward again with the writing of my memoirs. By February I had completed the fifth chapter, my first term in the Congo, and moved on to outline chapter six which dealt with my second term. About that same time I developed a bad cough which I couldn't seem to conquer. I didn't think too much about it since many folks in my church had similar coughs which wouldn't go away. I could not have been more wrong.

MY "DARK NIGHT OF THE SOUL"

When I began to feel pressure and pain in my chest, I decided I needed to see my doctor, Lesley Fernow, who immediately ordered a chest x-ray. She noted the build up of fluid in my lungs, tapped the left lung and sent a sample of the fluid to the laboratory. At the same time Dr. Fernow found a growth in my neck area. A few days later the growth was removed surgically and the pathology report came back as malignant. The lung fluid report also showed malignancy. Then came a bewildering round of cat scans, x-rays and blood tests, all showing that cancer had indeed attacked my body with a vengeance in a number of places.

For days I was stunned. I was facing cancer yet again. I just sat alone in my chair at home and stared into space. I couldn't read my Bible, I couldn't pray and I didn't write in my journal. I didn't feel well at all and I began to sense I might be facing the end of my life. I was not afraid to die, for I knew that I would go to be with Jesus, but there were still some ministries I wanted to do. I felt alone and cut off from my usual activities and from my friends. I reluctantly cancelled as the speaker for the Gorham ladies' April retreat. This was a huge disappointment because I had so looked forward to that event. I resigned as a member of the Dexter Library Board. I tried to keep going with the Bible study on prayer but finally asked one of the ladies to teach the last three lessons for me.

Gradually the Lord helped me to regain perspective and I felt His presence once again. I saw this trial as an assignment from Him. I knew that He loved me and I remembered the first great truth I had learned as a new Christian that "all things work together for good to those who love God" from Romans 8:28. I opened my Bible and began to read some of the cries of God's people and His promises to them:

"Why are you cast down, O my soul? And why are you disquieted within me? Hope in God; For I shall yet praise Him, the help of my countenance and my God."
(Psalm 42:11)

"Call upon Me in the day of trouble; I will deliver you, and you shall glorify Me." (Psalm 50:15)

"Blessed be God, Who has not turned away my prayer, nor His mercy from me." (Psalm 66:20)

"Fear not, for I am with you; be not dismayed, for I am your God. I will strengthen you, yes, I will help you. I will hold you with My righteous right hand."
(Isaiah 41:10)

"For I know the thoughts that I think toward you, says the Lord, thoughts of peace and not of evil, to give you a future and a hope." (Jeremiah 29:11)

"But may the God of all grace, who called us to His eternal Glory by Christ Jesus, after you have suffered a while, perfect, establish, strengthen, and settle you. To Him be the glory and the dominion forever and ever. Amen." (I Peter 5:10-11)

"Therefore we do not lose heart. Even though our outward man is perishing, yet the inward man is being renewed day by day. For our light affliction, which is but for a moment, is working for us a far more exceeding and eternal weight of glory, while we do not look at the things which are seen, but at the things which are not seen. For the things which are seen are temporary, but the things which are not seen are eternal." (2 Corinthians 4:16-18)

People who suffer from natural catastrophes and trials of fire, flood, financial loss, life-threatening illness or loss of a loved one have serious, soul-searching questions. Where is

God? Why did this happen to me? Why has God forsaken me? What is the purpose of all this suffering? We live in a world where these things happen to every one. For the Christian there is that underlying comfort that God is sovereign, He is in control of our individual lives and He designs what is good for His children. He blesses us with the good times and He carries us through the hard times. There are lessons to be learned in every life-situation. As Amy Carmichael said, "All weathers nourish souls." I gradually returned to the place where I wanted only God's perfect will for me and I wanted to learn all He had to teach me with this third diagnosis of cancer. After his prison experience in Russia, Alexander Solzhenitsyn said, "Bless you, prison, for having been in my life." I wanted to be able to say from a sincere heart, "Bless you, cancer, for having come into my life," and to be diligent in this new assignment that the LORD had entrusted to me.

TREATMENT AND RECOVERY

Dr. Fernow sent me to the city of Bangor, about an hour from home, to the Cancer Care of Maine at Eastern Maine Medical Center. All of my reports had been sent to an oncologist at the center. Some of my family were there with me and heard the oncologist say the awful word "chemotherapy" which was fully as scary to me as the word "cancer" itself. Without the chemotherapy I was told I had from six months to a year to live. He also told me that chemotherapy would not cure the ovarian cancer but that I would likely have some more quality time left to live. After several days of thought, prayer and encouragement from my family, I chose to submit to the chemotherapy treatment. My first treatment in Bangor was on April 8, 2005, with following treatments to be given by the Oncology Services of Mayo Regional Hospital in Dover-Foxcroft, only eight miles from my home. Once a month an oncologist from the Bangor center comes to Dover to check on the patients receiving chemotherapy. Dr. Fernow, as my primary doctor, was in charge of the Dover Oncology Services. I was very thankful to have these services so close to home.

My family was a great support and each one quickly fell into a routine to help, encourage and support me. Chemotherapy was scheduled for every three weeks. Bea drove me to Dover for the treatment, Mary Lou came to the clinic to eat lunch with me during the treatment and Charles drove me home when the treatment was complete. Marion brought roses to cheer me, food to nourish me and puzzles to amuse me. Cards began coming from all over the world and number just over two hundred at this writing. Phone calls meant so much and came from all over the country, even one all the way from Africa. Skip and Bea did not want to see me lose weight so they invited me to take my evening meals with them. Thanks to their love, thoughtfulness and good home-cooked food I have stayed healthy throughout the ordeal.

I had asked my friends to pray that the Lord would give me enough good days to complete the writing of my story. He graciously did this for me and I wrote the final chapter in mid-September, 2005. After six treatments the oncologist recommended two additional treatments for maximum benefit. As of this writing the final treatment is scheduled for September twenty-fourth. Two weeks after each treatment blood was drawn for the CA125 test, which gives what the medical people call the "tumor marker." My numbers started at four thousand eight hundred and have gone down consistently and steadily with each treatment. This writing finds my numbers down to only eighteen, which is well into the normal range. The doctors expect the numbers to stabilize in that general area. I am feeling so much better and have no regrets about my decision to choose chemotherapy.

GOOD DAYS AND BAD DAYS

Early in my chemotherapy, I learned that there would be a pattern to my treatments. After each treatment, which lasted from nine a.m. to mid-afternoon, there were seven to ten days when I really did not feel at all well. Those days were followed by some good days when I felt fine but was weak. Folks soon learned to ask if I were having a "good" day before they dropped by to see me. Even on my "bad" days I usually wanted them to come, although I did not feel able to leave my home and I definitely did not want to go out to eat. However, friends and family who made the effort to come to see me brought blessings and joy and those visits helped to pass the time which so often hung heavily over me. Many from the central Maine area came to see me; some brought lunch which we shared together, later others took me out for lunch, and there were times when we forgot food and simply enjoyed great fellowship, often sharing the Scriptures and prayer together. My friends are among my greatest treasures in life and their visits brought comfort, joy and encouragement in my time of greatest need.

Lunch with cousins Nelson and Alden

On my "good" days I tried to do something different, even if only to drive into Dexter to buy postage stamps. My home church is fifteen miles away and much of the time I did not feel stable enough to drive myself that distance. My sister Mary Lou committed herself to drive me to church and worship with me on Sunday mornings. This was a very great blessing to me and we missed very few Sundays. I shared the joy of the Psalmist who said, "I was glad when they said to me, Let us go into the house of the Lord." Psalm 122:1. Staying connected with my church family was very important to me during that time and receiving instruction in God's Word was vital to my continued spiritual growth.

In the spring of 2005 my home church had a missionary conference. Unfortunately it did not fit at all well into my "good day" cycle but I did manage to attend enough of the meetings to become acquainted with two young missionary families who were taking part in the conference. Don and Debbie Fisher are appointees to Ethiopia. Don is a former student of mine and a graduate of New England Bible College. Tim and Carre Gardner are appointees to Russia. Both of these couples are from Maine and I have a burden to help them discover their support. I have been contacting Maine pastors by phone and trying to encourage them to consider helping these Maine candidates on their way to the fields where God has called them. This has been a project that I could handle from my home on both good days and bad days. Having the support of Maine churches had meant so much to me when I was a missionary and I wanted the same for these Maine candidates. Some of the contacts I made opened doors for them to present their respective fields. Commitment for their support is gradually building.

My brother Charles was invited by Robert Wyllie, the music director of the Thomaston Baptist Church, to play his trumpet on a Sunday morning in August. I drove to Thomaston with him so I could enjoy the music and also see my friends, Quentin and Sylvia Johnson. The four hymns that Charles and Robert played together, Charles on his trumpet and Robert on the piano, were superb. After church the Wyllies, the Johnsons, and Charles and I enjoyed lunch at the Anchor Inn in Bristol on the Pemaquid Peninsula. I thoroughly enjoyed my first big outing in six months.

On a sadder note, I received news that my friend Marguerite Gay had passed away on August eighth. Her family encouraged me to try to come to Portland for the memorial service to be held later in the month. I knew I was not strong enough to drive that distance by myself but when I learned the date and found that it fit into my "good" days schedule, I arranged a shuttle to get me to Portland and back. Skip and Bea drove me to Augusta where Charlotte Russell picked me up and drove me to her home in South Portland. I spent the weekend with Charlotte and was able to attend Marguerite's memorial service with her. Along with others, I gave a testimonial in memory of Marguerite. I felt blessed to visit with the extended Gay family who have been such a source of joy and support to me for so many years. On Sunday morning I worshiped at my church in South Portland and saw so many of my church friends. After church, Frank and Gertrude Ham drove me back to Augusta where we connected with Skip and Bea for lunch and then the drive back to Dexter. I was so grateful for renewed

Pastor and Joline Inman with the prize winning Model T.

strength that allowed me to be with my special friends at that time. Once again here was another indication of God's loving mercy towards me.

On another "good" day Skip, Bea and I drove to Bangor to visit with our friend Shirley Chadbourne. The Sunbury Village apartments, where Shirley lives, sponsored a barbeque and an antique car show for senior citizens. Twelve of us ate lunch with Shirley. Pastor William Inman from Cambridge came in his 1917 Touring Car Model T Ford and won first prize. I treasured and enjoyed the opportunity to get out of the house on that lovely summer day. One other day I rode to Bangor where my three sisters and I met to enjoy a Chinese lunch in Brewer.

Another summer highlight was the celebration for Pastor Harold Wheeler's sixty years of faithful ministry, held at the First Free Baptist Church in Dexter. Many of his friends came from other churches in Maine where he had served as pastor. It was a delightful evening and I was so happy and blessed to be present and able to share in honoring this godly and faithful man and his wife, Mary Lou, whom I have known for most of those sixty years. Once again I was thankful that cancer did not hinder me from being with these friends for that special evening.

In between these events I worked hard on writing my story and set a goal to finish by the time I had my final chemotherapy session. I am a few weeks ahead of schedule, but there is a lot of work yet to be done. I need to make the corrections that my editor has pointed out and there are plenty! I will try to find pictures to enhance my story and learn how to put them into the proper space and time. Oops, I'm having a "good" day and I promised Mary Lou I would meet her in Dover at four-thirty for a chicken pie supper. I must go but I will return to write my reflections.

REFLECTIONS ON THE CONTINUING FAITHFULNESS OF MY GOD

" "Great is Thy Faithfulness," O God my Father,
There is no shadow of turning with Thee;
Thou changest not, Thy compassions, they fail not;
As Thou has been Thou forever wilt be."
— Thomas O. Chisholm (1866-1960)

When I retired from New England Bible College and

moved to Dexter I saw the faithfulness of my heavenly Father in so many ways. Housing was ready for me, loving family members were nearby, a church family was waiting for me and various ministries were open to me. I was so very happy and content those first two years and knew that I was where God intended me to be. I was especially thankful for the ministry opportunities that opened up for me. I delighted to serve in every instance.

Cancer struck me down again and I nearly gave up. When I began the chemotherapy treatments, hundreds of friends prayed for me, God was with me all the way and He restored my health. My doctors cannot tell me how long the restoration period will last but I intend to enjoy each day as a gift from God and trust Him for each tomorrow. He remains faithful no matter how I feel or what happens. I am ready for whatever new assignment the Lord chooses to give me. Always and forever,

GREAT IS THY FAITHFULNESS!!

Bunny and her editorial team: Carol, Bunny, Pam, Shirley and Rosemary.

Photo by Lindy

EPILOGUE

It is now late August 2006 and I am delighted to be able personally to bring you, my readers, up-to-date on my activities. The manuscript is formatted, the final checks are being made, and Pamela and I will take the disk and a hard copy of the story to the printer on September 8!

In September 2005, I was very happy when Dr. Fernow told me, following the blood check after my eighth chemotherapy treatment, that my cancer was in remission. I saw this as more of God's loving faithfulness to me and I looked forward to the new freedom. I was to have blood checks every three months and the oncologists made no promise of how long the remission would last. I was happy and wanted to enjoy every new day as it came along. To help build up my strength, some friends gave me a supply of the dietary supplement, Reliv. After drinking the twice-daily shakes for two months, I had new energy and felt better than before cancer. I have continued with the product.

The next months included some things I had hoped

for and looked forward to with anticipation. I was able to attend a women's conference where Cynthia Heald was the featured speaker. My annual trip to South Portland to spend New Year's weekend with my single friends was possible. I went on a bus tour to Lancaster County in Pennsylvania with my sister, Bea, and her husband, Skip, and our brother, Charles. I spent a profitable and enjoyable three months with the Dexter ladies as we studied together another Cynthia Heald guided Bible study, *Becoming a Woman of Freedom*. I delighted in a week at camp in Millinocket with my friend Shirley and a weekend in New Hampshire with the birthday girls of South Portland. Interspersed with these enjoyable and fun activities my editorial team and I worked steadily on revising and rechecking my manuscript. Finally, it was ready to be formatted and then there was more checking.

On July 18, 2006, I visited the oncologist to receive word on the blood test that had been done a week earlier. She gave me the sad news that the tumor marker had risen considerably. She spun into action with more blood tests, a CT scan, and on the third day I was given chemotherapy. Since I had been feeling so well for ten months, I was quite overwhelmed that cancer had so soon raised its ugly head. However, I was not in despair and remembered the good word I had read from Psalm 35:27 that morning, *"The Lord be exalted, who delights in the well-being of his servant."(NIV)*. Other Scriptures have encouraged me as I've entered another phase of the Lord's good plan for my life: *"I know, O Lord,...that in faithfulness You have afflicted me."* Psalm 119:75b. *"For great is your love, reaching to the heavens; your faithfulness reaches to the skies."* Psalm 57:10 NIV.

I know that I am in His care and I trust Him to take care of all the details of my life from now until the end. I fully expect that I will face periods of treatment followed by periods of remission until the Lord takes me home in His good time. Sometime ago I came across the prayer of an unknown old saint and, from time to time, I pray this prayer for myself and my aging friends:

"Prepare me for death that I may not die after long affliction or suddenly, but after short illness, with no confusion or disorder, and a quiet discharge in peace, with adieu to brethren." I continue to count on

HIS GREAT FAITHFULNESS!

August 23, 2006

EPILOGUE UPDATE

It was one year ago today that Pamela and I drove to Rockland, Maine with the manuscript and disk of *Great is Thy Faithfulness*. Two and a half months later the seven hundred copies were off the press. My home church sponsored a beautiful ceremony dedicating the books to the Lord. I worked hard to get the books out to those who wanted them and within several months the books were gone.

The cancer battle continues with just enough good days between treatments to complete the various assignments that the Lord gives me. I've had the privilege and blessing of speaking to a number of ladies' groups in our local area, teaching the women's class at our church and an evening Bible study in Dexter, discipling women and mentoring a delightful young couple who are candidates for the mission field. With each assignment I have seen evidence of the Lord's enabling grace.

There have been the fun times, too, this summer. A trip to historical Pittston Farm, north of Rockwood, with brother Charles in his new truck. Two sets of overnight guests brought blessing to my home. Cousin Gillie has driven from Farmington to take me out for lunch several times. Other friends have come for day visits which I have enjoyed so much.

Today sister Bea and her husband Skip hosted a surprise birthday open house for me. Fifty-five family members and very close friends came with cards, flowers, gifts and lots of love to help me celebrate my 81st! I didn't really expect to be here for this birthday. I face the unknowns of the new year with confidence that my heavenly Father's great faithfulness will continue to give me joy and hope during the good days and the not so good days that lie ahead.

*"All I have needed Thy hand hath provided—
Great is Thy faithfulness, Lord, unto me!"*

September 8, 2007

Cover Design
Pamela Nadeau